Unwin Education Books

Classroom Observation of Primary School Children

All in a Day

RICHARD W. MILLS
Principal Lecturer in Education, Westhill College, Birmingham

London
GEORGE ALLEN & UNWIN
Boston   Sydney

First published in 1980

GEORGE ALLEN & UNWIN LTD
40 Museum Street, London WC1A 1LU

© Richard W. Mills, 1980

British Library Cataloguing in Publication Data

Mills, Richard William
   Classroom observation of primary school chldren.
   1. Education, Elementary—England – Case studies
   I. Title
   372. 9'2'2   LA633   79-41799

   ISBN 0-04-372028-5
   ISBN 0-04-372029-3 Pbk

Typeset in 10 on 11 point Times by Red Lion Setters, London
and printed in Great Britain
by Biddles Ltd., Guildford, Surrey

Unwin Education Books

CLASSROOM OBSERVATION OF PRIMARY SCHOOL CHILDREN
All in a Day

Unwin Education Books

Education Since 1800 IVOR MORRISH
Moral Development WILLIAM KAY
Physical Education for Teaching BARBARA CHURCHER
The Background of Immigrant Children IVOR MORRISH
Organising and Integrating the Infant Day JOY TAYLOR
The Philosophy of Education: An Introduction HARRY SCHOFIELD
Assessment and Testing: An Introduction HARRY SCHOFIELD
Education: Its Nature and Purpose M.V.C.JEFFREYS
Learning in the Primary School KENNETH HASLAM
The Sociology of Education: an Introduction IVOR MORRISH
Developing a Curriculum AUDREY and HOWARD NICHOLLS
Teacher Education and Cultural Change H. DUDLEY PLUNKETT and JAMES
LYNCH
Reading and Writing in the First School JOY TAYLOR
Approaches to Drama DAVID A. MALE
Aspects of Learning BRIAN O'CONNELL
Focus on Meaning JOAN TOUGH
Moral Education WILLIAM KAY
Concepts in Primary Education JOHN E. SADLER
Moral Philosophy for Education ROBIN BARROW
Beyond Control? PAUL FRANCIS
Principles of Classroom Learning and Perception RICHARD J. MUELLER
Education and the Community ERIC MIDWINTER
Creative Teaching AUDREY and HOWARD NICHOLLS
The Preachers of Culture MARGARET MATHIESON
Mental Handicap: An Introduction DAVID EDEN
Aspects of Educational Change IVOR MORRISH
Beyond Initial Reading JOHN POTTS
The Foundations of Maths in the Infant School JOY TAYLOR
Common Sense and the Curriculum ROBIN BARROW
The Second 'R' WILLIAM HARPIN
The Diploma Disease RONALD DORE
The Development of Meaning JOAN TOUGH
The Countesthorpe Experience JOHN WATTS
The Place of Commonsense in Educational Thought LIONEL ELVIN
Language in Teaching and Learning HAZEL FRANCIS
Patterns of Education in the British Isles NIGEL GRANT and ROBERT BELL
Philosophical Foundations for the Curriculum ALLEN BRENT
World Faiths in Education W. OWEN COLE
Classroom Language: What Sort? JILL RICHARDS
Philosophy and Human Movement DAVID BEST
Secondary Schools and the Welfare Network DAPHNE JOHNSON *et al.*

By the same author

LOOK-OUT (with Gordon T. Taylor), Harrap, 1974: a package of material on the use
of film in English teaching
OCCASIONS, Longman, 1976: a series of thematic books on *Births, Weddings,
Funerals* and *Moments of Truth*, with accompanying slide sets and notes and a pupils'
Study Guide
TEACHING ENGLISH ACROSS THE ABILITY RANGE (ed.), Ward Lock Educa-
tional, 1977

Contents

For Robin, who has already probably
taught us more than we have taught him.

Acknowledgements

First, I should like to thank the pupils, teachers and headteachers who feature in these pages, for their co-operation in allowing themselves and their schools to be observed in the first place. They did not know at the time, and nor did I, that their words and actions would live on in book form. While anonymity protects their privacy, it also hides their hard work and expertise.

May I also acknowledge the kind permission of the following people and institutions to reproduce certain material:

Mrs Lorna Ridgway, for the maths teaching points made on page 165, taken from *The Task of the Teacher in the Primary School* (London: Ward Lock Educational, 1976).

Mr Mike Torbe, for his list of spelling hints on pages 159-60, taken from *Teaching Spelling* (London: Ward Lock Educational, 1977).

NFER for the chart of teacher activities on pages 205-6, from *The Teacher's Day*, by S. Hilsum and B. S. Cane, 1971.

The BBC for permission to include the text of the 'Carpenter's Song', broadcast on the BBC's 'Watch' programme on 22 October 1974

From *My Own Book for Listening and Reading*, pp. 55 and 69 published in the 1973 edition of the SRA Reading Laboratory® by Don H. Parker and Genevieve Scannell. © 1973, Science Research Associates, Inc. All rights reserved. Reprinted with the permission of the publisher and found on pages 116–71.

From *All About the Great Rivers of the World* by Anne Terry White, a specified adaptation of 'Junk in the Yangtze Gorges'. © 1957 by Anne Terry White. Reprinted by permission of Random House, Inc.

From 'The Golden Treasure', *Listening Skill Builder*, pp. 17, 18 and 19, published in the 1973 edition of the SRA Reading Laboratory® by Don H. Parker and Genevieve Scannell. © 1973, Science Research Associates, Inc. All rights reserved. Reprinted with the permission of the publisher and found on pages 127–9.

Every effort has been made to trace owners of copyright material and the publishers would be glad to hear from any further copyright owners of material reproduced in the book.

Several friends and colleagues have read the book in manuscript form and/or been good enough to offer detailed comments. I should like to thank them for their time, effort and enthusiasm. They include Tony Armstrong, Freda Cliff, Jenny Edginton, Michael Grimmitt, Gerald Haigh, Roger Harris, Hugh Wilcock, my brother Robert, and colleagues Marjorie Bilton, Hilda Fowler and Geoffrey Platt, who have kindly supplied information about appropriate fiction for Chapter 4, Sequel I.

Above all, my special thanks should be recorded to my wife, Jean, who knows every word of this manuscript, as she does those of my others, and who is the author of Chapter 2, Sequel I, 'Teaching English to Infants as a Second Language'.

R. W. M.

Setting the Scene

A VERY SHORT PLAY

Act I

Location: A primary school somewhere in England.

Actors: A teacher and thirty children, including John.

Action: A maths class is in progress.

Three masked raiders enter and demand the dinner money. Swift Kung-Fu-type blows from the deputy head render them helpless and they are carried off. Maths continues, with estimates first, then calculations, on the amount of money the thieves might have stolen. Lightning strikes the weather cock on the school roof. It crashes through the ceiling, scattering debris about the room. When the dust settles, the children sweep away the rubbish and then write about the experience in their daily diary.

During dinner time, a mad dog, foaming at the mouth, rushes around the dining room, savaging one of the infant's dolls. The art lesson in the afternoon captures the incident in paint, clay and collage.

Then, relaxation at the end of the day with the book, *Fearsome Frankenstein Fables*.

The bell sounds. Home time.

Act II

Actors: John and his mother at tea.

Action: Mother: What happened in school today, dear?

John: Oh, nothing.

Curtain

It is the mother's question that I have tried to answer in this book. I can record nothing quite so dramatic as the incidents just mentioned but, for those prepared to read on, there is mention of blood and tears, a dead man, a princess, Father Christmas, cannibalism, and The Boy Who Had No Pulse.

Each chapter tells of one day in the school life of the boy or girl whose name is the chapter title. Mike is a lively, extrovert 5-year-old gypsy boy in the reception class of a small rural Church of England school. Rashda is a 6-year-old Asian girl, with little command of English, in a multi-ethnic urban setting. David is a rather slow 7-year-old who needs very sensitive teaching at his city centre school. Lucy a very sharp Roman Catholic 8-year-old is outstanding in all she does. Lorraine, a member of the silent majority of 9-year-olds, is a quiet self-effacing girl in a suburban junior school. And Peter, aged 10, generates his own motivation in a semi-open-plan setting.

Another day, another boy or girl, another school, another observer, and everything might have been very different. So no unwarranted grand conclusions about the state of education should be drawn from these pages. The book is not a research report, but a microcosm of the educational scene. As such, its place lies in classroom interaction literature of the 'open-ended' rather than 'pre-ordained schedule' variety (See Open University Course E 201, Block 11, p. 29f.). There is some balance, I hope, in the selection, which was not random. The boys and girls are from differing backgrounds, have differing interests and different educational attainments. The schools from which they come are inner ring, suburban, rural; small and large; church and state. The teachers are like you and I. Thus, the boys and girls, schools and teachers are neither representative nor untypical.

My intention in observing them has been to record events as accurately and honestly as I can, but any classroom observer is constantly bombarded by a range of changing phenomena and, like a television cameraman, he must make some selection. What some might regard as trivial data is juxtaposed with more weighty matter, as befits a classroom. In any event, who determines what is trivial? Philip Jackson (1968) has some interesting comments on this matter.

> Considered singly, many aspects of classroom life look trivial. And, in a sense, they are. It is only when their cumulative occurrence is considered that the realisation of their full importance begins to emerge. Thus, in addition to looking at the dominant features of instructional interchanges and the overall design of the curriculum, we must not fail to ponder, as we watch, the significance of things that come and go in a twinkling – things like a student's yawn or a teacher's frown. Such transitory events may contain more information about classroom life than might appear at first glance.

The focus of my attention is not teaching style, or curriculum content, or class management, although all these are featured to some degree. The focus is the individual boy or girl to whom everything is happening. I have tried to look at a small part of the education process as it is experienced by the consumer. It is an impossible task and therefore worth attempting, as a theologian once remarked. With the exception of names and school-uniform colours, every detail and every word spoken is recorded as it occurred. Nothing has been invented.

The resulting data with commentary, and more extended information in the form of sequels at the end of chapters, are intended for students in teacher training, as an aid to linking theory with practice. As one reader of the book in manuscript form commented: 'It should be like learning chess from replaying games of the grandmasters in the security of one's home rather than in the highly charged, emotional atmosphere of the tournament room.' To this end, Chapter 7 provides a range of questions relating to theoretical and practical considerations, by means of which students in initial (and in-service) training can focus on issues which concern them all. One problem in teacher training is that tutor and students have rarely all witnessed the same events or taught the same children. One alternative is to discuss film and video-tape. This book will, I hope, offer another possibility, and serve as an introduction to life in the primary school, encouraging students to see events from the child's point of view, even in classes of thirty plus.

Finally, as an analogy with the classroom, let me briefly comment on a swimming lesson I observed recently.

The 10-year-old boys and girls were using a variety of strokes in order to move along in the water, changing from crawl to breast stroke to back stroke as the mood took them, and resting when they needed to. A tremendous range of attainment was evident, from the confident, competent experts to the splashers-over-five-metres with frenetic dog paddle; from those operating happily in the deep end, to those even holding the bar in water two feet deep; from those looking for help and assurance, to those oblivious of human observers; from those swimming elegantly for gold medal qualifications, to the beginners, engaging in watery scrambles in an alien medium. All were in the same pool, receiving individual attention and encouragement from a teacher walking beside them with a safety hook at the ready. All were aware of the inherently competitive nature of the setting, but making no fuss about it, and certainly not exploiting it. Those in the school who cannot swim come twice a week; others once a week. The headteacher insists that all boys and girls gain some kind of swimming badge from the school before they leave for their secondary education.

There are many educational lessons to be gleaned from this analogy. Some of them will be evident by inclusion in, or omission from, the pages which follow.

Chapter 1

Mike, Aged 5

Me dad likes pheasants the best

THE SCHOOL

Mike's junior and infant school has Church of England aided status. The church controls staff appointments, with the local vicar being chairman of the managers. An entry in that intriguing biography of any school, the log book, records the visit in 1890 of the vicar's wife, appropriately named Mrs Crucifix.

Some ten years ago, it was solely a school for the local village, but now its 142 pupils include 24 known as 'itinerants', loosely translated as 'gypsies'. Christopher Reiss (1975), outlines the problem of defining the term 'itinerant' and shows how such a term can include people from canal barges, fairgrounds, circuses, as well as gypsies and tinkers. Those designated 'itinerant' in Mike's school come from a nearby illegal caravan site and their parents are engaged in various casual labouring jobs such as fencing. They are, in fact, second- or third-generation gypsies, rather than true Romanies.

In addition to the headteacher, there are four full-time teachers and one part-timer. Each class is of mixed ability and there is no major reading problem. Nor is there any punishment other than disapproval and over the last thirty years two children only have been caned. For what crimes? one wonders.

THE DAY

I arrive at the school at 8.50 a.m. on a dull and rainy day near Christmas and the following exchange takes place in the small car park as soon as I get out of my car:

Boy (aged about 7):	This is a school, you know.
R. M.:	Is it? How do you know?
Boy:	Well, I'm here. We've been here for a hundred years.
R. M.:	Have you? That's a long time. What's your name?
Boy:	David.

One of the great pleasures of visiting infant and junior schools is that children will often initiate conversations quite unsolicited and tell you it is their birthday, or their mummy has had a baby, or the goldfish has died. It is good for the visitor's ego. Even a monster with one blood-shot eye in the middle of his forehead would find someone holding his hand at play time.

Lorna Ridgway (1976) quotes a headmaster, Mr Ron Waters, as he highlights what are, for him, crucial differences in outlook between young and old. He says:

> When parents and children follow each other into the Head's room, one cannot escape the comparisons. The children are curious, while parents know already; prejudice has replaced their curiosity. Children trust while parents are predominantly fearful and need to be put at ease. Children are spontaneously and intuitively honest in their appreciation of a situation, while parents tend to say what pleases. Lively optimism, curiosity, clear vision and a natural honesty that cuts through cant like a knife, mark the child's approach to life.

It is a view which has echoes of William Blake.

I go into the reception classroom where a few 5-year-olds are playing with toys and building apparatus. The room is fairly small with large windows wholly occupying one side. Christmas decorations are everywhere – a frieze of the Nativity; a Father Christmas cut-out; cotton wool on the windows; a small silver paper tree. There is a nature table area with cress growing and holly (not growing), cones and a log. A carpeted corner of the room serves as a story area and on one of the walls in this part are two newspaper cuttings of two pandas and a notice announcing, SUSAN BROUGHT THESE PICTURES. Occupying another corner of the room is a coat rack with named pegs. Like many modern infant school classrooms, this one has particular sections identified with various activities, so as to combine the best features of organisation and accessibility (see Gloyn and Frobisher, 1975, ch. 1).

As any reader of this book will know, it is customary in infant and junior schools for certain parts of the school year to be dominated by festivals which are a part of our Christian and cultural heritage. (A helpful teachers' guide to practical activities at such times is by Brandling, 1978.). Christmas and Easter clearly have considerable impact, both on the curriculum and on the children's consciousness, with related activities often extending over several weeks, and with classwork closely geared to each particular festival, as will be seen throughout these pages.

In such a way, the religious cultural traditions of the society are passed on from generation to generation. As Waller (1932) put it, 'Man and his heirs hold their common property in perpetuum'. Transmission of what has been found valuable in the past, and interchange of new but acceptable ways and ideas, are two sides of the cultural coin. It could be argued that, in an industrialised and suburban setting, with high social and physical mobility, such cohesive force as cultural continuity may be of more significance than in many rural, third-world areas where activities and attitude are often more homogeneous anyway. Key problems arise when there is a clash between the knowledge and values which are in accord with the 'general culture' of-a society, and differing knowledge and values which belong to a significant sub-culture within that society.

Such considerations will, at this point on a Thursday morning, be far from the mind of Mike's teacher, although they may, in a sense, inform what she does.

Mrs Hilton is an experienced teacher in her early 40s, with silvery hair and a pleasant, friendly face. She is very smartly dressed in a purple jumper and tweed skirt. A medallion hangs round her neck. While she is engaged in calling the dinner register, in walks Mike.

Mrs Hilton: Good morning, Mike.
Mike: Good morning.

He is a stocky 5-year-old. He has a chubby face with puffy cheeks and fair curly hair. It is a pleasant, open face with blue eyes and a good complexion. Underneath his thick coat he is wearing a floppy polo-neck sweater and long brown trousers, with a hole in the right knee. Brown boots. Blue socks. He takes off his coat and walks straight into the corner where the children are playing with building materials. He settles down instantly, an indication of the confidence and assurance he is to display throughout the day. 'Learning to live in a classroom', as Philip Jackson (1968) observes, 'involves, among other things, learning to live in a crowd.'

By 9.10 a.m. the attendance and dinner registers have been called and the twenty-three children, nine of whom are designated 'itinerant', move to the story corner. Such consistent localising of specific activities helps to develop a sense of security and order in young children. It also serves to heighten the ritualistic power of an occasion and, as we shall see throughout this book, ritual plays a powerful part in school life.

Mike has put his ruler in his trousers as a sword. He now takes a glove puppet but is skilfully and surreptitiously relieved of this by Mrs Hilton. It is done so quietly that no one realises it has happened. In such a way do sensitive teachers, and parents, avoid conflict where possible, and it is by no means as easy to put into practice as it may seem to the casual observer.

All the children are now sitting down on the floor, except Mike who walks about in an alert but nonchalant supervisory manner. Mrs Hilton begins the Nativity story with a short homily on the condition of the picture book she has in her hand. Notice the simple but effective narrative setting she adopts at the start, with quoted conversation between herself and Miss Barling. It makes the moral more immediate for her listeners, and virtually turns the torn book into an injured party.

Mrs H.: Well, yesterday afternoon, when you'd all gone home, will you listen please, Billy, Miss Barling came in the classroom and she very kindly said, 'Shall I put the book corner tidy?' So I said, 'Oh, yes please, because I've got so much to clear up'.

Mike: Today.

Mrs H.: Last night this was. So she made the book corner all nice and tidy and she found this lovely book for us. It's sad because some of the book has been torn, yes I'll tell you about this in a minute, sit down, I'll show you. I don't think it was you children because I haven't mended this book and somebody has. So I don't think it was anyone in this class. It's rather sad, isn't it, because a lovely book like that *(Mike explains that another teacher had already told them that story, and Mrs Hilton, not at all put out, says)* Did she?

Mike: Yeah.

Mrs H.: Well, I thought I'd read a little bit of it, because it's getting very near to Christmas and, do you know what it says there? *(pointing to the title on the cover).*

Child: Bethlehem.

Mrs H.: No.

Mike: Angel.

Mrs H.: No.

Child: Angels come from Bethlehem, don't they?

Mrs H.: Erm. Well, they went *to* Bethlehem, to tell the shepherds about Jesus.

Child: Fairies.

Mrs H.: No. It says, 'The Christmas Book'. 'The Christmas Book'. And the first part of the story, I'm sorry Natalie, isn't there, but that means you know the first part of the story don't you?

Children: Yes.

Mrs H.: Where did Mary and Joseph live?

Mike: In a shed. That shed there. *(He points to a picture on the wall.)*

Mrs H.: But where did they live before they went there, Mike?

Child: Bethlehem.

Mrs H.:	No.
Child:	In a cottage.
Mrs H.:	Well, I suppose you could call it a little cottage. It wasn't like the little cottages you know. A little house in *(pause)* NAZARETH. Can you say it?
Children:	Nazareth.
Mrs H.:	And what did Joseph do?
Child:	Carpenter.
Mrs H.:	He was a ...
Children:	Carpenter.
Mrs H.:	And what is a carpenter?
Mike:	What makes carps.
Mrs H.:	No, he doesn't make carps. He makes things ...
Child:	Wood.
Mrs H.:	Out of wood. Good boy. Don't shout.
Child:	And he makes some chairs.
Mrs H.:	He makes chairs and ...
Mike:	Tables.
Mrs H.:	Tables and ...
Child:	Bookcases ... book
Mrs H.:	Well, *(unintelligible)* ... wouldn't use today.
Child:	And and and he would and he would make a new book like this.
Mrs H.:	I shouldn't think so. He would make chairs like that ... Michele and Matthew and Sean are sitting on, wouldn't he, because that's made of wood.
Child:	And cardboard.
Mrs H.:	Are they? *(Several children talk at once.)* A wooden bench and tables. Very good, Warren. Well done. All right. And then they had to go on a long journey *(interruptions by several children)* ... to Bethlehem. And how did they get to Bethlehem?
Child:	On a donkey.
Mrs H.:	Well, Mary was on a donkey.
Child: *(shouting)*	And Joseph walked.
Child:	And Joseph walked a long way.
Mrs H.:	He walked a long, long way, and they were ...
Mike:	And they were so tired.
Child:	And they stopped.
Mrs H.:	So tired.
Child:	And they stopped in a layby.
Mrs H.:	They stopped in a layby? Oh, I don't think *(laughing)* they had laybys in those days, not like we have. They would stop on the side of the road. Yes, I suppose it was a layby really, wasn't it?

And so on. Mrs Hilton has superb, quiet control. She employs a considerable voice range, with a heightening of intonation and stress, almost automatic for talking with very young children. Perhaps dangerously so. Joyce Grenfell's splendid parody about Sidney and Co. reminds us of the thin dividing line between an intonation and manner which is accommodating and warm, and one which is patronising. It is a tight-rope which every infants teacher treads and, in an oblique way, calls to mind a curiously symbolic and oddly disturbing story told by John Holt (1974). A lady, shopping in a crowded New York department store, saw, walking in front of her, two charming small boys. Feeling affectionate, she patted them on the top of their heads, only to discover, when they turned round and looked up at her, that they were rather angry midgets. Presumably, in common with certain other minority groups, they could cope with such intrusions on their privacy and personality. Young children must often endure being addressed as if they were budgerigars, puppies, deaf, or senile.

But Mrs Hilton makes no such errors. She involves the children in the story, by using familiar language and constructions; by asking questions and then allowing time for reply; by showing pictures; by praising correct answers and by salvaging what she can from wrong responses; by laughing at errors; by displaying good humour. On reflection, it is generally the kind of approach which the psychologist B. F. Skinner* might endorse, as consistent with his theory of rewarding positive responses, thereby encouraging repetition of them.

Above all, Mrs Hilton has a high level of rapport with the children as she relates, where she can, the story world to their experience. This is an area explored more deeply in Sequel I at the end of the chapter. At one point, a little later, she says: 'Do you know, when I got home from the concert last night, there was a telephone message for me to say that my cousin had had a little baby boy, but he wasn't born in a stable.'

Mike: Where was he born?
Mrs H.:   He was born in a hospital. That's nowadays, that's probably where we shall find babies being born. Certainly not in a stable.
Child: I was born in a hospital.

The children, who are, of course, familiar with the story, respond to the teacher's prompting with enthusiasm and energy. Mike, meanwhile, has picked up a copy of Grimm's fairy tales and is now sitting above all the others on a cupboard, turning over the pages of this book,

*See the article by B. F. Skinner, 'The science of learning and the art of teaching', in E. Stones (ed.), *Readings in Educational Psychology* (Methuen, 1970). This is a reprint and abridged version of Skinner's original article of the same title in *Harvard Educational Review*, vol. 24 (1954), pp. 86–97.

but missing nothing of the Christmas story or the pictures in the teacher's book. He looks at the picture of the three wise men and exclaims:

Mike: Black man! Bat man! That black one was in the middle and now he's in the front.

Mrs H.:   Oh, yes. Well, they must have altered that. Yes, you're right, Mike. Well done!

The story continues and Mrs Hilton takes the opportunity, where it easily presents itself, as it did in the tale of the torn book, of developing or reinforcing the children's sense of morality. At one point a child says:

Child: I got some...I...I...I stole some treasure...two treasures.

Mrs H.:   You stole some treasure? That's not very good, is it? You don't steal things.

Child: You mustn't steal money from the bank.

Mrs H.:   You mustn't steal money from anywhere.

Child: That's bank robbers. That's bank robbers.

Children: *(General hubbub)*...robber...bank...terrible...bank ...I'm in the bank.

For a short while the Christmas story has to compete with the rival claims of bank robbers. It's touch and go for a moment, but the 2,000-year-old narrative reasserts itself (or the teacher has her own way). The story comes to an end. The picture book is put back on the shelf and Mrs Hilton says, 'Shall we sing "Away in a Manger?"'

Mike: No.

Children: Yes.

Mrs H.:   Not now, dear. Sit up. *(Various children's voices.)* Yes, I know. Oh, just a minute, please. Let's wait for Mike, shall we...*(unintelligible)*...Well, yes, he knew where I wanted to put it, actually. Thank you, Mike. That...Stand it up, that's it. Good boy. Come on, then. Dear, oh, dear. Come on, Andrew, sit down. Right. Stephen, will you... Ready...

Children and Mrs H. *(singing)*:
> Away in a manger, no crib for a bed,
> The little Lord Jesus laid down his sweet head.
> The stars in the bright sky looked down where he lay,
> The little Lord Jesus asleep on the hay.

Mike *(running his finger up and down the page)*: Up and down up and
          down up and down.
Children and Mrs H. *(singing)*:
        The cattle are lowing, the baby awakes,
        But little Lord Jesus no crying he makes.
        I love thee, Lord Jesus, look down from the sky,
        And stay by my bedside till morning is nigh.
Mike: Up and down up and down up and down.
Mrs H. *(to a child)*: You don't know 'The Cattle Shed'? Well, you shall
        sing it, you shall sing it. Put your hands together. Close your
        eyes.
        Thank you, dear God, for sending
Mike: Thank you, dear God
Mrs H.: Shall we just listen, Mike, please.
        Thank you, dear God, for sending baby Jesus to us at
        Christmas time. Help us to think of all babies and be kind to
        them.
Children: And be kind to them.
Mrs H.: Bless mummies and daddies and sisters and brothers and all
        the others in God's great family.
All: Amen.

After this prayer, which will be echoed at the end of the day, there
are two more short carols.
All (singing):
        Cattle shed, cattle shed,
        That's where Jesus lay;
        A manger bed in a cattle shed
        Was his shelter on Christmas day.
Mrs H.: That's lovely. You did do well. Well done! Let's sing erm . . .
Mike: 'Away in a Manger'.
Mrs H.: No. We've done 'Away in a Manger'. 'On a Lovely Christ-
        mas Night'. Right?
        All *(singing)*:
        On a lovely Christmas night
        Shepherds travelled far;
        Seeking baby Jesus,
        Following a star.
        Shepherds came to Bethlehem,
        Happy angels sing;
        Found a little manger
        And a new-born King

It is plain that Mike is a dominant character. He has already shown
several instances of initiative and leadership and is to show many more
as the day proceeds. I doubt if he has missed one word that has been

spoken. He has finished sentences begun by Mrs Hilton; interjected comments; asked questions; answered many, both right and wrong; made suggestions; been quick to do classroom jobs, such as making visible on top of the blackboard the picture book which Andrew had wrongly placed.

As an extrovert, divergent, independent person, he could on so many occasions, have been squashed by his teacher. Constantly in conflict and nagged *ad nauseam*. Instead, his energies are skilfully channelled and put to good use with an art which conceals the art. His antics with another teacher later this afternoon will highlight the expert handling he is receiving now from Mrs Hilton. To one teacher he is a lively and likeable leader; to the other, a pest.

King (1977) comments perceptively on the indirect techniques of social control used by infant teachers. His description monitors Mrs Hilton in an uncanny way.

> Little shaming and blaming are used. The verbal methods used instead include the no-need-to-answer-question, e.g. 'Are you getting on with your work?', said to someone obviously not doing so, and complete the sentence, e.g. 'And when we've finished our paintings we must?' ... pupils chorus, 'wash our hands.' Children quickly learn the nuances of meanings in the teacher's voice. These include the 'now we are going to do something exciting' voice, the 'slightly, aggrieved sad' voice, and the 'I am being very patient with you' voice (examples, perhaps, of restricted codes). Infant teachers also show professional equanimity, they are not upset when someone wets the floor; and professional affection, shown in their smiling faces and physical contact with children, holding hands and lap sitting, and in their use of endearments.

Only half an hour has yet gone by, and many of these features have been seen.

At 9.30 a.m. the children move to various tables for different activities. Andrew tries valiantly to approach a seat from under the table. As he comes up, rather like a bemused pot-holer, Mike, ever vigilant, squashes his face with his hand. It has the window pane effect of flattened nose and crumpled lips as he says, 'No. No. This is Billy's seat', and so it turns out to be.

There are three tables, each with about seven children. One group is finishing parental Christmas presents. Another is involved in a brick-building exercise whereby they fit together five small blocks, draw the shape on a piece of paper and write down the number of blocks. Mike's group is arranged as shown in Figure 1.1.

The children in this group are now involved in a matching exercise designed to encourage the skills of one-to-one correspondence; visual

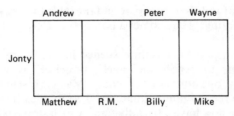

Figure 1.1

discrimination; sorting into sets; colour differentiation, and to develop some awareness of key terms, such as *more, less, greater, as many as, how many*. Plastic objects such as pigs, dogs, spanners, Land Rovers, are to be sorted according to colour or kind into a plastic tray, divided up into different compartments for the purpose. Mike settles down quickly to the work, making car noises as he plays with one of the racing cars, while sorting his objects into identical pairs. At one point, Peter addresses Wayne as 'You bloody pitch', with a change of 'p' for 'b', it could reflect his father's language.

Until now, the children have completely ignored my presence, either in the classroom or in this group. Having had a student teacher for the previous six weeks, they are apparently used to relative strangers. In any event, their own activities are much more interesting and engaging. And it allows me to record their activities more or less uninterrupted.

Led by Andrew, ('itinerant' in fact as well as designation having, at the age of 5, already attended schools in Scotland, Wales and Lincolnshire), four of the children in this group now decide to use their little plastic objects to play Cowboys and Indians. The green horsemen are lined up in battle formation and the children shoot each other with gun-shaped fists and fingers. Mrs Hilton works, for the moment, with the gift-making group, then, aware of these diversions, comes over to convert the children away from Cowboys and Indians and back to the matching task. Such rapid change of focus of attention by teachers will be familiar to all with experience. Philip Jackson (1968) found in one study of primary school classrooms that 'the teacher engages in as many as a thousand interpersonal interchanges each day'. Such an integral part of the job presupposes flexibility and sensitivity.

Mrs Hilton returns to her former table and, within a minute, battle formations again take precedence. Wayne says to Mike, 'Eh! you can have that spear for stabbing', and gives him a little plastic hand-saw, which Mike, entirely absorbed, accepts. Andrew and Billy start snatching each other's objects and off goes Mike, previously protective, you will remember, of Billy's territory, round the table to wreak vengeance on Andrew, chanting: 'Here comes a bomber ... Here's the Long [*sic*] Ranger ... '

There is, momentarily, absolute silence in the room, such as is thought by some to denote an angel's presence, as Tracy comes through the door, one hour late for school. Michele is sent to the head-teacher with the revised dinner numbers. Twenty plus three.

Billy and Mike now have a friendly fight, which stops suddenly after two or three seconds, when Mike observes, 'Eh! Tracy's come' (two minutes after her actual arrival). Billy and Mike are instantly the best of pals again. Mike picks up a folded card marked PEAS, says, 'This is an Indian's tent', and tosses it at Jonty who passively accepts it.

There is a compulsive quality about these plastic objects. The games vary from Matching, to Cowboys and Indians, to Bombing Each Other, and the objects are excellent vehicles for the children's imaginations. Duller objects might be preferred, on the grounds that the teacher-initiated activity would then stand more of a chance, but I think this would be proved false. At this stage in their development fantasy is more powerful than reality. The children are using real objects as symbols, endowing them with several attributes, and this would seem to indicate the pre-operational thought stage identified by Piaget. The children are handling small pieces, manipulating them into different relationships. When they have had adequate physical experience of this kind, they will, without immediately losing their interest in such activity, become more able to manipulate symbol and thought, where previously they could only deal in objects. The very process of reading involves such a transition, from the object to the word, which is a symbol, a conjuring up, of that object in the mind's eye.

There is, thus, intrinsic and extrinsic value in play itself which, as we know from Susan Isaacs's work (1930), can often bring about learning and thought and personal development of a high order.

The value and potential of the kind of play which leads to educational development is well summarised by Parry and Archer (1975):

> Play enables the child to test his competence in many ways without fear of failure, and this in turn builds up his concept of self and self-esteem. He faces problems in play and learns how to overcome them, since play provides an outlet for his strong feelings. He learns about his relationships with other children through sharing experiences with them, making friends, and observing how other children behave. He suffers experiences connected with being a boy or a girl, a leader or a follower, older or younger, stronger or weaker. Play encourages a child to use language, by providing a variety of first-hand experiences which stimulate him to develop skills which are necessary to cope with the complex world in which he is growing up.

Any teacher, like Mrs Hilton here, must make a judgement, in each instance, as to which kind of play is educational and which is merely time consuming. The work of Barbara Tizzard (reported in *The Sunday Times* 30 July 1978, commenting on a *New Society* article) clearly attempts to differentiate between these two. Free play can have the benefits outlined above by Parry and Archer. Equally, planned and careful, sensitive, professional intervention by the teacher should occur.[1]

At 9.55 a.m. Mike takes his tray off to Mrs Hilton who says, 'Good boy, Mike. That's splendid. There are one or two more down there'. He returns to the table and, within half a minute, he and Billy have a fight, actually punching each other. Mike says, 'I'm not going to play with you when we go out. I'm going to play with Wayne'. The teacher speaks patiently to the fighters and they calm down.

The apparently anti-social behaviour which has occurred so far – fighting, squabbling, pushing, bombing no less – may appear more serious when recorded in print than it seemed at the time. Perhaps these young children do not have the language to negotiate personal transactions and need to resort to physical contact which, within the context of this reception class, does not seem particularly inappropriate. Certainly, Mrs Hilton appears often to act on the behaviourist assumption that many of the misdemeanours may be ignored and they will die away, given time and the right atmosphere. Like Argos, she is well aware of everything that is happening in the room, but chooses her encounters selectively, rarely rebuking directly, for that would highlight the fault. Instead she diverts combatants into more acceptable forms of behaviour, by turning their attention to their tasks.

She now comes to join our group and asks Mike to show her two cars. This he does.

Mrs H.: Billy, will you show me three little pigs?
(Billy, hesitantly, counts three pigs into her hand.)
Mrs H.: Peter, you give me four little dogs.

Mike interrupts and counts six dogs into her hand, some blue, some red. The fact that he refers to one of them as yellow suggests that his understanding of colours is not yet clearly established. Although intelligent enough, he may have missed out on some kinds of pre-school experiences.

[1] A rationale for various kinds of play, with many practical classroom examples offered, is to be found in a book produced in 1977 by a Schools Council Project team, entitled *Structuring Play in the Early Years at School* by Kathleen Manning and Ann Sharp (London: Ward Lock Educational, together with Drake Educational Associates). Another helpful work in this area is *Play*, by Catherine Garvey (London: Fontana/Open Books, 1977). It is in the series 'The Developing Child', edited by Jerome Bruner, Michael Cole and Barbara Lloyd.

Wayne counts out five houses into Mrs Hilton's hand. Andrew is asked for three cars. He gives four, then takes one away. Jonty is asked to give two racing cars to Matthew; she gives him four. Matthew is asked for five little lambs. And so on, with each child getting a turn, not only at developing his counting and discriminatory skills, but also at working with an adult and with other children, thereby developing those social skills of accommodation and co-operation, of give and take (literally), which, it is hoped, will eventually minimise unacceptable behaviour.

Each child obviously needs to put a finger on each of the objects and not take his eyes off it. Memory and recall cannot serve for physical and visual contact, and there appears to be a security in touching. At such a transitional, pre-operational stage as this (see Sequel I to this chapter), their answers are characterised by inconsistency. They are sometimes right and sometimes wrong. They appear to have, as yet, no firm grasp of number concept.

For a short while now Mrs Hilton varies the routine with a different kind of activity: 'How many boats have I got?' She holds up two boats ...five race horses...and so on. Each time, Mike is the first to answer, thereby indicating not only his relative alertness, but also one of the inherent difficulties of asking questions of a whole group. It is the weak who need the practice.

> Reception age children and those still at the pre-maths book stage need to have lots of varied sorting, matching and number experience. When they are confident and able in these early maths activities, the groundwork for starting the progression of maths cards has largely been done (Gloyn and Frobisher, 1975).

All the children are now asked to clear away their materials. This is another aspect of their socialisation and of the classroom ritual. It helps familiarise the children with their own immediate environment and it gives them a sense of responsibility in caring for materials and tools. Once again one is reminded of Mrs Hilton's unfailing courtesy towards the children, by the manner in which she requests Andrew to get a tissue for his runny nose.

For a few seconds Mike lies under his chair, flat out, counting blobs of white plastic on the floor. Then he joins the rest of the children in clearing up and walks in triumph, like a proud butler, carrying seven white plastic trays to where they are stored. A little girl stops him en route and says, 'You're my friend, aren't you?' but the overture is rejected with a shake of the head. He is the last to finish and the teacher, instead of rebuking him, says, 'How are you getting on? Have you nearly finished down there, Mike?'

Most of the other children are now in the story corner. They sing a finger rhyme and then talk about the weather. Mike has permission to go to the toilet. The children are asked what weather it is and Helen says, 'It's snowing. No, raining'. In fact, it is neither. She finds the card which announces IT IS CLOUDY, which it is.

Mike's excursion has taken one minute. He returns and Andrew is allowed to go to the toilet. Andrew returns shortly and another child sets off. A kind of chain reaction. Mrs Hilton knows that toilet visiting, like confession, is best accomplished singly.

All the children are now sitting down in the corner but Mike is the only one with a book ('Ladybird'). It is news time and they are talking about what has happened to them. Such autobiographical news sessions are common in primary schools, but diminish as children grow older. They give an ideal opportunity for the children to relate the words of home and school and for them to use language in a natural and realistic context in that they are speaking of concerns and interests close to their hearts. Above all, perhaps, the message is implicit that the children's own interests have significance and importance. They have a validity at this stage which, somehow, seems to be rarely fully realised in secondary school. (For some implications of this approach, see Sequel II to Chapter 6.)

Tracy is about to tell us of her lion hunt. Can that really be the reason for her lateness this morning? We shall never know, for she fails to say anything. Mrs Hilton exhorts her to think about it tonight and tell us tomorrow.

Mrs H.:   Has anyone else got anything to tell us?
Sean.:   Barry gave me a new car.

This comment is missed by most in the general hubbub, but Mike, apparently absorbed in his book, has heard it and repeats it.

Mrs H.:   Katy, what have you got to tell us? *(No response.)*
Child: I've got a goldfish and its name is Deborah.
Stephen: Daddy's got a car and it's orange, red and yellow.

The teacher accepts what each child has to offer and repeats each response, thereby reinforcing it and establishing it as a piece of knowledge to be mediated to the others. Jonty is now sitting on her lap as she continues to ask the children, 'What have you got to tell us?' If a child cannot answer there is a slight chorus from three or four braver spirits: 'He's too shy, too shy.'

Helen: My mummy says one has to sleep at one end and one has to sleep at the other end.
Mike: My brother sleeps down the same end as my end and my sister sleeps down the other end.

Mrs H:	How many live in your trailer?
Mike:	Five. There's me mum, and she's called 'mummy'. And there's me dad. He's called 'Uncle Mike' and he specially likes eating pheasants. My dad eats them swans and when they got them long necks he eats everything off it.

Teachers are, inevitably, recipients of much personal information, sometimes mundane and dull; sometimes bizarre and contradictory; sometimes confidential and even embarrassing. The role, which may in secondary school be that of sympathetic counsellor, or dispenser of justice, is here that of gentle interviewer or facilitator.

Matthew, who, meanwhile, has been playing with a mechanical toy, is asked to show it to the rest of the children 'Then he won't need to play with it all the time, will he children?' It is a crafty, professional ploy for capitalising on his inattention. Further evidence, if it were now needed, of Mrs Hilton's excellent management techniques. Matthew winds up the car and off it goes, much to everyone's enjoyment. We next see Katy's mechanical mouse, which chases its own tail, and then the children briefly discuss the difference between mice and squirrels. Every incident is an occasion for language.

Helen now goes to open door number twelve on the cardboard cut-out of Father Christmas. She tells us what is inside: 'It's a little Bambi and a little rabbit and some snow.' Mike, who has been 'assisting' Helen, is diplomatically asked by Mrs Hilton to 'do a little job for me', i.e. distribute the straws. This he does carefully, one at a time, out of a London souvenir tin, while Matthew distributes the cartons of milk. By such simple but positive actions is the notion of corporate responsibility reinforced. No gifts were ever more welcome. However, there is one short and Mike goes off with Helen to fetch another carton. Infant messengers invariably hunt in pairs.

Reflecting teacher language, a child says, 'Shall we have our prayers?' and they do.

> Thank you for the world so sweet,
> Thank you for the food we eat,
> Thank you for the birds that sing,
> Thank you, God, for everything.

From then on it's suck-blow into the milk cartons. 'Nicely, please', says Mrs Hilton. Sounds of contented sucking and sighs. Some children try to blow labels across the table with their straws.

At 10.35 a.m. the bell sounds for break and the children put on their coats. Mike tries to claim sanctuary in the classroom on account of a cold, but is informed, 'The fresh air will do you good'. A euphemism for 'out you go', but more positive. He duly goes out with the others and Mrs Hilton and I take coffee and cake (a colleague's birthday) in the staff room.

While some schools vary breaktimes according to their activities, or even allow children to choose their own relaxation periods, most primary schools order their day along fairly similar lines. A common pattern, as indicated by Hilsum and Cane (1971), is as follows:

School Starts	A.M. Break Begins	A.M. Break Ends	Morning School Ends	Afternoon School Begins	P.M. Break Begins	P.M. Break Ends	School Finishes
8.55	10.40	10.55	12.00	1.30	2.30	2.40	3.30

This pattern, if not the precise times, is reflected in the first six chapters in this book.

At 11.00 a.m. we return to the classroom, where the children are hanging up their coats, before moving to the school hall for singing around the piano. Initially they sit on the floor, but, when Mike elects to sit on a chair, four others follow suit. The hall is narrow, small and cold. There are some climbing frames at the side, a Christmas frieze around the walls, and a stage prepared for a concert (which occurred the night before).

The children sing the song 'Say Little Squirrel', an appropriate choice in view of the earlier comparison between mice and squirrels. Questions are asked on the narrative of the song, with Mike, as earlier, foremost in answering. In this kind of context, comprehension becomes a natural and sensible activity. When the children repeat the song, Mike takes off his shoe and inspects his sock. Then a new song for them to learn:

> Here is a snowman, big and white.
> Isn't he a funny sight?
> Let's make a snowball,
> Toss it at his hat.
> Off it goes,
> Just like that.

Mike elects to clap in time to the music and says, 'I was clapping at the end'. He was, in fact, the only child to do so and, for most of the songs that followed, he adopted his own individual routine. Music is that kind of liberating medium for adults, as for children; it permits an imaginative response in terms of physical movement of some kind. Some current research indicates that music will even provoke movement from a foetus in the womb. How much more so from young children, although none of the others reacted quite in Mike's individual manner, except in imitation of him. During 'Yankee Doodle Dandy' (the most popular song, along with 'Jingle Bells') he danced in time to the music. One other child followed his lead. During the singing of 'Mary Had a Little Lamb' he mimed playing a guitar and was imitated by two others.

However, these activities did not dull his other responses. For example, when the children had sung

> Merrily, merrily over the snow,
> Merrily, merrily sleighing we go,

they were asked the meaning of 'sleighing'. Mike was the first to answer and replied, 'Ski-ing over the snow'. During another song he led the matching of finger counting with the appropriate line:

> Five little jingle bells fell in the snow.
> Four little jingle bells fell in the snow.
> Three little jingle bells fell in the snow.
> Two little jingle bells fell in the snow.
> One little jingle bell fell in the snow.

What such a song may lack in drama and excitement, it makes up for in security and familiarity perhaps.

The songs, seven of them in all, were punctuated by instructions to the children with regard to sitting down, singing louder and so on, all done in a very gentle, courteous but firm tone. The children were reasonably attentive for the most part, with the exception of Eddie, who spent his time and energy in trying to squeeze himself between wall and piano, an activity he accomplished quite successfully.

The music lesson finishes at 11.30 a.m., by which time the children have, unknowingly, had experience of oral comprehension and language development, of rhythm and rhyme, of exercise of memory. In addition to any intrinsic attraction, all these are useful pre-reading activities. They have also been involved in an interesting and enjoyable corporate activity, as well as exercising specific musical accomplishments.

Mrs Hilton now gives instructions for the next session. The red group will first go to the toilet and then back to the classroom for a puzzle. The yellow table will follow this sequence, but they should have their reading books ready. Very young children seldom find it easy to retain a future set of events in their heads, or plan in advance on the basis of verbal instructions. According to Piaget, it will not be until the stage of 'concrete operations' (i.e. *c*.7 to 11 years) is reached that, with the establishment of the sequencing of events, concepts about time will be clarified. These children have as yet a very hazy notion of time, and need constant practice, of the kind that the teacher is here giving, at anticipating events. Constant explanations and predictions of future sequences of activity are, perhaps, not too common in infant schools. It is language experience which may be unwittingly neglected.

We are now back in the classroom for the last session of the morning, which is related to pre-reading and pre-writing work.

The children on one table are given papers with patterns which they have to continue. Such work will, it is hoped, develop left to right eye co-ordination; awareness of shapes; visual discrimination; sequencing. The patterns they are given are shown in Figure 1.2.

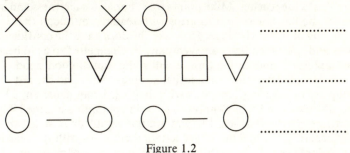

Figure 1.2

A second group is required to crayon a coloured line, following the arrows on the paper (Figure 1.3).

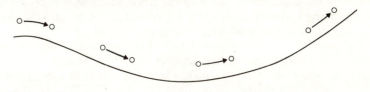

Figure 1.3

A third group is with the teacher responding to flash cards using words from the 'Happy Venture' reading scheme by Fred Schonell (Edinburgh: Oliver & Boyd). When news comes that some of the boys are playing in the toilets, that natural mecca for the more sociable in any school, Mrs Hilton sets off in missionary style to reclaim the lost, and soon returns with Mike and Billy, both of whom come skipping in.

Mike joins the flash card group and the teacher continues the activity of holding up cards with single words on them for the children to recognise. At this stage, it is a testing, rather than teaching, exercise.

here (no takers)

fluff (recognised by some children)

Dick (Mike says 'Jane')

Nip (Mike says 'ball')

Each time the children are wrong, Mrs Hilton laughs and says, 'No it isn't. What does it say?' Natalie, who has arrived from another group armed with her own reading book, despairs of such amateur guesswork and proceeds to point out to her peers the characters in the story – DICK, JANE, NIP, DORA, FLUFF.

The sentence on card, 'Here is Dick', is held up. 'Which word says *here*?' asks the teacher. Mike points to *is*. For all his alertness and intelligence, he has not yet got to grips with reading, although that is not surprising at this early stage. However, he does have the confidence to guess and, provided that can eventually be channelled so as to become less haphazard and unthinking, it will stand him in good stead.

Mrs Hilton determines on another strategy. Mike and the rest of the group are now each given cards with their Christian name on, a hardboard square, and a St Bruno tobacco tin containing a large lump of plasticine. If the flash-card letters are too small for some, then they may benefit from making larger letters themselves with the plasticine and seeing, perhaps, something of how the shapes are made up. At the same time, they will be engaged in something almost magical – a kind of creation of themselves out of an indistinguishable lump. Since Wayne is about to copy his name upside down, acting against my intention of trying to remain completely uninvolved, I turn his card the right way up, eliciting a look of utter amazement.

Billy says, 'I can't do my name', and Mike comments, 'Baby, baby, baby'. They elbow each other, smiling the while, and, after a few prods, return to the plasticine task, which grips them as they grip it.

Meanwhile, the arrow continuation and shape duplication groups carry on with their work, and all the children are actively absorbed for a quarter of an hour, a long time for 5-year-olds. During this time, the teacher has been constantly on the go – giving instructions and advice to individuals; focusing attention on the task in hand; moving from group to group and child to child, with the concern of an Olympics coach.[1] She remains courteous and pleasant, without being sentimental; firm and clear-headed, without bullying or nagging. The organisational skills and personal qualities required of a good infants teacher are quite considerable.

At 12.01 p.m., junior school prefects arrive heralding news of dinner and, with such an incentive, the children clear their desks remarkably quickly. A hundred and twenty children stay for school dinner and, such is the limitation of space, that classrooms and corridors have to be used, despite the intense cold. Over the decades, many schools have grown accustomed to tolerating unacceptable conditions.

While the preparations were being made, I talked with Mike for a

[1]A most helpful book which is full of practical pre-reading ideas for the teacher is *The Development of Reading Skills* by Frances Ball (Oxford: Blackwell, 1977).

few minutes, recording the conversation on tape. Billy was with us in the staff room, as moral support for Mike. It was strange that such an apparently extrovert and confident boy as Mike should have needed a companion, but he certainly was not going to talk without one.

The purpose of the chat was to learn a little of Mike's home and family, and it emerged that he lived in a white trailer, which he preferred to a house, with brother Peter, sister Chérie, mother (Aunt Jean) and father (Uncle Mike). In answer to my question about what he had done in school during the morning, he told me of a fight he had had some time earlier in which he and Billy and Eddie were matched against 'the big boys . . . the very big boys', and everyone won. Such information was obviously of much greater significance than anything that had happened in the classroom, and the only thing that he could or would recall from the morning was that Tracy had come in late. It is strange how odd incidents remain in the mind.

Telling me that his favourite dinner was jam on toast, we ended our somewhat bizarre conversation with an exchange about the preferences of his dad.

Mike: Me dad likes pheasants the best.
R. M.:   Yes, I heard you say your dad likes pheasants *(i.e. earlier in the morning in class)*. Does he catch them himself?
Mike: No. He kills them with these wheels.
R. M.:   How does he do it? How does he kill them?
Mike: Look. Look. He don't bib his horn. You just go . . . He just, he just let his motors run at them at them . . . when it's very far he goes brrrrrh!
R. M.:   And that kills the pheasants?
Mike: Yeah. He killed two this, four that time with one . . . one wheel . . . two went on his back wheels, two went on his front wheels.
R. M.:   Dear. Four pheasants.

This is a subject near to Mike's heart and he talks with enthusiasm and energy, describing the pheasants' manner of Boadicea-type death quite graphically. Language which closely involves the speaker is almost invariably richer, more vivid and more interesting. It also reveals more of the self. As Nancy Martin writes (1976):

As individuals we have to assimilate our experiences and build them into our continuing picture of the world; as social beings we need to legitimate the world picture we are continuously constructing and maintaining. So we hold out to others – in talk – our observations, discoveries, reflections, opinions, attitudes and values, and the responses we receive in the course of these conversations profoundly affect both the world picture we are creating and our view of ourselves.

Such a process as this is easier to observe in one's own very young children than in one's pupils, and there are parts of the statement we have to take on trust anyway. However, we are probably justified in believing that, as he talks and as he listens, this kind of assimilation and accommodation is occurring in Mike's mind throughout the day. The processes are two sides of the same coin, and operate simultaneously. The term 'assimilation' describes the adaptation by the mind of phenomena in the environment so as to render them capable of being absorbed into one's consciousness. 'Accommodation' refers to the actual incorporation of those new experiences.

After ten minutes' conversation, we are back at 12.15 p.m. in the classroom, where the tables have been laid for dinner. One teacher is using the waiting time in hearing a child read. Another teacher is doing finger rhyme songs with the rest of the children, 'hands and fingers/ knees and toes ... '

At 12.20 p.m. we all sit down to a lunch of mashed potatoes, sausages, beans, bacon; followed by apple pie and custard. I am sitting with Sean, Tracy, Katie, Peter, Stephen, Mike, Billy, and we chat about school and home, food and television, before getting caught up in a 'Can you do this?' sequence, i.e. we offer to each other for imitation ever more complex finger contortions.

After dinner the children play outside in the asphalt playground and I talk with the headteacher who, like many in schools, constantly has his break interrupted for a thousand and one reasons.

At 1.25 p.m. the class reassembles and, for a few minutes, most of the children play with toys and are supervised by the ancillary dinner lady. It is a useful settling-in period for the children to become adjusted once again to the classroom via the security of familiar and loved objects such as toys, as well as being part of their social education.

The class is to be taken for the first part of the afternoon by another teacher, Mrs Champion, an elderly, silver-haired, rather stately lady. The children are ready, grouped in the story corner, when Billy's father arrives to take him off to his grandmother's, some 120 miles away in Doncaster. It is a sudden, and perhaps permanent, move. So he misses the tale of Rodney, the hamster, who eats a good deal and likes wandering about the kitchen. This is an appropriate post-prandial story in which the children are absolutely absorbed, as they often are by fantasy about pet animals.

The food motif is continued in the poem of Mary Jane and her rice pudding by A. A. Milne. It is recited solely by Mrs Champion, who is concerned to promote skills of clear diction and elocution.

It is difficult to say how appropriate such verse is, for children like the strangest things. It has rhythm and structure, and allows scope for a reasonable intonation range. But, apart from the weakness of at least two of the rhymes, its chief problem seems to be that it echoes a middle-class, early-twentieth-century world, remote from this one. Its language and context are foreign to Mike and his peers. Moreover, it does not say very much of interest.

Furthermore, reception-age children do not listen easily unless they are physically involved in some way. So, from poetry to mime, and the children stand around the teacher holding up imaginary dandelion flowers, which they blow when appropriate for the words.

> One o'clock, two o'clock, three o'clock, four;
> I've got a fairy clock close to my door.
> Five o'clock, six o'clock, seven o'clock, eight;
> I blew and I blew and I found it was late.
> I blew and I blew till I counted to ten,
> And now I begin all over again.

The rhyme ends and the children have almost blown themselves into extinction, such is the enthusiasm of willing participants, who practically need to be protected from themselves. In fact, they are becoming rather restless and noisy, and the tape recording of the next poem is only partially audible. The problem is, again, their lack of involvement in what is a monologue, recited without pictures, and with physical actions related only tenuously to a difficult text. The poem, 'The King's Breakfast', is again by A. A. Milne, and both may be found in his volume, *When We Were Very Young*, published by Methuen. The mistaken substitution at one point by Mrs Champion of 'Dairymaid' for 'Alderney' only exacerbates language problems which are taxing enough anyway.

Mike, all this while, has been following the teacher with his eyes and performing such actions as there were with his hands, but he does not know the words. It is a similar pattern to that he adopted during the morning's music in the hall.

He is given permission to go to the toilet and, on return, decides to seek his own amusement among the coats hanging on their pegs. While the other children are involved in a variety of poems and mimes – banging imaginary cymbals on the march; hammering 'bing, bang, bong' on the floor; reaching up into the air and down to the ground, as teddy bears; walking about chanting 'tick, tock, tick, tock'[1] – Mike is hiding away behind the cupboard, moving in and out of the coats, lying on the floor beside a box.

---

[1]Useful collections of infant songs, finger plays and rhymes are *This Little Puffin* by Elizabeth Matterson (Harmondsworth: Penguin, 1969) and *40 Action Songs and 40 Finger Plays* (available from Pre-School Playgroups Association, 87A, Borough High Street, London, SE1).

Three or four other boys follow his lead, forming an energetic if, as yet, rather cautious splinter group. Observing this withdrawal, or diversion, of labour, Mrs Champion remains very patient throughout, occasionally retrieving one of the recalcitrants, only to lose another. Her class is disintegrating and she adopts the efficacious tactic of dramatising 'Twelve Currant Buns in a Baker's Shop'. Under the guise of seeking *more currant buns*, i.e. children to take parts in the narrative about to unfold, she manages to retrieve most of them. The promise of physical involvement wins over all but the hard core of coat dodgers and the song begins.

> Twelve currant buns in a baker's shop,
> Nice and round with sugar on the top.
> A boy came in, with a penny one day,
> Bought a currant bun and took it away.

A child, alias a currant bun, is led away beaming with pleasure, and the song runs its inexorable course for twelve verses, much to the delight of all but the two or three deviants. One of these is Mike, and another, 4½-year-old Peter. This boy had been very quiet all morning, but became quite lively during the coat campaign, enjoying himself, finding his feet, and getting acclimatised. It is a credit point to salvage from the afternoon session so far. Some of the children would obviously enjoy, and benefit from, a large play area where they could hide – a Wendy House or its equivalent.

Towards 2.20 p.m., the children are becoming particularly buoyant and the titles of the last two songs assume an ironic significance: 'Where Are You? Where Are You?' and 'I Hear Thunder. I Hear Thunder'. However, ten minutes later, having donned cardigans, jumpers and anoraks, they are out in the playground, where they need to be.

The benefit of such a break is clear at 2.45 p.m., when the children reassemble with Mrs Hilton for the last session of their day. They are spoken to courteously but firmly and, duly chastened (such news and noise travels fast), sit in the story corner to await further developments.

A similar sequence of activities to that before break now begins, with the exception that all the children act, sing, mime, move, as a group, fully integrated into the activity. They are the same children, but not the same, such is the effect of teacher on pupils and the interaction between them. There are no coat dodgers now, no noisy wanderers, as they all go through their paces and sing 'The Farmer's in His Den'; 'Fair Rosie was a Lovely Girl', 'Here We Go Luby Loo'. Mike plays a major role now in these dramatisations, galloping around the circle as a prince; weaving in and out as an elephant; giving Stephen a kiss. When a messenger comes in for a brush and pan, Mike, quick as a lizard's tongue, darts off to get it for her. 'Thank you, Mike. That was very sensible', says Mrs Hilton.

Then, at 3.15 p.m., came one of those golden moments in an infants' classroom, when any unoccupied adult who is present might meditate for a moment on lost innocence and the transience of human life. All the children were standing in the middle of the floor, with their hands together and their eyes closed, as they sang with their teacher the home-time prayer:

> Jesus taught
> That his children ought
> To forgive one another each day,
> And to give and take
> For his dear sake,
> So help us all we pray.
> And it's rough and tumble,
> Rattle and noise;
> Mothers and fathers,
> Girls and boys;
> Baby in the carry cot,
> Cat by the stove;
> A little bit of quarrelling,
> A lot of love.

Thus, the afternoon is rounded off as an occasion, with ritual and order, and a reinforcement of Christianity and morality, the last two lines of the prayer serving as an appropriate summary of what has happened this December day.

At 3.18 p.m., the bell rings and, one by one, the children either go out to find their parents or wait in the classroom to be collected. It is a natural, regular and valuable contact between parents and teachers. One parent asks about a reading book for her child. Another comes to complain. He tells Mrs Hilton that she has gone over time; that time is money to him; and that she should release his son immediately on the bell. Mrs Hilton is as courteous with this man as with her infants and explains about the danger of running straight outside into the road. The father is unimpressed and clearly appreciates nothing of the problems of buttoning coats, tying shoes, zipping up anoraks.

After a day with 5-year-olds, the adult world has reasserted itself.

Sequel I.   Religious Understanding and Piaget

Mrs Hilton's comments early in the chapter clearly indicate her intention to discuss the Christmas story at its narrative level. Many of the questions and comments are related to factual information from the Gospel accounts. The prayers and carols which follow these comments recall part of our cultural heritage, but are also intended to suggest something of a link between the Bethlehem story 2,000 years ago, and events here and now. Presumably, they are generally successful in this, although the level of understanding of this relationship reached by young children cannot be more than a dimly preceived one, based on the teacher's juxtaposition of these two acts, rather than any deeper awareness.

Children's religious thinking (i.e. normal thinking directed towards religion) has been interestingly explored by Ronald Goldman (1964) and his work is still highly influential. His researches indicate that, when questioned about Bible stories, children's thinking appears to reflect those stages which Piaget (1958) had earlier outlined. A brief reminder of these may be helpful and, for further information, reference could be made to some of the many summaries of Piaget's finding, for example, those by Lovell (1958) and Beard (1969).

Bearing in mind that the ages given here are merely approximate, and that the movement from one phase to another is gradual and tentative, rather than dramatic, the stages are as follows:

(1)   Sensori-motor (i.e. birth to 2 years)
This stage is not precisely relevant to the present discussion. It is the period during which a child, by movement and physical manipulation of objects around him, builds up his view of the world as containing objects which continue to exist even when unseen, and which retain their same shape even when seen from different angles. At the end of this stage, the child is able to work out in his mind how to do something before he actually does it. In other words, prospective actions have become internalised, anticipated in thought.

(2)   Pre-conceptual thought (c.2 to 4 years)
This is the period when individual objects are not yet appreciated as members of a class. A daffodil, for instance, may be recognised as a daffodil, but not as a flower sharing common characteristics with other flowers.

(3)   Intuitive thought/pre-operational (c.4 to 7 years)
Here there is greater internalisation of action into thought, but the child can only appreciate one relationship at a time (i.e. he thinks transductively), and this may lead to illogicality (in adult terms) and a preference for insignificant detail over and against important and relevant factors.

> This leads to unsystematic and fragmentary thinking, which in turn leads to illogical and inconsistent conclusions, because all the evidence has not been considered. But the major disability is the lack of reversibility of thought, the inability to work back from an inconsistency to check on the evidence in the light of conclusions reached. (Goldman, 1964).

Chapter 4 of the same book contains many fascinating examples of children's comments on various biblical narratives, and shows how the characteristics of intuitive thought, mentioned just now, reveal themselves. For example:

R. G.:   Why do you think the ground on which Moses stood was holy?
Pupil: Because there was grass on it.

A reflection, one imagines, of public park-type prohibitions such as KEEP OFF THE GRASS.

(4)   *Concrete operations* (*c*.7 to 11 years)

'Operations' is Piaget's word for actions which can be brought about in thought and which are reversible. During this stage the child is aware of sequences of thought in his mind and is capable of logical deductions. But his thinking is limited to concrete situations and personal visual experience.

R. G.:   Why didn't Jesus turn the stone into bread?
Pupil: He thought the devil might take the magic away. Jesus might have it hidden, and if Jesus used it, the devil would know where it was and take it one night.

(5)   *Formal operations* (*c*.12 to 15 years)

At this stage, all but the least able of children now have a much greater repertoire of responses in their minds (i.e. 'operations') to any thought or idea which presents itself. Generalisations may be derived from a number of specific instances. More abstract concepts may be grasped.

R. G.:   Why was Moses afraid to look at God?
Pupil: The awesomeness and almightiness of God would make Moses feel like a worm in comparison.

It will be plain that any teacher who tries to take account of Piaget's thinking is going to find his practice radically affected. You do not knowingly attempt to teach children what they cannot understand. Therefore, according to Goldman, you 'avoid instruction in ideas far too difficult for the child to grasp'. You do not seek to 'reinforce crude immaturities but to wean the child away from them; and, while allowing a child's religion to be childish, will prepare him for a more critical and rational approach to religion with which to face the years of adolescence' (1964).

This means, in practice, a more child-centred approach to the teaching of religion, with material appropriate to the conceptual understanding of the children.

Themes such as Our Home, People who help us, People who put things right (doctors, builders, gardeners), Friends, Farm animals and the farmer, are some examples of what might be attempted at the top end of the Infant School. This will be an enlargement of general experience with perhaps the occasional 'religious' focus, but would not necessarily come under a narrow 'religious knowledge' label on the time-table. (1964)

Such an approach has now been absorbed into much infant and junior teaching. Exposure to appropriate influences (such as those discussed in Chapter 5, Sequel I), with investigation of everyday concepts and life themes is acceptable to many teachers of young children (see Cliff, 1967), as will be evident from the chapters in this book. The fear amongst some teachers is that religion is being relegated to the substitute's bench, to be brought on when something goes wrong or when the match is being lost. In fact, in this kind of teaching, a religious viewpoint is seen to be at the heart of things. Religion is not transcendent, but immanent.

REFERENCES

Beard, R. (1969). *Piaget for Teachers* (London: Routledge & Kegan Paul).

Cliff, F. and P. (1967). *A Diary for Teachers of Infants* (London: Hart-Davis).

Goldman, R. J. (1964). *Religious Thinking from Childhood to Adolescence* (London: Routledge & Kegan Paul).

Also, for more practical classroom ideas, see

Goldman, R. J. (1965). *Readiness for Religion* (London: Routledge & Kegan Paul).

Lovell, K. (1958). *Educational Psychology and Children* (London: University of London Press).

Piaget, J. and Inhelder, B. (1958). *The Growth of Logical Thinking* (London: Routledge & Kegan Paul).

For further information about the changes in religious education thinking which have taken place since Goldman's work, see:

Grimmitt, M. (1973). *What Can I Do in R.E.?* (Mayhew-McCrimmon).

Holm, J. (1975). *Teaching Religion in School* (London: OUP).

Chapter 2

Rashda, Aged 6

I saw the Indian no [sic] television.

THE SCHOOL

Rashda attends a large infants school of 350 children in a now decaying, residential suburb of an industrial city. Gradually, the poorer Edwardian houses are being demolished and replaced by smart council houses and flats. In this area the school is a focus for stability, although the demolition and rebuilding, with concomitant change and mobility, produces constant alterations on the school roll. Not merely in the names of the children attending, but in their ethnic origins and social backgrounds. It is not unknown for stray dogs to roam the streets and rubbish dumps, but the school itself forms something of an oasis, with its neatly laid out gardens and buildings contrasting markedly with the nearby untidy railway yard, where lorries off-load scrap. Not far away can be seen small factories and metal-smelting works.

The main school building is twenty-five years old, and a number of mobile classrooms and a nursery unit of fifty places have been added more recently. Eleven infants staff are complemented by three and a half extra teachers who cope with special remedial reading classes and English as a Second Language, the only occasions when children are grouped according to their ability.

The school intake is composed of 20 per cent white children, a slightly smaller proportion of children with West Indian origins, and a majority of children whose origins are Asian. In the main, these are of Sikh background, but there are also some Gujeratis, some Pakistanis, and some Indian Christians.

THE DAY

It is 9.00 a.m. on a fine, cold autumn day and the children whose turn it is (i.e. about half of all those in the school) have come straight into assembly, by-passing their classrooms, many fully dressed in coats and anoraks. This is one way of saving useful time in the school day. The hall seems large because the children are so small, sitting cross-legged in rows, with the choir on a dais, facing inwards towards the teacher in the middle, who is to conduct the service.

Rashda is pointed out to me, sitting with a smile, gripping one of the legs of the chair which the teacher of English as a Second Language is sitting on. Her name indicates Muslim culture. The family originated in the sub-continent, but Rashda herself was born in England. She is rather chubby, with dark eyes and black hair, done in two plaits, tied with orange ribbons. A fringe on her forehead sticks up as though it has just been washed. She is well dressed in a dark purple trouser suit, partially covered by a green cardigan. Her shoes are black, yellow and green. I am told that she had been ill the day before with earache.

The assembly teacher now asks, in a very quiet voice, to see everyone's hands. Silence descends immediately. It is a simple but highly effective ploy, and some such method is needed by all teachers, particularly when handling large numbers of children. She now asks to see everyone's face.

Teacher: Put down everything in your hands. *(They do so.)* Good morning, children.
Children: Good morning, Miss Francis.
Teacher: Good morning, everyone.
Children: Good morning, everyone.

After this formal and courteous beginning, we sing a hymn which, from one point of view if not another, might be thought appropriate for a multi-ethnic school. The children are accompanied by a member of staff on the piano.

> Jesus loves the little children,
> All the children of the world;
> Red and yellow, black and white,
> All are precious in his sight,
> Jesus loves the little children of the world.

Teacher: Hands together. Eyes closed. *(They do so.)*
            Let us pray together and work together to make our school and the world a happy, lovely place.
            Think of the children in your class and the teachers and the ladies about the school. Mr Morgan. The lollipop lady. Your mummies and daddies and nannies.[1] *(A coin drops.)*

---

[1] One could legitimately expect the children to understand this prayer, since its concerns are close to their experience and they know the people being referred to. One might even speculate on whether the reference to 'nannies' is intended to reflect the extended family influences which many of the children here will be familiar with. Often the language of prayers in school may represent sheer confusion to many young children. Witness the 6-year-old who prayed:

> Thy deliberately faith I full,
> Faith against almight worship God,
> And faith all unto you,
> Faith against they holy prayer. (Goldman, 1964)

It is a kind of computer's prayer, gone wrong.

	Amen.
Children:	Amen.
Teacher:	Do you all think of ways you can help people? Yes?
Children:	Yes.
Teacher:	Well, I shall be round the school all day, seeing if you are helping people. And, Class 10, *All day*!

This injunction to good behaviour is reinforced by the next hymn, with the children performing appropriate hand movements.

The wise man built his house upon the rock	*(Children place fist on fist)*
The wise man built his house upon the rock	
The wise man built his house upon the rock	
And the rain came tumbling down.	*(Hand-waving motion)*
The rain came down and the floods came up	*(Outstretched fingers moved*
The rain came down and the floods came up	*up in stages)*
The rain came down and the floods came up	
And the house on the rock stood firm.	*(Fist on fist)*
The foolish man built his house upon the sand	*(Waving hands)*
The foolish man built his house upon the sand	
The foolish man built his house upon the sand	
And the rain came tumbling down.	*(Hand-waving motion)*
The rain came down and the floods came up	*(Outstretched fingers again)*
The rain came down and the floods came up	
The rain came down and the floods came up	
And the house on the sand fell *FLAT*!	*(Loud clap)*

The loud clap, made by everyone with great enthusiasm, marks the end of the assembly.

Teacher:	You're going to have to watch me very carefully to see if your class should go out. *(She signals to one boy who stands up.)* If you're in the same class as this boy, stand up. *(No one moves.)* What class are you in?
Boy:	Class 7.
Teacher:	Oh! You shouldn't be here anyway. Off you go.

The routine is repeated, with rather more success, and one class goes out to the words and music of 'Baa Baa Black Sheep'; another to a verse from 'Humpty Dumpty', and so on.

Apart from the establishment of a respectful atmosphere, the sense of corporate identity and individual concern, and the calming influence at the beginning of the day, the assembly may well have achieved other aims too. Notice the valuable language activities which have occurred – the co-ordination of hand movements with appropriate words; the enjoyment of rhythm and repetition; the simple narrative with a clear sequence and ending; the reinforcement of verbs in the past tense; the reminder of well-loved rhymes, which are a part of the English cultural heritage. Such considerations are taken further in Chapter 5, Sequel I.

However, there is time to ponder on them a little now in the classroom as the children queue outside. The room is quite large, with windows on two sides, one side frosted and the other looking out on to the playground. There is a Wendy House in one corner and reading materials, including a lockable cupboard full of books, in another. A nature table contains a picture book about THE BULB, and labels such as BLACKBIRD'S NEST; ROSEHIPS; LAUREL; TANGY; GRANDFATHER; BLACKBERRIES.

Around the walls are various pieces of equipment and school work, including self-portraits with the children's names, to make identification possible; butterfly cut-outs, made and coloured by the children; a teacher-made colour chart with lists of months of the year, days of the week, and words for a story (such as: *girl, boy, witch, wizard, giant, castle, king, queen, prince, princess*). There is also a list of words with significant parts highlighted. For example:

hot   not

got   dog

In each case, the short *o* is printed in a different colour from that of the other letters. Its pronunciation is exactly the same in the four words listed. Such a presentation may reflect the influence of C. Gattegno (1962) and his colour-coding ideas. It certainly suggests a stress on phonics in the teaching of reading in the school. As further support for this material, there is a professionally produced alphabet chart, with letter, plus word, plus drawing, as shown in Figure 2.1.

f

fish

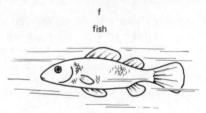

Figure 2.1

There is a table of maths materials, including boxes of work cards, counting equipment, magnets, model clocks, games such as 'Lego', and a cupboard of children's boxes, each neatly labelled with their names, and containing their own work. Also a cupboard of open shelves, with scissors, paper handkerchiefs, chalk, rulers, etc. Such equipment can serve as the springboard for a child's interest, or the facilitator of a task in progress. A stimulus balance is necessary. As Brown and Precious observe (1968):

> Care must be taken to see that the amount and variety of materials is not so great that the child is overwhelmed by the formidable task of choosing. Too wide a choice would seem, paradoxically, to be almost as limiting as too little and many teachers feel the need to withdraw certain things from the classroom and reintroduce them at what seems a more appropriate moment.

The teacher's desk is at the front of the room, to the side of the blackboard, and the tables are arranged in six groups with six chairs and one line of pencils (see Figure 2.2).

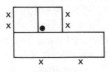

Figure 2.2

A boy of Indian origin comes into the room and looks at my note-book. 'All the boys and girls', he says, even though that is not what I have written. Strangely enough, he said exactly the same thing a week ago, when I came on a preliminary visit. Doubtless, it is his way of drawing attention to himself and establishing some kind of contact.

The rest of the children now enter, leaving their coats on a rack outside the classroom door. They sit on a mat in front of Mrs Parsons, a slim, quietly spoken teacher in her mid-20s, who now calls the attendance register, boys first, followed by the girls.

Mrs P.: Joseph . . . Stephen . . . Sukhjinder . . . Raj . . . Peter . . .
Amarjit . . . *(and so on)*.
Inderjit . . . Dawn . . . Kuldip . . . Jenny . . . *(and so on)*.[1]

Thirty in all, and in each case the child answers, 'Yes, Miss Parsons', not considered inappropriate for a married lady.

The practical purpose of calling the register is to identify absentees. Part of the hidden curriculum of such a ritual may well be to heighten the significance of the occasion, and to help develop a corporate identity, by making each pupil more aware, if only slightly, of his classmates.

---

[1] *A Guide to Asian Names* is available free on request from the Commission for Racial Equality, Elliott House, 10/12 Allington Street, London SW1E 5EH. Tel. 01 828 7022. CRE also publishes a monthly broadsheet.

During the marking of the dinner register there is a knock at the door and Tina enters, carrying a small brown bag which had been left in the hall by one of the boys. Some schools seem to have a constant traffic in such messengers, for a variety of purposes. Perhaps to trace lost owners, or lost articles; to bring items of news; trace a boy or girl; check milk or dinner numbers; advertise school events. The interruptions may be annoying for some teachers, and time-wasting for some pupils, selected because they are nuisances. On the credit side, are the potentially beneficial effects on the messengers trusted with the task. In any event, the transactions of any institution must go forward and, short of installing a classroom intercom system (such as is done in the occasional large secondary school), there seem few practical alternatives to human message-carriers.

Soon registers give way to more exciting possibilities, as the teacher says: 'Have any of you got raffle ticket money before you go?' One child has, and he pays up. Then Rashda and five others are off to a small annexe for thirty minutes of English as a Second Language, i.e. special daily language work for those children whose grip on English is tenuous or non-existent. Many live in at least two language worlds and switch from one language to another, when met at the school gates each day, perhaps twice a day, by parents or relatives. However adaptable and resilient, as children are traditionally supposed to be, one wonders at the effect on them of such abrupt transitions. What, too, of the effects on their parents?

The annexe is a cramped and cold space, partitioned off outside a classroom, but made to look attractive with plenty of pictures on the walls, cut-out figures, books, objects, a clock, and a weather chart. The language teacher, Mrs Matthews, a member of the city's peripatetic team, but based at this school all the week, is a slim, medium-sized, dark-haired person in her late 20s, with a quiet and efficient style.

First, there is a brief preliminary chat about the days of the week and the weather that day. Such talk of the weather may help to develop language and powers of observation by sensitising children to their environment. At this stage the language is simple and the judgement global, for example: 'It is raining'; 'It is sunny'.[1]

After this initial acclimatisation for the children, the main part of the session begins. It is a revision lesson to reinforce language structures involving the words *on, in,* and *under.* Each time a phrase is used it is highlighted by an action with an object, and the six children sitting round the table are consistently involved. Here are the opening exchanges, with the girls – Rashda, Inderjit and Kuldip – being referred to as R.; I.; K.; and the boys – Alwis, Sukhjinder and Balvant – being referred to as A.; S.; B.

[1]For more sophisticated ideas on the weather, appropriate for juniors, see the Schools Council Project materials *Science 5–13* book *Change, Stages One and Two* (London: Macdonald Educational, 1973), pp. 16–24.

Mrs M.:	Right. Here's a pencil. The pencil is in the tin. The brush is in the cup *(Actions and objects are used.)* The scissors, sc the scissors are in the box. The crayon is in the box. Now, Balvant, tell me about the pencils.
B.:	Pencils in the tin.
Mrs M.:	They're in the tin. Right.
B.:	They're in the tin.
Mrs M.:	Inderjit, tell me about the brush.
I.:	In the cup.
Mrs M.:	It's in the cup. It's in the cup.
I.:	It's in the cup.
Mrs M.:	Tell me about the crayon. Tell me about the crayon.
S.:	The crayon's on
I.:	The crayon's in the cup.
Mrs M.:	The crayon's in the box. It's in the box.
B.:	Box
Mrs M.:	It's in the box.
B.:	It's in the box. It's in the box.
A.:	It's in the box.
Mrs M.:	You say it. Good. It's in the box.
S.:	It's in the box.
Mrs M.:	Good. Tell me about the scissors.
A.:	It's in the box.
Mrs M. *(whispers)*:	They, they. They're in the box.
A.:	They're in the box.
Mrs M.:	Right. They're in the box. In. Now all those things are in. In. In. Now then. Where's my hand?
I.:	On the table.
R.:	On the table.
Mrs M.:	Right. My hand's on the table. The picture's on the wall. That picture's on the wall. This picture's ...
B.:	On the wall.
I.:	On the ...
Mrs M.:	... on the board. On the board.
A.:	On the blackboard.'
Mrs M.:	My coat, it's ...
R.:	On, on ...
Mrs M.:	... on the peg.
I.:	On the peg.
Mrs M.:	The bin, it's ...
Children:	On the floor.
Mr M.:	... On the floor. It's on the floor. Right.
B.:	Where's that book?
Mrs M.:	Let's look at some cards.
K.:	Where's that book?

Mrs M.:	What book?
B.:	A book we made.
K.:	Me first.
Mrs M.:	Ah! We'll finish that another day. Tell me about the saucepan *(holding an appropriate drawing on card)*.
B.:	Saucepan.
R.:	It's in the sink.
Child:	In.
A.:	In the sink.
Mrs M.:	It's in the sink, good. It's in the sink.
Child:	The sink.
Mrs M.:	Tell me about the mirror.
R.:	It's on the wall.
Mrs M.:	Good. It's on the wall. Tell me about the baby.
Child:	It's on the pram.
Mrs M.:	Where?
Children:	In the pram.
Mrs M.:	It's in the pram. Good. It's in the pram.
K.:	It's in the pram.
Mrs M.:	Tell me about the glasses.
R.:	It's on the ...
Mrs M.:	The glasses are on the sink. On. On.
Children:	On.
Mrs M.:	On the sink. Tell me about the orange.
R.:	It's on the glass.
I.:	It's in the glass.
Mrs M.:	In. Yes. In.
I.:	In the glass.
Mrs M.:	Tell me about the lamp.
B.:	It's on the table.
Mrs M.:	It's on the table. Good. Tell me about the pencils.
R.:	It's on the box.
Mrs M.:	Sh. Kuldip.
R.:	On the box. In the box.
Mrs M.:	They're in the box.
Child:	Box.
Mrs M.:	They're in the box.
R.:	In the box.
Mrs M.:	They
K.:	They're in the box.
Mrs M.:	They're in the box. Tell me about the dog.
R.:	It's in ... on the box.
Mrs M.:	It's on the box. Tell me about the clock.
A.:	In the box.
Mrs M.:	It's in the box. Good. Tell me about the telephone.

Set out on paper like this, these first few minutes may read like some ghastly laborious language treadmill, but this is certainly not the reality when the words are seen in their real context. The children obviously enjoy the session and are highly motivated, participating constantly. One can almost chart Rashda's progress, from uncertainty and diffidence, to a rather more secure understanding of the structures being revised, even though they are not yet entirely grasped. The teacher energetically moves about, relating language structure to meaningful action. She adopts the systematic structural/situational approach to second language learning which would be endorsed by many experienced in this field. If the structures are clearly established, so the argument runs, then varying items of vocabulary may be slotted in as required. How such an English as a second language (E_2L) programme may be developed with young children is described in Sequel I at the end of this chapter.

Notice the regular reward ('right', 'good', 'yes') and repetition of the structure to be taught, and the fact that the teacher's own language must necessarily be very precise and uniform. It would be matey but confusing to say to a child: 'Now, I don't suppose you can tell me what this is, can you, me old friend?' Imagine yourself as a second language learner, trying to cope with that in, say, Russian, or Serbo-Croat.

The teacher's words at one point may appear to be a summary dismissal of Kuldip's suggestion about the book, but in fact she allows time to be spent on the book later in the lesson. At this stage she wishes nothing to interfere with the particular language structure under consideration, as she moves from real objects to representations on small cards. Each time a child answers correctly when the card is shown (for example, 'Tell me about the saucepan'; 'It's in the sink'), he is given the appropriate card for his collection. Unlike the gambling casino, here every child wins something and, at the end of the game, they count out the cards as they return them.

There were two blemishes in the lesson which Mrs Matthews later pointed out to me. One was her undue emphasis in pronunciation of the key items, *in, on, under*. These should have been said with perfectly normal intonation and stress, rather than highlighted, as they were from time to time. This fault is not evident from reading a transcript, but the other one is, namely, the use of both singular and plural subjects in the practice examples (*pencil; scissors; crayon; glasses*). You will notice the confusion they cause. It would be better to use only singular or plural subjects, rather than mix the two. The fact that such points were noticed at all testifies to the value of occasionally taperecording and transcribing one's own lessons. (See the last suggested assignment in Chapter 7.)

After revision of *in* and *on*, Mrs Matthews moves on to the word *under* and now asks each child: 'Where are your hands?'; 'Where are your legs?' Alwis makes an interesting and acute observation. 'Like cutting', he says, 'like cut hands', indicating that his own hands have been 'cut off' under the table. It is what might be termed 'creative talk', based on real perception.

Then, the same procedure as earlier follows, with objects (e.g. a bag, a bin) and picture cards. This time, by using the present continuous tense, a greater narrative element can be introduced.

Mrs M.:	Right? The mouse is going under the gate. Now then. Look at the boy. He's going under the fence
I.:	Fence.
Mrs M.:	He's going...
I.:	Under the fence.
Mrs M.:	...under the fence.
I.:	Under the fence.
Mrs M.:	Now look at those boys. They're going...
I.:	under the...
Mrs M.:	...under the fence. They're going under the fence. Now look at that book. It's under the table. *(B. laughs.)* Look at...
S.:	I'm froze.
Mrs M.:	...the girls. They're sitting under the tree.
Child:	The table.
Mrs M.:	The girls are sitting under the tree.
I.:	Under the tree.
Mrs M.:	The girls are sitting under the tree. All right?

This leads naturally to a more extended narrative and the popular story, in the illustrated 'Ladybird' version, of the three goats in which, you will recall, the troll lived under the bridge...under the bridge ...under the bridge. Balwant, perhaps rather afraid of the picture of the ugly troll, says, 'He could that one could bash him up in the water'. It is one of several indications in this lesson of how non-English speakers call upon other sources for the language they use. Perhaps the comment reflects playground talk.

After more repetition of *under*, in various contexts, Mrs Matthews moves to the next phase of the lesson, again intended as reinforcement. The children are now required to complete drawings on cyclostyled sheets, putting a brown dog *under* the table...a blue book *under* the chair...a black cat *under* the television. As they complete the sheet, illustrated in Figure 2.3, working quite co-operatively in exchanging coloured crayons, they have an opportunity to practise rather different kinds of language, i.e. instrumental (see Chapter 6, Sequel II) for getting jobs done, and interactional, in the social context, as you will see from the exchanges, which follow the worksheet.

Write, draw and colour.

A brown dog is under the table

A boy is under the tree

A blue book is under the chair

A red pencil is under the book

A black cat is under the T.V.

Figure 2.3

Mrs M.:	A black cat, yes, and now a black cat under the television.
R.:	We can have brown cats if we want.
K.:	It's my black black cat.
B.:	Can you colour can you colour the tele?
Mrs M.:	Yes. You can colour the television.
K.:	Black and white.
S.:	I want yellow.
A.:	I got a yellow.
B.:	I got orange.
R.:	Purple.
S.:	Me yellow.
A.:	Noo!
R.:	You're a big one, you got big ones.

I.:	Here y'are, Rashda.
R.:	Thank you.
A.:	There y' yellow.
R.:	A yellow and a black.
S.:	Finished.
B.:	What we gonna do on a these?
Mrs M.:	Right. Now you colour in the rest of the picture.
B.:	What we goin a do?
Mrs M.:	Red pencil.
R.:	Red pencil.
I.:	I can colour it.
A.:	Miss, Miss, finished.
Mrs M.:	Right, Alwis. Can you write your name?
A.:	Yes.
Mrs M.:	Put your name at the top then.

There is a clear easing-up here, rather like putting on slippers after wearing tight shoes. The children are now freed from the earlier constraints involved in answering the teacher's carefully controlled questions. There is some initiation by the pupils, and more pupil to pupil interaction. It is almost the language of commentary – on their own actions and on the task itself.[1]

All through the lesson Rashda has been concentrating and involved, enjoying each different activity, and making oral contributions on no less than forty-one separate occasions. So many more comments than would have been possible in a full class, and highlighting one of the advantages of such small group language work.

I should like to think that all such non-English-speaking children regularly received language teaching of this kind which, given time, will pay dividends in terms of classroom and home relevance. If the children were left to their own devices to pick up the language as best they may, the result might well be a hideous mish-mash of words and phrases, such as one hears from some refugees who have been in England thirty years. Such pidgin English may indeed be glimpsed in the last exchanges of this lesson now that the children, no longer operating under strict language control, are departing one by one.

Mrs M.:	Bye bye, Alwis.
A.:	Bye bye.
B.:	There's black black
K.:	Black

[1]Much of the language used in this exchange would fall into Categories One and Two, i.e. 'Self-maintaining' and 'Directing', of Joan Tough's classification. See Chapter 6, Sequel II. For information on the spectator and participant roles in language, see Open University Course E 262, 'Language and Learning'.

Mrs M.:	Right. Now, when you've finished colouring in your picture, it's time for you to go. You can do the writing in the classroom, if you ask Mrs Parsons. Off you go then. Kuldip, have I got your crayons? Right. Bye bye, Kuldip.
K.:	Bye bye.
B.:	Here it is, it's finished.
R.:	I . . .
Mrs M.:	Right. Off you go then, Balwant.
B.:	I gone write my name yet.
S.:	This yellow?
Mrs M.:	You can colour the television yellow, if you want to.
I.:	Green, I got this colour.
R.:	Miss, I did finish it. Miss, I finish it.
Mrs M.:	Good.
B.:	I finish it
Mrs M.:	Right.
B.:	Look at this.
R.:	Inderjit
B.:	Where you going?
Mrs M.:	Thank you, Inderjit.

Their daily half-hour lesson is over, and they return to their class-room as Mrs Matthews prepares for the next six.

Rashda is now (i.e. 9.55 a.m.) back with her original class, this time sitting in a group around three double desks with Jindo, Balwant, Dawn, Narrinder and Darryl. Virtually all the children in the class are quite well dressed and appear to be well cared for. There are two girl twins of West Indian origin, identically clothed in yellow dresses, grey cardigans, black shoes, blue socks, white ribbons in their hair. There are two West Indian boys; six English girls; one English boy; and the remainder of the children are of Indian and Pakistani origin. The atmosphere in the classroom is of purposeful activity as the children copy from the blackboard sentences intended to reinforce work they had done with Mrs Parsons on the *i* sound, and the distinction between *i* and *j*. Some children are sitting working; others half standing; others kneeling; others waiting around the teacher's desk to have their work checked.

Rashda, with one shoe on and one off, struggles with flagging concentration. She has copied the teacher's sentences, but has not invented any of her own, which was part of the exercise. As an aid to invention and retention, each of the children has a small, alphabetic-ally arranged, word book in which to put words they encounter, for example:

fly	*football*	*fighting*
pen	*paint*	*pencil*
tie	*tall*	*tent*

Each letter having a separate page.

Rashda looks at her word book and asks others in her group to read words to her, which they do. Such co-operation is a common feature of the class, as is unsolicited entertainment. 'Look!' exclaims Darryl, 'I've got a loose tooth', and, with a tentative stabbing movement, proves his words to the admiration of two onlookers. Sometimes the bustle and activity exceed educational limits. 'Er, Joseph, if I have to speak to you once more . . .', says Mrs Parsons. The incomplete, unspecified threat is effective, and silence descends for a while.

It is 10.17 a.m. and Rashda goes off to stand in the queue for teacher's desk. There are eight children in front of her. Her work is shortly checked and Mrs Parsons stands with her hands up, palms outwards, and says, 'Children!' The children copy her actions and silence reigns in a second, as though vocal and physical systems are linked. The same superbly effective method, you will recall, occurred in assembly and it is interesting to find evidence of a common approach throughout the school. While every teacher will have her own range of such invaluable devices for calling her group to attention without undue fuss and noise, if colleagues share the same methods they are likely to be more powerful.

There is generally a clear relationship between teacher's noise level and class's noise level. One provokes the other in an ever-increasing spiral of decibels. Quiet teachers often make for quiet classes. Mrs Parsons explains quietly that the children are to put their books in their tables and prepare for milk, which they do.

Rashda now sits with arms folded, straining backward, with the index finger of her left hand on her lips, presumably exhorting everyone else to silence. No other child adopts this position. One by one, a boy or girl from each table goes to the front of the class and collects two bottles of milk at a time for his or her group. Rashda collects bottles, already strawed, for her group, serving herself last, as is the courteous custom.

Now there is industry of a different kind as the children sit sucking milk and eating biscuits and sweets. Concentration never wavers until all is gone, when each child returns his bottle to the crate and puts his straw and bottle top in the waste bin. Such rituals are the medium by which social learning occurs. As R. S. Peters comments (1966): 'Rituals as well as the use of authority are a method by means of which the importance of a practice can be marked out and children made to feel that it is something in which they should participate.'

What characterises a ritual seems to be consistency of detail, repetition of operation, with the understanding on the part of all participants (or, perhaps, on occasions, the teacher only) that its enactment has some other kind of outcome. There is, in other words, a prospective power behind the present action. 'Children have to be initiated into forms of thought and behaviour, the rationale of which they cannot at first properly understand' (Peters, ibid.). Hence the devices described throughout this book for gaining attention, exerting authority, organising children, enlisting participation and involvement, locating the individual within the community. A perfect example of this last device will be found in the next chapter.

The children on Rashda's table now show each other how to sit with arms folded, and again she adopts her individual Buddha-like stance before skipping to sit on the mat in the same manner. Mrs Parsons hands her a work book; she reads the name on it and takes it to its owner. It is a subtle way for reading practice to have an immediate practical outcome.

More children now have finished their milk and are occupying the mat in front of the teacher, who sits in her chair holding the hand of a boy at her side. Some children mill around the classroom coat rack, collecting anoraks before joining the others on the mat. To see them squashed together, but uncomplaining, on this small piece of territory reminds one momentarily of ominous visual representations, seen from time to time on television, warning of overpopulation.

That thought flits by as one of the boys spontaneously begins to sing 'One two three four five, Once I caught a fish alive', and the song is taken up by several others. When it is over, there are a few moments of silence as we wait for the bell. It sounds and, one by one, the children are given permission to go to the playground. On her way, one of the girls says to me, 'My big sister . . . after Father Christmas . . . we got toy roof . . . ' but we shall never really know what information she intended to convey. Another girl endows me with all her worldly goods, 3p, saying that unless I guard it 'someone will pinch it'. She will retrieve it after the danger of breaktime is past.

Mrs Parsons is on playground duty and has arranged for another member of staff to provide coffee. Mrs Heal duly arrives with the coffee and tells me of the interest aroused among the children by the tall sunflower which one of the teachers has been growing just outside in the garden. Apparently some of the children who have seen it talk of Jack and the Beanstalk, and I heard later that this innocent gardening idea had blossomed into a means of raising money for the school fund. Each child who participated in the scheme backed a sunflower seed for 2p. Named pegs in the ground linked seeds with their promoters and, at the end of a prescribed period of time, the backer of the tallest sunflower won the prize of a packet of felt-tipped pens and a colouring book. Not only did the scheme raise attractive sunflowers, useful money and considerable interest in growing things, it also gave the children opportunities for estimation and measurement in a matter close to their hearts.

The classroom is now empty of children, enclosed in a kind of echoing silence, heightened by the morning's bustle. The sounds of the playground – distant screams and muted shouts – can be heard over against the noises of metal being dumped and lorries unloaded. Schools and classrooms are dead places without their occupants.

At 10.55 a.m. the children are back in class and the remedial reading teacher has arrived to collect a group of six, of whom Rashda is one, for a short period of concentrated attention on reading. Mrs Renshaw is a teacher in her late 20s, of medium height and with auburn hair and freckles. She has a quiet voice and a warm manner. Off we go to another mobile classroom and, before the lesson proper begins, the children slide their ink-well tops backwards and forwards, chanting 'close . . . open . . . close . . . open'.[1]

Mrs Renshaw begins some letter recognition work. She holds up a card and the children call out the sound of the letter displayed: *a . . . buh . . . kuh . . . duh . . . e.* Next she uses a collection of neat, home-produced, pink cards, each with a drawing and a label: *dog, axe, egg, ambulance, boy, doll, elephant, baby, car, boats, arrow, bee, duck.* As each card is displayed and named, so the children cover up the corresponding picture on their larger master card which has eight sections. It is a form of word bingo, as the children soon indicate.

Mrs R.:	I'm going to give you eight of these. *(The children count out loud one to eight with the teacher as she distributes the cards.)* Now, I'm going to call out the sound and the word that's on the other side. If you've got the thing that I call on your card you cover it up. And the first one to . . .
Child:	It's like Bingo.
Mrs R.:	It's like Bingo. The first one to have them all covered up is the winner.
Child:	Just like Bingo.
Mrs R.:	This one?
Children:	*e*
Mrs R.:	For?
Children:	Egg.
Mrs R.:	Egg. Egg. Cover it up if you've got it. Cover 'egg' if you've got it.
Children:	*e . . . e . . . e.*
Mrs R.:	You've got an egg, cover it up. Cover it up like that. That's right. Next one.

[1]An ingenious book by John Gregory entitled *The Tinker and the Cobbler* (Oxford: Pergamon, 1967) contains poems, songs and music related to various classroom sounds such as ink-well-top-clicking; chalk-squeaking; shoe-scraping; ruler-twanging.

Children:	*a ... duh ... buh.*
Mrs R.:	For?
Child:	Ball.
Mrs R.:	Doll. Doll.
Child:	Doll.
Mrs R.:	You've got it, Joseph. Put yours on the desk. Put it on the desk.
Child:	Put it on the deks [*sic*].
Mrs R.:	Put your card on the desk. This one?
Child:	*cah.*
Child:	*kuh.*
Mrs R.:	*kuh* for?
Child:	Car.
Child:	Clock.
Mrs R.:	That was dog not doll, doll not dog. Clock. You've got it.
Child:	I've got.
Child:	I haven't got it.
Mrs R.:	Next one is ...
Children:	*a.*
Mrs R.:	*a* for axe.
Children:	axe.
Mrs R.:	axe.
Child:	Easy for axe.
Child:	Miss, I got it.
Mrs R.:	Draw that arrow. You've got axe, yes. That's arrow. Next one.
Child:	*buh.*
Mrs R.:	For? ... baby ... baby.
Child:	Ah! I nearly finish.
Child:	Don't look at mine.
Mrs R.:	Next one.
Children:	*buh.*
Mrs R.:	*duh* for daddy, daddy.
Child:	I've got daddy.

At first Rashda does not see what is required of her but watches the others and soon grasps the idea. She does not shout out 'I've got ... ', as others do, but quietly consults her card and looks at the cards of those near her. After one or two rounds the children take over from the teacher as callers and Rashda has her turn. '*kuh* for cat', she says, '*a* for apple' (and is corrected when the word is seen to be *ambulance*); '*duh* for dog; *kuh* for clock; *buh* for baby' (the picture is, in fact, of a boy).

She is guessing the formula without reading the words and needs help at breaking down a word into its constituent parts, something in which there will be practice later in the day back in normal classwork. In any event, it needs to be done carefully, so as to avoid the pitfall of separately pronouncing distinct elements which then do not add up to a proper word. *Duh . . . o . . . guh* does not add up to the word *dog*. If the method is to be used at all – and it may well assist good spelling and interest in words – it should be employed at the appropriate time, and not forced on children before they can cope with such phoneme separation. Bullock (1975) is wary and believes that we should go back to using traditional rhymes and jingles (such as were seen in abundance in Chapter 1). The Report's words, in para. 6.17, are worth quoting:

> What the variations within each phoneme have in common is some kind of preparatory position in the speaker's vocal apparatus, but this configuration changes as the sound is produced, depending on which sound is to follow. If, then, we teach a child how to pronounce a series of sounds and ask him to run them together to form a word he will indeed learn the trick of saying those separate sounds and of then saying the related word. But he has certainly not built up the word from the sounds he has pronounced first . . . The process is not yet fully understood by which children learn to imitate the sounds of speech and discriminate between them. To break up a word into what are thought to be its constituent elements does not, however, seem to us the best means of developing this process. We believe a better way is for teachers to rely upon methods that have a long history in the infant school but which have unaccountably fallen out of favour; namely, the use of rhymes, jingles and alliteration. These focus attention on the contrastive elements in words while avoiding the inevitable distortions of the more analytic approach.

Many teachers of reading, I imagine, would agree with the second point made by Bullock, regarding the use of rhymes, etc., but would be most unhappy about rejecting a phonic approach. Even allowing for the validity of the first point, it does not automatically follow that no value can then stem from a method based upon an apparently false premise. While such a seemingly illogical procedure is not generally to be endorsed, in the matter of reading there are so many unknowns and imponderables that a method which practising teachers feel is valuable cannot be easily set aside.

Meanwhile, Rashda continues to make every effort. She is quietly confident and assured, and smiles each time she reads a word. There is no fuss when she makes an error. The children, as a whole, are very keen and enthusiastic, often guessing words (e.g. *egg* for *elephant*). They are sharply competitive, each being concerned to win, and this is where the emphasis of the session falls, rather than on the actual reading. So much so, that occasionally feeling runs high, as in this seemingly Old Testament confrontation:

Joshua: You was teasing me.
Joseph: I weren't teasing you, you liar.
Joshua: You was.
Joseph: I weren't teasing you, you liar.
Joshua: You shut up.
Joseph: I don't have to.
Joshua: You shut up.

Having reached this impasse, the rest was, fortunately, inaudible on the tape.

At 11.10 a.m. the last round of the word bingo finished, with three simultaneous winners, and it is time to move on: 'Put your chairs [*sic*] and don't forget your watch, Surinder. Off you go.'

The children move to rejoin the rest of the class, who are now sitting on steps in the school foyer, watching the end of a television programme for schools on their black and white set, about a carpenter who is making a zither. The children participate by singing the words of the chorus, performing appropriate actions, such as sawing and hammering, and clapping in time to the music at the end of the programme. The song goes as follows:

> Here is the carpenter to make something new
> A saw and a piece of wood
> Now watch what you do.
> Saw saw saw the wood
> Saw saw saw,
> Saw saw saw the wood
> Saw saw saw.
>
> This is a wooden saw
> And each one is rough,
> You use a plane to make it smooth
> Until it's smooth enough.
> Saw saw saw the wood
> Saw saw saw,
> Saw saw saw the wood
> Saw saw saw.
>
> Now we've got a compass
> And a circle he can draw,
> And then he'll use a brace and bit
> And slowly start to bore.
> Bore bore bore the hole
> Bore bore bore,
> Bore bore bore the hole
> Bore bore bore.

Through the hole that's in the wood
He puts a special blade,
To saw round the circle
So a bigger hole is made.
Saw saw saw the wood
Saw saw saw,
Saw saw saw the wood
Saw saw saw.

Join the wood together now
But how will he begin?
He'll first pick up the hammer
And some nails to hammer in.
Hammer hammer hammer the nails
Hammer hammer hammer,
Hammer hammer hammer the nails
Hammer hammer hammer.

Next to the wooden box
A peg and some screws,
A screwdriver is the tool
That he'll have to use.
Turn turn turn the screw
Turn turn turn,
Turn turn turn the screw
Turn turn turn.

The last verse is rendered inaudible by the movement of other children, but it includes notes from the new zither.

Announcer: Do you know what the carpenter was making? It's a zither *(she plucks the strings)*. You have to be a very good carpenter to make a zither.

Singer: But you could try making a splinter. *(He demonstrates the sound of this simple instrument.)*

Announcer: Or a pair of claves. *(Again a demonstration.)*

Singer: And you could make a Jingling Johnny too. *(Another demonstration.)*

Announcer: And then you could use them all to accompany the carpenter's song.
Goodbye.

Singer: Goodbye.

Children: Goodbye. *(Music plays out the programme.)*

Television can be such a gripping medium that children are often completely captivated by a programme, good or mediocre. And to see television in school may, even now, be sufficient of a change to be regarded as a treat, and therefore respected all the more. Precisely what value a programme has is difficult to determine. Often they seem to be interludes within the school day, unrelated to anything else, but they can be used as a springboard for a variety of creative activities, or as a booster to work in progress. The lack of video-tape-recording equipment in most schools restricts viewing to prescribed times and this has a strait-jacket effect.

Rashda and her peers seem to enjoy the singing in the zither programme but one doubts its further language and cultural value, although the repetition of *say, hammer, bore, turn*, may help the non-English-speaking children. Clearly, no child here will be in a position to make the rather exotic musical instruments mentioned at the end, although older children might. (Sequel II at the end of the chapter offers sources for television material and programmes.)

It is now 11.18 a.m. The boys and girls line up separately and walk back to the classroom, where they continue with the sentences which they were previously working on, rather than use the opportunity to follow up parts of the television programme. Perhaps they will do so on another occasion, although infant memory spans are short.

Rashda is having her work checked at the teacher's desk. She is actually with Mrs Parsons for forty-five seconds and returns with two ticks against the sentences she has copied, but still without having written any of her own. A word from me to her:

R. M.:   Where's your daddy?
           (No reply.)
           Is he at the factory?
           (She nods her head.)
           Where's your mummy?
Rashda: At home.

She now writes: 'I saw Indian' in her book and returns to stand in the queue near the teacher's desk. I look at her number book while she is away and another girl, ever vigilant, asks me: 'Have you copied them?'

After three minutes in the queue Rashda returns to her desk merely to write her name on her word book before rejoining the teacher queue. Shortly afterwards she returns with the word *television* in her alphabet book and this enables her to complete the sentence, 'I saw the Indian no [*sic*] television', in a few seconds before returning to the teacher's desk yet again, this time with ten children to be seen before her.

I later queried this procedure with another teacher on the staff, who operated in a similar manner herself, although she had never done so in her previous school. She maintained that if she moved around the class from table to table, then it had a Pied Piper effect and children wandered about after her. At least if she was at her desk, she felt, they all knew where to find her. So, despite the apparent time-wasting involved, the staff clearly felt such a procedure was right for this school.

One boy in the queue says, 'Thomas, Thomas', and, having caught that boy's attention, dramatically stabs himself with a pencil and, in best Old Vic tradition, 'dies' on the carpet. No one is unduly disturbed by his demise; some children are mildly amused and merely smile. Perhaps he expires in this way quite often.

Some children are now doing simple addition sums from arithmetic work cards prepared by the teacher; others are still engaged on their sentences. Individuals make a point of checking on my movements. A girl approaches, looks at my notepad, satisfies herself there is no danger, and goes away again. A boy keeps wandering near chanting, 'I'm going by again'. One girl confides, 'Sometimes I get my sums wrong because I've got the wrong number'. A boy counters, 'Today I got them all right'. In the role of teacher, a girl asks, 'Are you doing your homework?' The situation is not unlike that of the anthropologist, who descends with camera and notebook on unknown peoples, to be treated with friendliness and mild amusement.

After three minutes Rashda has had her work marked. The *no* has been changed to *on* and a tick given. One is reminded of the 'pattern practice' for the prepositions *in* and *on* earlier in this chapter during the E_2L lesson, and of the three mistakes which Rashda made when using these words. Clearly, the differentiation between the prepositions *in* and *on*, and between the letter sequences *on* and *no* has not yet been established beyond all doubt.

She spends a moment at her own desk and then returns, for reason unknown, to the teacher. Perhaps she needs constant reassurance and contact; perhaps her concentration is waning; perhaps she has become inextricably involved in an unthinking process.

This time five others are in front of her, and the teacher is working steadily, thoroughly and unhurriedly. The children in the queue are generally well behaved, only one or two occasionally pushing or remonstrating. Others crowd around Mrs Parsons, leaning on her desk as she helps an individual. Two boys in another part of the room are sword-fighting with pencils. Without pausing in her work, and apparently viewing them with eyes in the top of her head, Mrs Parsons says gently, 'Joseph, what have you got there? Come and give me that book', and the combat is over.

Rashda returns after four minutes this time, with a sentence to copy: *I saw an insect crawling on a leaf.* Seconds later it has been done and back she goes, nine children in front of her. Quite clearly, she enjoys the queue.

At this point Mrs Parsons says, 'Children!' She holds up her hands. The children follow suit and again this piece of magic has brought instant quiet. The sixteen dinner children come out to sit on the mat for a minute, before going off to school dinner, while the others are allowed a little more time to finish their work. The mat has been established by custom in this classroom with distinct territorial status. However crowded this magic carpet becomes when the whole class is grouped on it together, no child will tolerate being so cut off that he has no physical contact with even a small part of it. There is power in the connection and the child who was adrift would feel himself an outsider, cut off from the life-raft. That seems to be one of its functions. To define, and thereby strengthen, a sense of corporateness. At other times it is a kind of staging post or launching pad, from which the children move to other activities. They appear to benefit from the security of a clearly understood logistic routine, and there is orderliness in this classroom without excessive, or even overt, inhibition. As adults, of course, we like our own territory to be clearly defined. Hence our habit of often occupying the same seat in a lecture room or church. The place seems to confirm our identity or, at the least, give us a familiar bearing on our surroundings.

It is now very quiet. Four or five children are working at their desks; six are queuing for the teacher; two or three are around me. One of these reads his own name on his book, three times: 'Jaswan Singh . . . Jaswan Singh . . . Jaswan Singh.' He is actually called Peter! When asked what he is to have for dinner, he replies, 'Pachati [presumably, chapati] and curry and tomatoes'.

Rashda is now with Mrs Parsons who elicits from her, with help, the sentence: *I put the milk into the jug.* Each word is said out loud as it is written in her book. Again the same sequence: return to desk; few seconds of copying; back to queue; now three children ahead of her.

This kind of activity and attainment clearly places Rashda in the fifth stage of what Gloyn and Frobisher (1975) identify as a progression of five stages of writing for children in a reception or vertically grouped class. Their description of this copy-writing stage indicates, however, Rashda's tenuous grip, as yet, on the activities normally associated with this stage

> where children draw and colour interesting pictures, have a lot to say about their pictures and can copy reasonably accurately. The 'news' or 'free expression' book is supplemented by copy-writing in maths and as part of the reading programme. There are also many opportunities for children to communicate through writing when pictures and models are displayed.

The Schools Council 'Breakthrough to Literacy' material offers ideal opportunities for such an experience-based approach to reading and writing.

The final version of Rashda's work, which earned her a star, is shown in Figure 2.4.

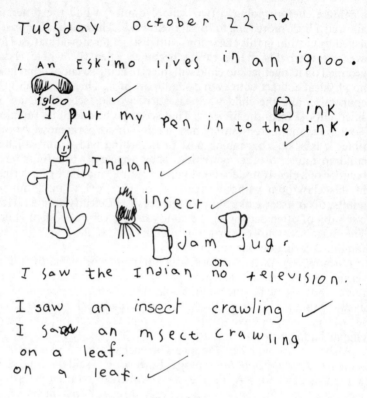

Figure 2.4

I ask her what she is to have at home for dinner and, after some hesitation, she quietly offers: 'Meat . . . carrots . . . drink water.'

R. M.:   Are you going to have potatoes?
Rashda: Potato in the carrots.

She says 'Bye bye', and is off home to her lunch.

It would be easy to calculate the number of minutes Rashda spent merely waiting for Mrs Parsons to check her work, and to assume that all such time had been wasted. It may have been. However, perhaps one could also argue that Rashda's concentration was, in any event, flagging as the morning wore on; that she would not have been able to sustain any more solitary effort; and that queueing up with other children has socialising benefits.

Lunch of sausage, chips, beans, bakewell tart and custard. I sit on a table of five reception-class children who regard me with awe. Ultimately, their fondness for beans overcomes their wonder but, even

I put jam on my
I pur jom on my
bread.
bread ✓

I put milk into the
I pur milk into the

jug ✓ Very good try
jug

★

Figure 2.4 *continued*

while eating, they continue to stare with silent inscrutability and my attempts at conversation fail.

1.30 p.m. The door of the classroom bursts open and, in a second, the children spill inside, full of life and vigour and, presumably, dinner. They put their coats on hooks and sit on the mat, preparing to answer their names. One or two children arrive late, looking rather pleased.

Mrs P.: Samuel.
Samuel: Yes, Miss Parsons.
Mrs P.: Mark.
Mark: Yes, Miss Parsons.
Mrs P.: Darryl.
Darryl: Yes, Miss Parsons.
Mrs P.: Balwant.
Balwant: Yes, Miss Parsons.

Mrs P.: Narrinder.
Narrinder: Yes, Miss Parsons.
Mrs P.: Raj.
Raj: Yes, Miss Parsons.
Mrs P.: Mark.
Mark: Yes, Miss Parsons.
Mrs P.: Sukhjinder.
Sukhjinder: Yes, Miss Parsons.

Mrs P.:	Harjinder.
Harjinder:	Yes, Miss Parsons.
Mrs P.:	Thomas.
Thomas:	Yes, Miss Parsons.

And so on. The girls' names follow the boys' and, when this ritual is over, all on the mat turn to face the blackboard on which are written two letters together – *sm* – as a starter for some phonic work.

Mrs Parsons asks for words beginning with *sm* and the first three suggested are: *mouse, Samuel, mud*. Then a child offers the word *smile* and this is written on the board. Next comes *smoke* and then Rashda suggests *something*.

Mrs P.:	'Something?' No, the letters aren't next to each other. Sukhjinder?
Sukhjinder:	Smith.
Mrs P.:	Yes, that's somebody's name, isn't it?
Child:	Smudge, because my Auntie Ellen at the shop has a cat called Smudge.
Mrs P.:	Oh! and that's the cat's name. Yes. Good.
Joseph:	Snow.
Mrs P.:	'Snow?' What letter is that?
Joseph:	suh.
Mrs P.:	suh and a nuh, isn't it?
Child:	Smell.
Child:	Dr Smith.
Child:	Small.
Mrs P.:	'Small'. Good girl.
Child:	Smack.
Peter:	Smack on your botties. *(Several children chuckle.)* Dr Smith.
Mrs P.:	We've had that three times now, you're not listening. Thomas?
Thomas:	Sums.
Mrs P.:	No. You're not thinking now.

At the end of the activity, which lasts about three minutes, the children repeat with Mrs Parsons all the words on the blackboard, going down the list and emphasising the *sm* sound: *SMile . . . SMoke . . . SMudge . . . SMack . . . SMell . . . SMith . . . SMall*. It is work to which they will evidently return, time and again, since the sound is by no means clearly identified by the children.

Most teachers today, as indicated earlier, would argue that the 'Look and Say' approach to reading needs to be allied, at the appropriate time, to such a phonic approach as this, where words are broken

down into their constituent parts, in order to be built up again. A kind
of Meccano set principle, with a child ultimately able to break down
and fit together varying sequences.

Next, the teacher holds up a pencilled drawing on cardboard of a
prospective puppet (Figure 2.5) of various geometrical shapes, and
questions are asked for three or four minutes about these shapes.

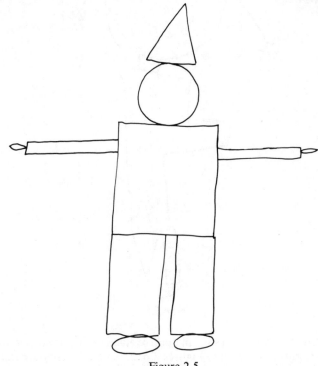

Figure 2.5

Mrs P.:	What shape is his face, Sukhjinder? What shape is his face?
Sukhjinder:	Round.
Mrs P.:	Round. What's another word?
Child:	Circle.
Mrs P.:	What shape are his legs?
Child:	A tetrangle.

After questioning, some children are allowed to colour the puppet
shapes on paper. Others must first finish their number work.

I ask Rashda to draw a picture of herself; of the teacher; and of me.

Figure 2.6

A little reluctantly she does so, in approximately one minute per drawing. The results are shown in Figures 2.6, 2.7 and 2.8. They are flattering to no one, but they do give sufficient information for Rashda to be assessed as slightly above average on the Goodenough–Harris *Draw-a-Man Test* (London: Harrap, 1963). This test requires the child to draw a man, a woman and herself. Each drawing is evaluated by totalling the number of items it shows, according to the check list (e.g. head, eyes, nose, nostrils, ears, mouth, body, arms, hands, legs, feet). An average of the three scores gives the total score and this can then be reckoned against chronological age. You will notice that Rashda's drawing of Mrs Parsons shows her with eight fingers, whereas the other two drawings reveal no fingers at all. Averaging out such items over three drawings permits account to be taken of bodily features which are only tentatively established in the child's mind.

Clearly, such a test can only be a rough guide to intelligence, since it

Mrs parsons

Figure 2.7

omits any assessment of language, reasoning and number, and it has come in for severe criticism. In fact, its omissions are, in a sense, its strengths. In my view, its very simplicity and unusualness make it worth using and worth recording.

Having disposed of this diversion, Rashda returns to serious work and settles immediately to a green sum card, standing up as she works, and using her fingers to count, along with the dots on the paper. She achieves two correct answers and three reversals, as the following will indicate.

2	+ 6	+ 2	=	10
3	+ 6	+ 3	=	21
4	+ 6	+ 4	=	41
5	+ 6	+ 5	=	61
1	+ 9	+ 2	=	12

Figure 2.8

Class 8 is now fully occupied. Some children are colouring in parts of the geometric puppet, with a different colour for each separate shape; others are working on a variety of sum cards; others are queueing again by the teacher's desk to have their sums marked. The door is constantly opening and closing, as people come in and out. Mrs Parsons says, 'Because you're all using such great big voices, there'll be quiet for two whole minutes'. And there is.

Rashda finishes her sums and has them marked. Whether or not the fact of reversing the answers for sums two, three and four was pointed out to her is uncertain. She then collects her puppet shape for colouring. Some of the children have already decorated their puppets with buttons, eyes, eyebrows, noses, coats, etc., instead of merely colouring them in one uniform colour for each part. She begins by colouring the triangle hat in dark red, but then comes under the influence of the others and draws in some eyes, holding her picture up to me with the triumphant smile of an innovator.

As in the morning session, so now, children are constantly coming to make contact with me. 'Look! Look!' they say, offering their work ... 'I live at 131' ... 'I live in another place' ... 'Do you count?' asks Kuldip. When I nod, she commands me to count, which I do, up to twelve. Smiles and laughs from the group. Even these anthropologists use our numbers. I ask Rashda if she has a television at home. She nods her head.

R. M.:   What programmes do you like?
Rashda: Dance.

It is now 2.15 p.m. Rashda has copied Balwant's clown who was crying. In answer to the teacher's question regarding the crying, she explains, 'He's lost his mother'. Her own puppet drawing is now approved by Mrs Parsons and she is called for reading practice with the story *A Home in a Tree* (The McKee Platform Readers A3, by D. Castley, K. Fowler and S. Carstairs, London: Nelson).

Mrs Parsons points with her biro to one word at a time and Rashda pronounces most of them correctly, but whether she understands what she is reading is not certain. For example, the word *tall* occurred in the story and, when asked for the meaning of this word later, she replied *little*. Errors often tell us more than right responses. Such an error could be noted by Mrs Parsons in her reading records for subsequent attention, either by herself or by Mrs Matthews in an E_2L session. Such liaison between staff is vital, and exchange of information can take place either outside teaching time or, when possible, by occasional observation of, and involvement in, each other's lessons. (For more comment on reading, see the document 'Hearing Children Read' in Chapter 7.)

Rashda's voice, incidentally, is much louder when reading than speaking. Up to this point it has been like Cordelia's in *King Lear*, 'soft, gentle and low'. While I am listening to her, one of the other girls tries to cut my hair with her scissors and smiles seraphically when I tell her I had it cut only the day before.

At 2.33 p.m. Rashda has finished her reading of pages ten to thirteen, and is sitting on the floor cutting out her puppet. All around children are busily occupied in lawful or semi-lawful pursuits. One child is playing with some bricks; one with Lego; another croaking for fun. There is a group around the teacher with their cut-out puppets; a number sitting at tables colouring theirs; a few sitting on the floor cutting out their puppets; one mooing like a cow, or howling like a banshee, it is difficult to say which; three with a bowl of sand, playing happily.

This idyllic scene obtains for a few minutes until the teacher repeats the formula: 'Children!' She holds up her hands, the children follow suit, and there is silence in a second, which permits the clearing-up jobs to be distributed. All Class 8 move into action, hunting out scissors, crayons, bits and pieces of waste paper. It is obviously a popular activity and appears to be done very conscientiously. Rashda carries five tins of pencils. Mrs Parsons sets a time limit on the clearing up, and counts to five in order to speed the process: 'One ... two ... three ... four ... four and a half ... four and three quarters ... '

All except three or four children are now on the carpet and the corporate identity of the class is confirmed with a song in which they all participate. Perhaps it confirms their physical identity also, since it is one of those marvellous cumulative songs about parts of the body, which forces the children to concentrate very carefully as they perform actions appropriate to the words. For the non-English speakers, such relevant language repetition, of the kind that now follows, is excellent.

Mrs P.:	One finger, one thumb, one arm, one leg
	Keeps moving,
	One finger, one thumb, one arm, one leg
	Keeps moving.
	One finger, one thumb, one arm, one leg
	Keeps moving.
	We'll all be merry and bright.
	One finger, one thumb, one arm, one leg,
	One nod of the head,
	Stand up.
Children:	Sit down.
Mrs P.:	Keeps moving.
	One finger, one thumb, one arm, one leg,
	One nod of the head,
	Stand up.
Children:	Sit down.
Mrs P.:	Keeps moving.
	One finger, one thumb, one arm, one leg,
	One nod of the head,
	Stand up.
Children:	Sit down.
Mrs P.:	Keeps moving.
	We'll all be merry and bright.

Such is the atmosphere in the room that they do indeed all appear to be merry and bright. When the song is over there is a momentary pause until the bell sounds and the children go out to play for fifteen minutes before returning at 3.05 p.m. for story time.

Mrs P.:	*(very gently)*: I'm waiting to start the story and I don't want to have to wait for you. *(Pause.)* Once upon a time, there lived a king and a queen who were very happy. Except for one thing ...

The children are again sitting on the mat in front of Mrs Parsons. Rashda occupies the same piece as earlier, sitting still, concentrating;

now looking up at the teacher, now with her head on her folded arms. The story of *The Sleeping Beauty*, Ladybird version,[1] continues.

Mrs P.: They both longed to have children, but they had none. Every day they said to each other, 'If only we had a child.' Now, it happened one day, when the queen had been bathing, a frog crept out of the water and spoke to her. It said, 'Your wish shall come true. Before a year has gone by, you shall have a daughter.'

We are in the fantasy realm of kings and queens, magic wishes, and talking frog obstetricians.

Mrs P.: *(showing a picture)*: There's the frog, talking to the queen.
Child: Can frogs talk?
Mrs P.: No. It's a magic frog.
The queen was delighted and she hurried to tell her husband the good news.

Mrs Parsons reads well, with good stress and intonation, following the text very closely, with additional questions of her own about the pictures ('She looks wicked, doesn't she?') and about particular words:

Mrs P.: She was furious. What does that mean?
Child: Ugly.
Child: Wicked.
Child: Angry.
Mrs P.: Angry. Yes. Good girl. Angry.

One boy is playing with his teeth; another is picking his nose; a girl is doing her hair; two boys are sucking their fingers. But, despite these slight physical activities, all except one have their eyes firmly on the teacher and are concentrating on the story. Their attentiveness hardly wavers until, at 3.26 p.m., 'They lived happily ever after'.[2]

Coats and anoraks are collected, first by boys and then girls, as has been the sequence throughout the day.

Mrs P.: Hands together and eyes closed.
The children do as asked, sitting cross-legged on the mat. Mrs Parsons sings one note and they all join in:

> Loving Father of the Children,
> I belong to you.

[1] *The Sleeping Beauty*, re-told by Vera Southgate-Booth, with illustrations by Eric Winter. A Ladybird Easy-Reading Book (first published Wills & Hepworth, 1965).

[2] Stories figure prominently throughout this book and Chapter 4, Sequel I suggests appropriate ones for each age range.

> Through the day-time
> And the night-time,
> You take care of me. Amen.

There is the same satisfying sensation of completeness at the end of the school day as occurred in Chapter 1 with Mike's experience.

We all now sit and wait for the bell, the children still cross-legged with arms folded, 'reaching up tall', as the phrase is. On the bell:

Mrs P.:   Goodnight, children.
Children: Goodnight, Mrs Parsons.
Mrs P.:   Say goodnight to Mr Mills.
Children: Goodnight, Mr Mills.
R. M.:   Goodnight, children.

Sequel I Teaching English to Infants as a Second Language

PART ONE

Most native speakers of English face a psychological difficulty when it comes to teaching their own language. They have probably never looked upon it as a language to be taught, like French or Latin, and cannot remember being taught it themselves. Moreover, they have usually learnt foreign languages through the grammar translation method. That is, for example, by having French future tenses translated into their English equivalents. This method has some drawbacks. Primarily, of course, not many teachers speak Punjabi, Urdu, Chinese, Greek or Italian well enough to teach by translation. Also, the method gives the impression that there are always one-to-one equivalents between languages. This is not so. Each language has some concepts which are impossible to translate adequately into another language, besides rules of grammar which are quite alien to the language learner. Moreover, the fact that grammar translation often relies heavily on reading and writing, the memorising of rules and irregular patterns, etc., makes it obviously inappropriate for young children, who are not yet at the level of such abstract thought, and who need immediately useful oral skills.

The direct method of teaching English is perhaps particularly appropriate for young children as it emphasises contact and communication between teacher and pupils, and uses meaningful and realistic situations, rather than translations of the 'Caesar's campaign in Gaul' type. The teacher does not translate English into Punjabi or Chinese, but uses the particular item he wishes to teach in a situation that makes its meaning obvious. Put this way, it sound impossible. However, let us take some items from the language list in Part Two.

(1) *It's a box.*
> Teacher has a box. She points to it: 'It's a box. What is it?' Child replies, with encouragement, 'It's a box' (or, more likely at first, 'It a box').

(2) *Going to* (i.e. future tense).
> Teacher says: 'I'm going to draw on the board'.
> (Teacher draws on the board.)
> Teacher says: 'I'm going to shut the door.'
> (Teacher shuts the door.)

(3) *I feel . . .*
> Teacher smiles and says: 'I feel happy.'
> Teacher pretends to cry and says: 'I feel sad.'
> Teacher glowers and says: 'I feel angry.'

These are very crude examples, but it is hoped that they convey the core of the method. Naturally, the infant and junior teacher will use her whole repertoire in teaching English language, e.g. drama (acting of repetitious stories; mime;

situation dialogues); PE (think of all those imperatives); art (colours, preposi-tions, adjectives); maths (emphasising concepts in particular); sand and water play ('It floats; It sinks; It's wet; It's dry'). Thus, all one's work cards, games, models and graphs need not be put away when one teaches English as a second language. They are used for their potential in eliciting and reinforcing particu-lar language items. In my experience, it is possible to teach all the language on the list in such ways.

It is important, however, that the teacher does not do all the talking. She has, after all, had plenty of practice already. The aim must be to get the children to respond as much as possible in full sentences. This last point is a personal preference. Some people would say it is more natural to answer 'No', when asked 'Have you got the card?' rather than, 'No, I haven't got it'. I feel that, if one insists on the full pattern, it gives more practice. On the other hand, shortened forms such as: he's, she's, I've, what's, are taught where appro-priate, as they are more common in actual speech than their longer counter-parts.

Continual repetition and revision are vital. Once you have taught the date 1066 in history, that is usually that, but, in language teaching, structures can be used in many different combinations. For example, question forms need to be practised with all the different tenses. A useful rule to remember is: when teaching a new structure (part of grammar), use old (i.e. already learnt) lexis (vocabulary). When teaching new lexis, use an old structure.

Again, it is very easy to teach vocabulary items, but these are only the bricks. The mortar, which will bind all the bricks together, are the structures. These structures – i.e. involving verb tenses, pronouns, prepositions, question tags, singulars and plurals, etc. – are more difficult to teach, but vital for children with language problems.'

I also feel it is important to stress concepts in the language we teach. (See the separate section in Part Two under B(8) below which is simply the basis for many more.) The first language of the children may not have these concepts. Anyway, the child may not have had the opportunity to learn them in his own language and/or in English. The teaching of concepts is, of course, part of a wider educational and linguistic aim for the infant teacher.

It is worth remembering, too, that the first language of the child may well interfere with his learning of English. For example, Italians pronounce *ce* as *che, ch* as *k, ci* as *chi* (as in Cinzano). In Punjabi, *bus* expresses the idea of enough, no more, thank you; it also means *bus*, as in English. There are also similar-sounding words in Punjabi for pen, coat, button, gloves. If the child tries to apply the rules of his own language to English he may be confused or misled.

A final point. The list which now follows could be used with a wide range of age groups with a similar language attainment, e.g. a newly arrived infant and a 16-year-old. However, children differ not just in age, but in ability in language learning, and length and type of exposure to English. Therefore, we must keep in mind the different needs of different pupils and teach them appropriate language. On early acquaintance, children should be tested, either using the NFER tests (London: Ginn, 1973) or (for experienced teachers) a simple test of your own devising, using picture cards and tape recordings to evaluate aural and oral ability.

PART TWO

The list of structures in Part Two is intended as a guide for the teaching of language to non-English-speaking infants. A different sequence of items is possible and the list of vocabulary and structures is by no means exhaustive. They have simply been found to provide a useful framework for the work of one teacher. The grammatical names of structures are used in the list for clarity; they are, of course, never taught to the children.

The list is divided up into what seems to the writer a rational, logical and convenient order. First, language is centred around the immediate classroom situation that the child will have to cope with. Secondly, there is language which will help the child to talk about himself. Finally, language which will help him understand the outside world. Thus, the language taught will, we hope, be immediately meaningful and useful to the learner.

The 'syllabus' – although it is not intended as such – should give new teachers of E₂L an idea of what to teach and in what order. Any teacher using it as a guideline would find, as she grew in experience and confidence, that it could easily be supplemented or rearranged, according to the difficulties the children face. I personally feel it is important to start with some kind of language list, in order to avoid confusion and incoherence for teacher and children, and to give a feeling of order and progression, as well as assisting record-keeping and testing.

Structure and Situation	*Examples*
Section A. Language centred around the classroom.	(T. = Teacher's language). (C. = Child's response).

(1a) Introductory sessions to enable the child to cope in the classroom situation.	T.: What's your name?
	C.: My name's . . .
	T.: Who's got a . . .
	C.: I've got a . . .
	T.: This is a . . .
	    What is it?
	C: It's a . . .
	Hello. Goodbye. Listen. Look.
	Classroom vocabulary:
	  box; blackboard; table; book; pencil; chair; numbers; pen; ruler; brush; school; towel; soap; tap; sink; hat; toilet; coat; shoes; buttons; milk; door; clock; man; lady; girl; boy.

(1b) Practice of classroom vocabulary by instructions.	T.: Give me a . . . T.: Pick up a . . . T.: Can I have a . . . Yes, please. No, thank you.
(2) Pronouns	T.: Whose is this? C.: It's mine/his/hers. T.: Is this yours? C.: Yes it is. C.: No it isn't.

(3) Imperative. Run; walk; jump; stop; come; go; sit down; stand up.

(4) Personal pronouns plus verb. He('s); she('s); I('m); it('s); we('re); they('re).

(5) Present continuous tense. I am (Am I?); You are (Are you?); he, she is (Is he?) ...
cutting; painting; drawing; reading; writing; eating; drinking; hopping; jumping; running; walking; skipping.
T.: Where's he going?
C.: He's going home/to school/shopping.

(6) Possessive pronouns. His; her; my; your.

(7) Prepositions. In; on; with; to; up; down.
T.: Is it on the ...
C. No, it's in the ...

(8) Simple mathematical terms. Numbers 1 to 10.
It's the same. They're different.
Big/small.
Circle; triangle.
This one; that one.
T.: How many are there?
C.: There are six books.
T.: What are these?
C.: They're ...
Red; blue; green; yellow.

Section B. Language centred around the child

(1) Parts of the body. Head; arm; leg; foot (feet); hand; hair; eye(s); lips; teeth; mouth; chin; neck; nose; nails; fingers; thumb; elbow; shoulder; chest; back; tummy; knees.
T.: You're touching your ...
What are you touching?
C.: I'm touching my ...
T.: Is this your nose?
C.: No, it's my chin.
Curly; straight; long; short.

(2) Clothing. Gloves; pants; scarf; belt; trousers; vest; hood; buckle; boots; pyjamas; tie; laces; skirt; nightdress; collar; cardigan; slippers; zip; shirt; jumper; anorak; dress; socks;
A pair of ...
T.: What are you wearing?
C.: I'm wearing ...
T.: Who's wearing a ...
C.: I am. I'm wearing a ...
T.: Why are you wearing an anorak?
C.: Because ...

(3) More prepositions. Under/over; inside/outside; behind/

		in front of; off; by; across; after; along; through; between.
(4)	Irregular simple past tenses.	Saw; was; went; had. T.: Did you...? C.: Yes I did/No I didn't. T.: Tell me where you went. C.: I went.... T.: Tell me what you saw/had/bought.
(5)	Family.	Daddy; mummy; husband; wife; son; daughter; sister; brother; auntie; uncle; cousin; granny; grandad. Married.
(6)	Home.	Names of rooms in the house. Names of items in each room, e.g. pillow; blanket; sheet; bed; light; curtains. Appropriate verbs: He's sweeping, cooking, washing. Upstairs/downstairs. Into/out of.
(7)	Emotions/illnesses plus simple present.	I feel; he feels. He is sad/happy/angry. I've got a headache/toothache/an ear-ache/tummy-ache. Like. Want. Need.
(8)	Various concepts.	Long/short; hot/cold; old/young; heavy/light; fat/thin; near/far; fast/slow. High; deep; strong. Very. Too.
(9)	More questions and negative answers	T.: Am I...? C.: Yes you are/No you aren't. T.: Are you/we/they...? C.: No/Yes I'm/We're/They're... T.: Is he/she/it...? C.: Yes/No... T.: Have you...? T.: Has he...? T.: Can I/you/he...?

Section C. Language centred around the outside world

(1)	The weather.	Types of weather. T.: Yesterday it was... Today it is... Sun; moon; stars; clouds; wind; sky; rain; snow; fog.
(2)	Day and night.	Morning; afternoon; light; dark; breakfast; dinner; tea.
(3)	The street and road	Bridge; subway; zebra crossing; kerb; pavement; lorry; car; bus; bicycle; bike. Stop. Look. Listen.

		Cross the road.
		Safe; dangerous; fast; slow.
(4)	Shops and shopping.	Money – names of coins plus simple calculations. Fractions.
		Full/empty.
		Names and different contents of shops, e.g. fruit shops; an apple; orange; pear; banana; some grapes; onion; potato; cabbage; carrots.
		Never/sometimes.
		Bought.
		Each; altogether; a bunch.
(5)	The park and more of	See-saw; swing; pond; slide; leaf; fence; grass.
	the simple past tense.	Hopped; jumped; played; ran; walked.
(6)	Comparative and superlative.	Big; bigger; biggest; bigger than.
(7)	Future.	Going to.
(8)	Further topics to develop vocabulary and understanding.	Animals – farm/zoo/domestic.
		Farming – seasons and crops.
		Town and country – different types of scenery.
		Fires and firemen.
		Doctors and hospitals.

BOOKS FOR FURTHER REFERENCE

Aplin, Y. *et al.* (1978). *Scope Handbook 3 (English for Immigrant Children in the Infant School)* (London: Schools Council Longman).

Butterworth, E. and Kinnibrugh, D. (1970). *Scope Handbook 1 (The Social Background of Immigrant Children from India, Pakistan and Cyprus* (London: Schools Council Longman).

Derrick, J. (1966). *Teaching English to Immigrants* (London: Longman).

Manley, D. (1978). *Plays and Dialogues* (eight small books to supplement the Schools Council's 'Scope Stage One' series of readers) (London: Longman).

Ridge, J. *et al.* (1969). *Scope Teachers Book for Stage One* (London: Schools Council Longman).

Rudd, E. (1971). *Scope Handbook 2 (Pronunciation for Immigrant Children from India, Pakistan, Cyprus and Italy)* (London: Schools Council Longman).

Schools Council Working Paper 31 (1970). *Immigrant Children in Infant Schools* (Evans /Methuen Educational).

Shiach, G. M. (1972). *Teach Them to Speak: A Language Development Programme in 200 Lessons* (London: Ward Lock Educational).

Stoddart, J. and F. (1968). *Teaching English to Immigrant Children* (London: University of London Press).

Note:
For a rather different approach from the 'structural-situational' one described in Chapter 2, see D. A. Wilkins, *Notional Syllabuses* (Oxford: OUP, 1976). This book outlines approaches to a functional syllabus based on a number of categories of communication, such as: asking questions to obtain information; controlling others; persuading; understanding and telling stories. Such a 'notional' approach is now attracting considerable interest.

Sequel II Television and Radio Information

PART ONE: BBC

There is a vast range of educational broadcasting designed for particular purposes and with defined age ranges indicated. Anyone interested to know what provision is made for schools' programmes and who wishes to obtain information about specific series should write for the BBC Annual Programme leaflet to:

School Broadcasting Council for UK, The Langham, Portland Place, London W1A 1AA. Tel: 01 935 2801.

Teachers' notes and pupils' pamphlets for each series may be obtained from:

BBC Publications, 144-152 Bermondsey Street, London SE1 3TH.

Inquiries about the hire and purchase of records and films should be sent to:

BBC Radio and Television Enterprises, Villiers House, The Broadway, London W5 2PA.

Radio and radiovision programmes for sale from BBC Publications can be seen at:

The National Audio-Visual Aids Centre, 254-6, Belsize Road, London NW6 4BT.

For any teacher who fails to record a school radio or radiovision programme, a tape of it can be bought from:
Stagesound (London) Ltd, 14 Langley Street, London WC2H 9JG.

Education Officers, whose job it is to receive and relay information about BBC television and radio programmes, may be contacted locally for the following regions:

England

Northern Division I and II: Broadcasting House, Woodhouse Lane, Leeds LS2 9PX. Tel. 0532 41181.

North-Western Division: New Broadcasting House, Oxford Road, Manchester M60 1SJ. Tel. 061 236 8444.

South-Western Division: Broadcasting House, Whiteladies Road, Clifton, Bristol BS8 2LR. Tel. 0272 32211.

Midland Division I and II: BBC Broadcasting Centre, Pebble Mill Road, Birmingham B5 7QQ. Tel. 021 472 5353.

London North: Villiers House, The Broadway, Ealing W5 2PA. Tel. 01 743 8000.

London South, Eastern, and South-Eastern Division: The Langham, Portland Place, London W1A 1AA. Tel. 01 935 2801.

Southern Division: BBC, South-Western House, Southampton SO9 1PF. Tel. 0703 26201.

Northern Ireland
Broadcasting House, Ormeau Avenue, Belfast BT2 8HQ. Tel. 0232 44400.

Wales

The School Broadcasting Council for Wales, Broadcasting House, Llandaff, Cardiff CF5 2YQ. Tel. 0222 564888.

North Wales Division: Bron Castell, High Street, Bangor. Tel. 0248 2214.

Scotland

The School Broadcasting Council for Scotland, Broadcasting House, 5 Queen Street, Edinburgh EH2 1JF. Tel. 031 225 3131.

Glasgow Division Broadcasting House, Queen Margaret Drive, Glasgow G12 8DG. Tel. 041 339 8844.

Aberdeen Division Broadcasting House, Beechgrove Terrace, Aberdeen AB9 2ZT. Tel. 0224 25233.

BBC Local Radio Stations broadcast special programmes for schools. They are to be found in: Birmingham; Blackburn; Brighton; Bristol; Carlisle; Cleveland; Derby; Humberside; Leeds; Leicester; London, Manchester, Medway, Merseyside, Newcastle, Nottingham, Oxford, Sheffield, Solent, Stoke-on-Trent.

Any inquiry should be sent to the station concerned, or to: The Education Organiser, BBC Local Radio, Room 232, The Langham, Portland Place, London W1A 1AA. Tel. 01 935 2801.

PART TWO: ITV

The annual ITV programme leaflet is available from: ITV Education Secretariat, Knighton House, 52–66 Mortimer Street, London W1N 8AN.

   ITV Education News is a free publication sent each year to all schools and colleges known to be viewing ITV programmes. It contains information about series transmitted during the previous year, with details from practising teachers on their organisation of, and follow-up to, the programmes.

   Inquiries concerning ITV schools broadcasts should be sent to the Education Officer of the appropriate company, as follows:

Borders and Isle of Man: Border Television Ltd, Television Centre, Carlisle CA1 3NT. Tel. 0228 25101

Central Scotland: Scottish Television Ltd, Cowcaddens, Glasgow G2 3PR, Tel. 041 332 9999

Channel Islands: Channel Television, Television Centre, Jersey, Channel Islands. Tel. 0534 73999

East of England: Anglia Television Ltd, Anglia House, Norwich NR1 3JG. Tel. 0603 28366.

Lancashire: Granada Television Ltd, Manchester M60 9EA. Tel. 061 832 7211.

London: Thames Television Ltd, 306–16 Euston Road, London NW1 3BB. Tel. 01 387 9494.

Midlands: ATV Network Ltd, ATV Centre, Birmingham B1 2JP. Tel. 021 643 9898.

North East: Tyne Tees Television ltd, The Television Centre, Newcastle upon Tyne NE1 2AI. Tel. 0632 61 0181.

North-East Scotland: Grampian Television Ltd, Queen's Cross, Aberdeen AB9 2XJ. Tel. 0224 53553

Northern Ireland: Ulster Television Ltd, Havelock House, Ormeau Road, Belfast BT7 1EB. Tel. 0232 28122

South of England: Southern Independent Television Ltd, Northam, Southampton SO9 4YQ. Tel. 0703 28582

South-West: Westward Television Ltd, Derry's Cross, Plymouth PL1 2SP. Tel. 0752 69311

Wales and West of England: HTV Ltd, Television Centre, Bristol BS4 3HG. Tel. 0272 770271

Yorkshire: Yorkshire Television Ltd, The Television Centre, Leeds LS3 1JS, Tel. 0532 38283

David, Aged 7

When there's a fire they ring the bell,
like a bell when you go into school.

THE SCHOOL

David's Church of England school was built in 1961 in the middle of an industrial city, and is surrounded by small factories – plastics, auto-crome, press work. It has some 144 children and there is a nursery unit, a junior school and a comprehensive school, all in close proximity. The infants school is multi-racial, with more children of West Indian origin (30 per cent in David's class) than Indian or Pakistani, but a predominant number of white children.

David himself is first pointed out to me in assembly. He is well dressed in new, smart, patterned long trousers, a grey shirt, green pullover, brown shoes, blue socks. He has longish mousey hair and is taller than those around him, being a term or so older. His class teacher says that he was very unsure of himself when he first arrived from Yorkshire two terms previously, that he was slightly aggressive and ready to burst into tears at a moment. Miss Bennett felt that his attitude had improved enormously since that time.

THE DAY

Outside is a dull, rainy, gloomy day. Inside the large, light school hall there is a warm atmosphere as the headmistress, a well-dressed, smiling lady with greying hair, welcomes two visitors to the assembly, the local Anglican curate and myself. The hall is set out with children grouped in rows around the central open square, and teachers at strategic intervals, as in Figure 3.1.

Mrs Manders, the headmistress, immediately involves different children in the assembly. First of all, several individuals display certain objects they have brought into school, such as books and dolls. A 'birthday boy' has brought a tin of Kit-e-Kat which he donates to Mrs Manders. John has an announcement regarding the stamp club; it will meet the next day in the afternoon. Such clubs (as stamp, chess, drama, music, model making, art) operate in many a primary school on one afternoon a week. They give the children opportunity to get to know a wider range of children than merely those in their own class.

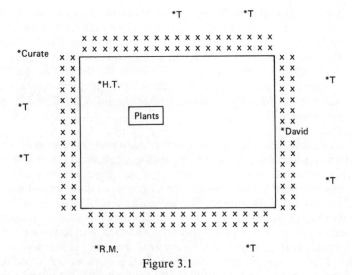

Figure 3.1

After such individual activity there is corporate involvement with a sung prayer, the children's own silent prayer, and then hand gestures appropriate to gramophone music, i.e. first swaying like branches in the wind, then rain-like movements. David looks carefully at what others are doing and joins in tentatively for a second or so every now and again. He is obviously unused to this activity. When the music is finished it is named, by the children, as *Aquarium* and there are a few questions about the nature and appearance of an aquarium. No such opportunity for a widening of vocabulary would be missed by any experienced teacher.

Then the curate tells his story:

There was once a magic pair of boots and each boot believed itself to be the shinier of the two. They didn't realise that they were going to have to live together all their lives. A soldier bought them and went on guard at the Tower of London, dressed in a very smart red and gold uniform and a new pair of black boots. The left boot didn't like the fact that the right boot was always told to go first when they started marching and it leaned across and tied the laces together. The soldier fell flat on his nose. *(Laughs from the children.)* The soldier was very annoyed and told his boots how naughty they were. But the boots merely tried to outdo each other for speed and the soldier went faster than all the other soldiers. The right boot was jealous that the left boot was overtaking him and the left boot complained that the right one had hit him when the Commanding Officer called 'Attention!' and all the soldiers were meant to click their heels together. So an argument started between the two boots and they were fighting each other, just like children having a quarrel in the playground. The soldier was in trouble now and all because the boots hadn't learnt to get on with each other; not to be jealous of each other; not to stop saying 'me first.' At the end of the day the soldier sold the boots and the shopkeeper put them on the second-hand shelf. And if you invite me back again, I'll tell you if anyone else bought the boots.

The curate has told the story with good humour and an easy manner, at an appropriate speed and with much eye contact. He has used mime, where relevant, to illuminate his words and thus cater for a wide range of listener, and he has interspersed a number of questions to which the children readily responded. There was an excellent atmosphere and the children, sitting cross-legged on the floor, were silent and attentive. None more so than David, who followed each turn in the narrative as carefully as if he had been a foreigner in a strange country listening to directions. There is marvellous power in a good story well told, and the curate has taken care not to kill it by over stressing the moral element.

Moreover, it is good for children to have regular contact with adults from the local community outside the school walls. Section 7 of the 1944 Education Act recognised the local education authority's responsibility to contribute to the 'spiritual, mental and physical development of the community' and such responsibility is mutual and cyclical. Children are a part of the community; they can give and receive, and the Plowden Report (1967) comments in para. 121f. on the progress made in this respect, particularly in certain European and American schools. Para. 107f., incidentally, indicates the part which local parents may play in the life of their school.

The assembly continues and we now witness the full ritual accorded a 'birthday boy'. The birthday boy mentioned earlier had had his celebration at a previous assembly. Now it is the turn of James, who has brought a packet of birthday cards to show the children. These are held up one by one and Mrs Manders says something about each. The children laugh as they see pictures of long-trunked elephants and furry tigers, and then all join in the sung greeting: 'We wish you many happy returns of the day, James.' Everyone counts as seven candles are lit in the middle of the hall. Another song. Seven claps by everyone in the hall, and then single staccato claps as James blows out his candles one by one. It is a highly effective ceremony, which has delighted James, gripped all onlookers, and marked the end of assembly.

The message of the ritual is clear. In this brief moment in the school year, the whole community downs tools to acknowledge James's existence. He and, by implication, every other individual has significance within this group of people. He is made to feel important and valued.

Next day, or next week, will be someone else's turn. As you will see at the end of this chapter, David acknowledges that he has not yet felt able to face this public expression of belonging. That, in itself, is significant.

The children stand, class by class, clapping to the accordion music on the gramophone, and depart leaving a class behind which contains David. He has been highly involved throughout the proceedings and adapted well to the change in rhythm of the various claps.

It is 9.40 a.m. and David's class awaits their movement lesson. One girl approaches and asks me to write 'Beverley number 20'. When this is done she points it out to a group of her friends. It seems to be part of a testing-out process which some young children employ with a stranger. Evidently this one can write; he might be useful to me. David tells me he lives in the fire station and his number is 14. I assume, wrongly, from this that he is a fairly confident boy, since I have not yet spoken to him and he does not know that I am to spend the day monitoring his activities. Another boy tells me that his father is the school caretaker. Yet another is the local vicar's son. These isolated introductions have been made while the rest of the class was preparing for the register.

All now sit at the teacher's feel while names are checked, girls first. Miss Bennett, who has been Class 4's teacher for three weeks, accomplishes the task quietly and efficiently. She is a teacher of Welsh origin and one year's experience, being in her early 20s. She has recently been ill, and for anyone feeling even slightly unwell teaching is miserably remorseless. She tells the children that there are only five minutes left for them in the hall and they are to take off their shoes and socks. David does this very quickly and lines up with the others, all carrying shoes, socks, pullovers, which are deposited in a long line at the side of the hall.

Each child now finds a space and moves about the hall to the noise of the tambourine as 'wibbly wobbly jellies'. They 'reach up tall' on tiptoe several times. They run round the hall, weaving in and out without touching anyone. 'Use your mind', says Miss Bennett, 'come on, Andrew, you're being silly.' They run to the sound of the tambourine; they stamp 'like great heavy giants, very slowly'. Now they shout 'STAMP!' as they stamp, and they laugh when they stop in the middle of the word 'st ... ' They are exhorted to move with 'twirling and twisting tiny quiet feet, like the snowflakes yesterday', and they do so. Then they race round the hall to the noise of the tambourine and prove the unwritten law that, in such a situation, children always move anti-clockwise, as any teacher knows. One boy, Dean, is sent to stand by the door for sliding. Finally, as a winding-down exercise, they go round 'like trotting horses with knees up high', as the teacher taps out the rhythm on a piece of wood.

The potential of this kind of range of physical responses is clearly recognised and endorsed in official circles, as a Department of Education and Science document will indicate. *Movement: Physical Education in the Primary Years* (London: HMSO, 1972) states:

> Movement provides a two-way channel of learning, being both a way of finding out and a form of accomplishment. It may result from other experiences and learning situations, or it may lead into them. As an expressive art, it shares and reinforces the contribution of music, drama and the visual arts. It has close links with literature, science and mathematics, and a teacher should constantly be on the lookout for opportunities for children to use movement in its many different roles and connections.

There is also a view that physical education may be especially of value to many children retarded in their reading and writing. The theory is that the fine physical and visual control needed for handwriting and reading can develop from a refinement of large, crude movements in PE and drawings in art which precede it. This is akin to the kind of progress a baby makes in his third year of life, when he can unscrew bottle tops, manipulate 'Lego' materials, hammer a small peg with accuracy and control. Such thinking has underpinned the development by A. E. Tansley of a screening device for identification of clumsy children in need of special help (see Lambert, 1976).

Having had practice, then, in the co-ordination of movement and sound, experienced a variety of rhythms, and possibly developed their language a little, as well as enjoyed themselves, the children line up in the middle of the hall, without a sound, and collect their bundles of clothes, like refugees, before standing by the door, boys and girls in separate ranks.

The importance of an understood and ordered routine in much of what goes on in school would be accepted by most teachers. This is not an argument for mindless regimentation. Quite the reverse. Good organisation and management is a prerequisite for innovation and there should certainly be opportunities throughout any school week for children to exercise initiative and learn how to manage freedom and choice. However, in PE a precise framework is an essential in its own right, as a condition of health and safety. To organise a good PE lesson, so that all children operate enjoyably in safety and with confidence, being prepared to extend their physical skills and accept new tasks, is one of the most demanding challenges a student teacher can face.

The children now make the short walk down the corridor to the classroom, David being last in line and closing the door. It is 10.05 a.m. and the children sit very quietly on the floor, putting on shoes and socks. One of them is crying. 'Oh!, Conway, be brave', exhorts Miss Bennett and continues to issue rebukes, questions, advice, encouragement to individuals. David has pulled his lace out of one shoe and a girl, quite unsolicited, comes to his aid and threads it for him. He later pulls the laces out again, for Miss Bennett to re-thread them. Perhaps he feels it is a job for experts, or perhaps it is one of his ploys for gaining adult attention.

A question and answer session now develops as they continue to dress themselves. Miss Bennett, who is lacing another pair of shoes on her lap, says that so far they have only two items for their class news book – a picture of a hamster called Tich, and Beverley's story about King Kong. What other news can they add? Contributions are offered with the confidence of hesitant salesmen unconvinced of the value of their product. Nicola watched Donald Duck and Mickey Mouse television cartoons with her Mum and Dad, Grandad and Grandma. Neil merely 'watched tele'. Julie went to the doctor with her mother and then watched television but, like Neil, cannot remember the programme. The teacher asks Brian if he played with his brothers and sisters, but this elicits no response. He only reacts when television is mentioned and he speaks of Woody Woodpecker. Lynn tidied up her toys but is informed by Miss Bennett that 'that is not very interesting'. Hugh says he helped Elizabeth to make Louise's bed and then they played with a very small dolly, catching it on the back of their hands. David sits on his knees at the back, saying nothing. Sharon tells the world that her mother is going into hospital to have a baby.

Miss B.:	But I saw your mother this morning. When's the baby going to arrive?
Sharon:	I dunno, I ain't seen it yet.
Miss B.:	And where's it going to come from?
Sharon:	I dunno.
Child:	Out of mummy's tummy.

Such an open forum for children's news is a common occurrence in infant and junior schools and, provided that each item, however trivial apparently, is accepted and used as a growth point from which a little more discussion may stem, then it can be a very valuable activity indeed. At best, it relates the worlds of home and school; it convinces the children that their experience matters and is worth talking about; it gives them the opportunity to get a better grip on that experience by putting it into words.

At 10.17 a.m. the children move into seven groups all round the room (see Figure 3.2). There are twenty-one boys and thirteen girls and the tables are loosely ordered in terms of ability, David's group being the slowest. In this way, non-streaming within the basic structure of the school's organisation becomes streaming within the confines of the classroom, as the 1978 HMI survey, *Primary Education in England*, pointed out.

The room is very attractive and, amongst other items, contains notices which which give it a domestic warmth, such as:

> SHARON'S PATTERN REMINDS HER OF CHRISTMAS

> CONWAY SAW SOME WEDDING TAXIS IN THE STREET

> HARDEEP LIVES IN THIS RED HOUSE

> CAN YOU SEE THE BUDS OPENING INTO LEAVES?

> ROBIN HOOD IS FIGHTING PRINCE JOHN

Such notices as these, drawing as they do on children's own experience, comments and interests, can serve as a prelude to the development of individual books or folders of personal news or information.

There is a star chart on the partition and all Class 4 children have been awarded stars except Neil, Dean, Beverley, Donna, Conway, Hardeep and David. Ridgway (1976) urges caution in the use of such external rewards and incentives. She writes: 'A child's self-esteem is very dependent on the view the teacher takes of him: the response of the teacher to what he does is often interpreted by him as an assessment of his own value . . . Star and no-star may be interpreted by children as "I'm good and he's bad".' Certainly, praise and rebuke may be received by many children as moral judgements upon them, and a school, like no other institution, issues both with the profligacy of a busy machine gun. As Philip Jackson (1968) observes: 'Schools are places in which rewards and punishments are administered in abundance. Smiles, compliments, special privileges, good grades, and high scores on tests are occasioned by certain kinds of classroom behaviour. Frowns, scoldings, deprivations, poor grades, and low scores on tests are occasioned by other kinds.'

Books and materials are ready on each set of tables, and tasks are distributed, group by group. One is to copy sums from the blackboard; another to do some writing; another, including David, to match words (on yellow cards) with pictures (also on yellow cards). His partner, Stacey, first announces: 'Look at me. I've got a star', and then adopts a more altruistic stance by showing David the cards.

David: What's the word?

Stacey: *Kuh . . . a . . . ruh. (This is no help to David and he asks the teacher.)*

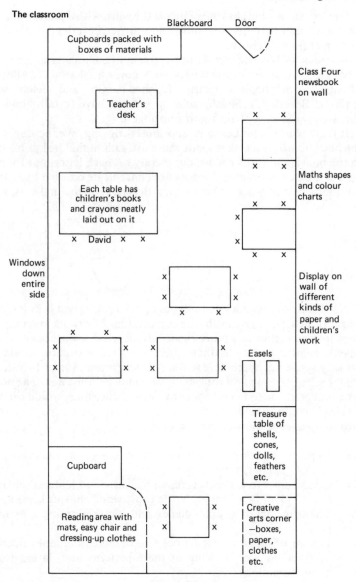

Figure 3.2

David: *Kuh.*
Miss B.: What do the next two letters say? *(No response.)* aaah...
         What do *kuh* and *aaah* say?
David: Car.

Success at last, but, having matched the word with a picture of a car, he is uncertain as to his next move and watches Beverley, who is drawing a picture of a clown.

Meanwhile, Miss Bennett issues a stream of comments as she moves from group to group round the room: 'Come on, Sharon . . . All right, Maxine? . . . Stephanie's nearly finished . . . Go and fetch some crayons, Beverley . . . Shush, Julie, you don't have to talk about it.' 'Miss', says Stacey, 'I ain't gorra horinge'.

It is 10.30 a.m. and David is laboriously copying 'Wednesday' from the blackboard. His task is made more difficult in that he has his back to the board and turns round, not merely for each letter, but for each part of a letter. Moreover, he does not concentrate on what he is doing but looks first at Stacey's book, then Beverley's. His final version is:

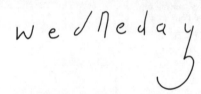

No labour of Hercules caused more problems. David is in the early stages of getting to grips with the complexities of writing and may still need much practice at a more elementary level. A sequence of writing development activities as that which I will now outline would be, broadly speaking, acceptable to many teachers and, for further detail, Chapter 2 of Gloyn and Frobisher (1975) may be consulted. The points are numbered one to twelve for convenience since there would often be no clear dividing line between them. Each child would need to dovetail into the sequence as and where appropriate.

(1) Opportunity for play with manipulative toys and materials, e.g. 'Lego', jigsaws, plasticine.
(2) Opportunity to make pictures with a variety of materials in addition to paint, e.g. leaves, bottle tops, wood shavings, wool.
(3) Colouring in of simple shapes and pictures, using crayon or pencil.
(4) Tracing of shapes and letter patterns of increasing sophistication, followed by free drawing of these patterns and, later, proper letter formation.
(5) Copying of own name in large letters. Later, this from memory.
(6) Close copying on top of (and later underneath) teacher's writing. Accompanied by appropriate and attractive decoration of the page.
(7) Constant and on-going discussion of activities and content.
(8) Written captions for child's own paintings or pictures.

(9)   Class and/or individual news book, based on real experience.

(10) Close copy of teacher's writing, eventually followed by close copy of material from work card and, later, far copy from blackboard.

(11) Development and use of word banks, whether in shoe pockets, 'Breakthrough to Literary'-type folders or, later, notebooks arranged in alphabetical order.

(12) Free writing, based on child's own activities, model, drawings, etc., with increasing sophistication of style.

David would appear to be operating on activity number ten. Perhaps he should be allowed to regress in order to consolidate.

At 10.35 a.m. the milk has arrived and the children collect it from the front of the class, group by group. They sit on the floor, drinking it and eating their crisps.

David has now realised that he can copy the date, 29th January, more easily from Stacey than from the blackboard and this he does before wrestling with drawing and writing.

Miss B.:   Come on, David, it's taking you a long time.
David *(to Stacey, twice):* Do you have to do it in pencil or crayon?

Like many a diffident child, he is afraid of making mistakes. Receiving no answer, he tries Miss Bennett.

Miss B.:   What do we usually do our pictures with?
David: Crayons.

He now chooses a purple crayon to draw his car. He is the only child not to have had his milk, in fact, the only one still working at his table. Suddenly he looks at my notebook and says, 'You've done two Davids'. It is true enough, but if he really has recognised the words from my scrawl, then he possesses talent far beyond what is apparent. He asks me why I write like that (presumably he means scribble) and, when I tell him it is quicker, it reminds me that there is no very good reason why he should be forced to work at an unnatural pace. He is neither lazy nor naughty. Merely slow.

Miss B.:   Have you finished, David?
David: No. *(Shakes his head.)*
Miss B.:   Hurry up.

The rest of the children collect their coats one by one and line up by the door before going out to play. On his way, Brian tells me, 'All that writing is yours, isn't it?' and, by this simple means, makes the brief human contact he needs.

Only David and I are left in the classroom. He is standing at the front of the room, sucking his milk through a straw; I am finishing my notes before coffee in the staff room. Outside in the corridor Miss Bennett may be heard organising children.

At 11.00 a.m. break is over and a group is extracted from the class for special remedial attention. Such a withdrawal policy can be an effective way of coping with individual weaknesses (and strengths) as was seen in Chapter 2. In order to work successfully, the withdrawal time from normal classes should not be excessive; the composition of the groups should change to meet differing needs; and, above all, the attitude to the system itself should be right. On one occasion, in another school not discussed in this book, as weak readers were going out of the classroom to their separate lesson, I heard a remaining pupil comment, 'The mentals are off'.

The nine extracted children here, including David, go to a brightly decorated and attractive classroom which has a variety of pieces of equipment strategically spaced about. In this room Mrs Wilder, a smartly dressed, dark, clearly spoken teacher of considerable experience, provides intensive work throughout the day for group after group.

She begins today's session by organising the children in a semi-circle on the floor in front of her. Then she tosses cardboard shapes down on the floor and the children call out the correct name – oblong, square, circle, triangle. At one point Derek says painfully, 'Oh! God, I've forgotten it'. A moment later Mrs Wilder asks David the difference between [   ] and □. Pointing to the oblong, he says, 'It's got two little sides and two big sides'.

There is an excellent atmosphere and work proceeds at a steady pace, underpinned by unobtrusive yet clear discipline. The teacher is kind and quietly spoken and accepting. Above all, she has planned the work carefully, knows precisely what she is doing, and the children inevitably fall under the spell of the clear framework for activity. They are to attempt tasks appropriate for their ability and interests. Here, then, are at least eight ingredients which, when skilfully combined, could hardly fail to produce a successful lesson.

Mrs Wilder shows the group a card on which are printed three shapes, as shown in Figure 3.3.

Figure 3.3

Stacey has the opportunity to match single cardboard shapes on the floor with those on the card. She manages the triangles but tries to superimpose a square on top of the rectangle. New boy Brian now tries the card shown in Figure 3.4.

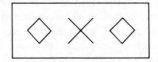

Figure 3.4.

When he succeeds, the children 'give him a big clap'. The approval of one's peers is a powerful incentive.

David attempts the card shown in Figure 3.5.

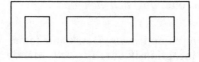

Figure 3.5

He is rewarded, like Brian, by applause when he succeeds. By such means the sense of corporate identity and desire for group success is strengthened. He now tries another (Figure 3.6), with words of encouragement from Derek, 'Think very hard, David'.

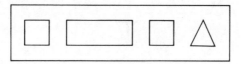

Figure 3.6

But he fails to remember the triangle at the end.

The activity, which is very popular, continues for another minute or so, punctuated by constant and genuine advice from dominant Derek, who is very proud of his own attainments in this area and, like all of us, needs to be successful in something.

After this practice of visual discrimination, which is also a pre-reading and pre-writing activity, Mrs Wilder moves to tactile experience, and tosses on to the floor small blue cards which have different pieces of material pasted to them. In threes the children are told to feel them. Derek says, 'This one is much softer and this is a little bit rough'. In this way, the tactile discrimination finds expression in language which, as the activity progresses, should be of increasing refinement. Virtually everything that happens in school is capable of being used as a language opportunity.

The children attempt to test what they have experienced and Beverley is the first to stand up, feel a texture behind her back, without seeing it, and then attempts to locate that same texture on one of the blue cards in front of her on the floor. She succeeds first time and earns a clap. David tries but, although close, is not quite right. Only the teacher knows which is correct, as each child has a turn.

At 11.16 a.m. the activity changes to sound discrimination. Mrs Wilder calls out some words – *catch cat cot pot can* – and the children try to spot the odd one out. Brian thinks *cot*; James *pot*; David *catch*; Derek *pot*.

Mrs W.:	Why are Derek and James right?
Derek:	Because it's got a '*p*'.
Mrs W.:	Try this one: *dog den hen dad dig.*

Beverley and Brian plump for *dig*; Derek and James, drunk with their previous success, incautiously vote for *dad*; Mandy and David settle for *hen*.

After four minutes several rounds of this new game have been played and it is time for pair work. Two children use the Bell & Howell Language Master machine;[1] two are completing unfinished shapes such as:

Two are joining dots to follow a pattern. Stacey and David work together with two cards of shapes. They have to repeat the sequence of shapes on the paper, which is so constituted that anything drawn may be easily erased. The card is shown in Figure 3.7.

When David has completed his card he reads the shapes to the teacher; gets them all correct; rubs them out and returns to his seat for the next exercise, which involves visual discrimination of a more subtle kind. He has a chart on which he will ring repeats of words found in the left-hand column (Figure 3.8).

---

[1]Made by Bell & Howard A/V Ltd, Alperton House, Bridgewater Road, Wembley, Middlesex, this is a kind of tape recorder which uses professionally produced and home-made 'talking cards'. Oblong cardboard pieces carrying magnetic strips, with visual and/or written material on them, are fed through the machine which 'speaks' the appropriate words, allowing for the pupil then to repeat them. Although rather heavy to be easily portable, the machine is easily operated independently by children of any age, and allows them to work conveniently at their own speed.

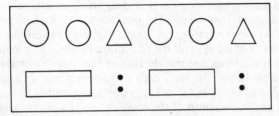

Figure 3.7

four	fuor	four	foru	rouf
left	left	lfet	telf	felt
boil	biol	loib	boil	doil
skin	inks	sink	skin	skim
limp	limb	linq	limq	limp
pots	tops	pots	bots	stop
doll	ball	dall	doll	boll

Figure 3.8

David counts the words in my notebook as I have been copying the chart – seven – and checks them with his own, which he has all correct. In answer to his question, I tell him I have finished the card and he takes it off for checking. He has, in fact, been very solicitous for my welfare all morning, seeing to it that I have a chair, opening the door, checking my work, and so on. Such consideration for others is rarely as noticed or rewarded in schools as academic success.

There is now a hint of trouble as Beverley says, 'That boy's putting his tongue out at me'. In some circumstances such a statement could be easily glossed over, but Beverley, so I was told later, is prone to work herself into a frenzy at the slightest provocation and will then spend up to an hour rocking herself to and fro, a clear indication of disturbance. Mrs Wilder takes her on her lap and cuddles her back into a good mood, while two of the boys look on sympathetically. It is as natural an act within the context of the lesson as holding up a flash card, and it succeeds in solving the problem before it has really had time to develop.

Mrs Wilder's treatment of Derek is similarly skilful. He is known as a volatile child, who will react with violent aggression at any hint of criticism from another child, such as 'You've got it wrong'. With praise and encouragement he is a delightful person, co-operative, warm, and good humoured. He now says, 'Miss, I'm getting too clever'. 'Yes, you're getting too clever for me', replies Mrs Wilder, without a trace of irony, and his self-image receives a welcome boost.

Beverley and Derek are merely two of the nine who have obvious personality problems. In fact, each of the nine seems to have some degree of disturbance, but is skilfully contained within the security of this lesson and the warmth of the relationship. I was told later that 30 per cent of the children in David's class come from broken homes, and it is information for reflection rather than immediate action. What should a teacher do about such knowledge, when the simple stereotype of 'the broken home' may be as dangerous as that of 'The West Indian child' or 'The underachiever'? Perhaps the key point is that while relevant background knowledge about a child's domestic situation, family relationships, attitudes, interests, health, and so on, helps to make that child more of a real person in the eyes of the teacher, it will not lead instantly to the panacea of a perfect teaching programme. But, it must, in some way, inform the entire educational experience, and assist in the process of turning teaching fodder into whole persons, with independent integrity. With such thoughts in mind, some words of A. S. Neill (1939) have even more force than usual. He writes: 'A good teacher does not draw out; he gives out, and what he gives out is love. And by love I mean approval, or, if you like, friendliness, good nature. The good teacher not only understands the child, he approves of him.' There is no sentimentality here, for the 'love' finds expression in professional concern and expertise.

Meanwhile, two of the recipients of this concern and expertise, David and Stacey, have moved to the Language Master corner and they begin their work here with a question and answer session designed to clarify certain preposition problems. David shows Stacey a card which has on it a picture of some children jumping above a box. Stacey says that the key word is *under*; the card number is matched with the mark card and her answer is seen to be incorrect. She puts a cross by number six; the original picture card is fed through the Language Master and the word *above* is spoken by the machine. This process is repeated seven times with other cards designed to teach the words *under* and *above*. Stacey gets seven out of eight correct, retaining the correct ones, and her card records her success (Figure 3.9).

Having finished this, the two children take the card to the teacher. Stacey, skipping her way there and looking very pleased with herself, says, 'Miss, I only got one wrong'. When their work is marked they return to the machine, taking a quick glance at the Wendy House *en route*, and change chairs. They now reverse tasks and Stacey asks the questions. When David answers correctly she comments, in the role and language of teacher, 'That's a good boy', unwittingly investing

```
Prepositions
1 ✓
2 ✓
3 ✓
4 ✓
5 ✓
6 ✗
7 ✓
8 ✓
```

Figure 3.9

academic success with a moral dimension. When David sees card number six of the children jumping above the box he says, 'jumping', for which he gets a cross since the word spoken by the machine is *above*. I tell him he was right, in a way, but both children are, not surprisingly, rather baffled. When they have their work checked I notice that he explains about *jumping*. Mrs Wilder spots that his two incorrect answers should both have read *above*, and she notes down this information in her records, no doubt for next time.

David and Stacey now move to their last activity of the morning, which is to transfer different coloured shapes on one piece of squared paper to another piece of squared paper. It is a matching exercise involving shape, colour and location. David's original document, which he endeavours to copy, is shown in Figure 3.10, with colours indicated as follows: purple for the square of four blocks; yellow for the cross of four blocks; green for the vertical four blocks; orange for the two horizontal blocks to the left of the vertical column; brown for the two horizontal blocks to the right of the vertical column; black for the two horizontal blocks in the top right hand corner; and red for the L-shaped three blocks in the bottom right-hand corner.

He begins with purple, counting carefully across the centimetre-squared paper to find the correct location. He tells Stacey that hers is wrong (which is true) and that his brother is called 'Chatterbox'. The two facts do not appear to be significantly related. However, if Stacey is in difficulty, then so is David, particularly with the colours, although that is not all. He realises that the green shape is wrong (he started one square too high) but he continues on brown without making any attempt to correct his original error. I know, from having tried it, just how much care and co-ordination the exercise involves, and it is interesting that David did not try to correct the error he had made. The acceptance of such error seems to imply a kind of fatality. Either that, or a lack of concern, and this would seem to be uncharacteristic.

However, he is saved from further exertions as time is running out and the children are told to write their names on their papers so that the exercise may be finished the next day. And that is, apparently, that, when Mark tells the teacher that there is a dead man in the Wendy

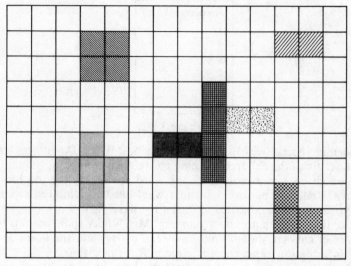

Figure 3.10

House. My immediate reaction, rather a callous one, is to speculate on this as the theme for a television play. Who is the dead man? How did he get there? How should he appear to a child looking in through the Wendy House window? How do the children react when they see the body? Such clinical and hard-hearted reflections are ended by the sober truth. Mrs Wilder, who has clearly encountered many such dead bodies in her time, takes us all to inspect the corpse. But, peer as we may through the door and windows, not one dead man can we see. Nor even a dead fly. I must confess to a mild degree of disappointment. Even so, that Wendy House was never quite the same for me, and perhaps the children, too, endowed it with some peculiarly dramatic quality thereafter.

The incident provides a rather macabre ending to an otherwise normal sequence of events. It should not draw attention away from the high-quality teaching which these children have experienced over the past hour. In general terms, they have had teaching and reinforcement in the basic skill areas of shape, texture, sound and word recognition and discrimination, as well as development of the senses of sight, touch and hearing. All have experienced some success while engaged in a variety of interesting language and number activities in a secure atmosphere. (Even the prospect of a dead man shook no one's equanimity, except perhaps mine.) They have, at times, been responsible for their own progress, as well as being encouraged to co-operate together and develop important social skills. A good time has been had by all, and learning has undoubtedly been achieved. What kind of learning was it?

For a consideration of this, and related matters, please see Sequel 1 at the end of this chapter.

It is now lunchtime, but before we eat, David and I talk for a few minutes about his home (he says he has a dad and a brother) and interests. He lives in the local fire station and really comes alive in our discussion as he talks of the work his dad does.

R. M.: Now, David, did you tell me this morning that you lived in the fire station?

David: Yes.

R. M.: Is that right?

David: Yes.

R. M.: Tell me about that. What's it like living in a fire station?

David: When you first got there?

R. M.: Yes.

David: Me dad's working like a fireman. There's a big built tower. A man in it. When the fireman comes just pretends dead he's dead. There's smoke coming out of it. Then you get firemen get some hose on. They put water in it and the fire engine and the water comes out the pipe and . . .

R. M.: Yes, go on.

David: . . . and when there's a fire they ring the bell, like a bell when you go into school.

R. M.: I know. And when the bell rings, what can you see from your window?

David: When I'm playing out fire engine up at the firemen go up in the tower and they go really fast and or like cars`in the way they move out the way, don't they, sometimes?

R. M.: They do.

David: And fire when er . . . ambulance goes fast when somebody knocks some people over. They go really fast. Put the sirens on when they meet cars in the way they just go vroom!

R. M.: It's exciting, being a fireman, isn't it?

David: Yes.

R. M.: What do you want to be when you grow up?

David: A fireman.

R. M.: Do you?

David: A bird shooter.

R. M.: A bird shooter?

David: Yes.

R. M.: Yes.

David: A horse rider.

R. M.: Horse rider, yes.

David: And . . . Indian.

R. M.: And an Indian, yes.

David:	Cowboy.
R. M.:	Cowboy, yes.
David:	And erm . . . ambulance man.
R. M.:	An ambulance man.
David:	And erm car driver.
R. M.:	A car driver.
David:	And er . . .
R. M.:	Well, can you be all those things?
David:	Yes.
R. M.:	Can you? Heavens. That's a lot, isn't it? You're going to be very busy *(laughs)*.
David:	Have to go whowhowho *(Indian yodelling noise)* . . . tch! *(the sound of a cowboy gun firing)*.

If asked to write about his father's job, it is doubtful if David could have produced more than a line or so. But the experience is there and shows itself, not only by what he says, but in the way he says it. He is more animated at this point than at any stage during the morning and his enthusiasm is indicated in the broken sentences, the onomatopoeic utterances, the clear if disjointed narrative sequence and, above all, the helter-skelter sensation of movement and excitement.

It is a useful strategy for a teacher occasionally to tape record the spoken words of a poor writer and transcribe them later, thereby giving him the satisfaction of having produced a piece of 'written work' which, in our educational system, is a form of higher status than spoken language. Given the opportunity, David would readily respond to the invitation to talk about his world. Apart from his obvious enthusiasm for the fireman's life, he has many other interests, witness his list of prospective occupations. Such experience will remain vague and shadowy unless given flesh in spoken language. There need to be constant opportunities in school for all children to talk about their experiences and interests and, thereby, get a better grip on them and on themselves. (Chapter 6, Sequel II, elaborates on these matters.) Perhaps, in the process, our notion of what constitutes a 'remedial' child will undergo radical modification. We are all remedial in some area.

However, now we move from one branch of the public services, the fire brigade, to another, the schools meals sector, and an excellent lunch of hamburgers, parsnips, potatoes, Yorkshire pudding, cabbage, gravy, and chopped-up fresh fruit (i.e. apples, bananas, oranges) with custard. All this punctuated by conversation between Samantha, Maria, Wayne, Hugh, David and myself about teeth, dentists and fillings. It began, as good conversations often do, with an observation drawn from real life, and one of the children commenting on the gold tooth which I have. Actually, it is a filling between two front teeth made of National Health gold. The conversation then continued with each of the children, at intervals, opening his mouth and stuffing his fingers down his throat, along with the hamburger, to point out various natural and acquired phenomena, for my benefit. All very entertaining, but not for those of a queasy disposition. Teeth, accidents, animals, babies, being sick, seem to be topics of great interest to young children.

After lunch I return to the classroom, outwardly unscathed by the mealtime encounter, to prepare for the afternoon session. The door opens.

Child: *(shouting from the doorway):* Are you a doctor?
R. M.:   No, dear, I'm not.

But the suggestion is reasonable and, to a child, it would make more sense than any true justification one could offer for such observation and note-making. Certainly, the children are rightly curious regarding my presence among them. When they come in at 1.30 p.m., many of them sliding on their knees across the wooden floor, a number crowd around asking, 'What are you writing?' ... What are you doing?' ... 'You're always writing, aren't you?' You may remember from Chapter 1 that Mike's 5-year-old contemporaries completely ignored their classroom intruder. By the age of 7, such insularity is less likely. It will reappear later, but for different reasons.

The children group themselves on the floor in front of Miss Bennett's desk. David is sitting in the same position as this morning, territorial stability being an important thing, as was noticed in Chapter 2. Silence falls and the teacher calls the register, girls first. Someone knocks at the door and a few of the children call out, 'Come in'. The visitor (the same Derek as appeared before lunch), enters but is turfed out immediately by Miss Bennett who explains, 'I'm the one who says "Come in"'. A few seconds later, to prove the point, she repeats the open sesame formula, 'Come in', and Derek re-enters to ask for the next of Mrs Wilder's groups. Three boys and a girl go off and the remainder of Class 4 moves into Neil's group, Mark's group, Julie's group.

It is customary in many schools to organise children in small groups, presumably so that a wider range of activities may be followed with only limited resources, or that it may be administratively convenient for the teacher. There is, too, the opportunity for more social learning to occur and for interaction between the group members. As Williams (1970) observes:

The once familiar weight of children in serried rows of desks, furtively attempting to communicate with friends at the far side of the room, has given place to an arrangement whereby children are encouraged to interact, to make friends and to learn to resolve their own differences. In addition to desks arranged in fours and sixes, moveable cupboards and bookshelves form nooks and alcoves within which groups of children are working.

Such an arrangement of the environment does promote easy communication and interchange of ideas but, on occasions, opportunities for co-operative work and mutual discussions are overlooked. The children may be physically grouped together, apparently for some corporate purpose, whereas, in reality, they are often pursuing solitary activities. In such a case, there may be little interaction between them. Close physical proximity does not lead automatically to all benefits; teacher attitudes and beliefs are crucial and paramount.

Moreover, even where pupils are working corporately, is the quality of their interaction, and particularly their language, sufficient to justify the method of grouping? In this respect, Douglas Barnes asks some pertinent questions (1976) which are applicable across a wide age range. Here are four of them:

(1) Are your pupils really discussing the meaning of what they are doing? For example, in science are they talking about how their 'experiment' relates to the principle in question, or is their talk mainly at the 'Pass the matches!' level?

(2) Can they find problems and formulate them, put forward explanatory hypotheses, use evidence to evaluate alternatives, plan lines of action?

(3) Can they cope with differences of opinion, share out the jobs to be done, move steadily through a series of tasks, summarize what they have decided, reflect on the nature of what they are doing?

(4) Have the topics which they have chosen, or you have prescribed, led to useful discussions?

Clearly, such questions are important even, with a liberal degree of interpretation, at this 7-year-old stage. Clearly too, the teacher's level of language awareness must be high, if David's performance in a group is to be adequately monitored. The rough level of social skill may be immediately apparent – either by presence or absence – but to assess spoken utterance competently requires a finely attuned ear. This concept of 'appraisal' of children's language is interestingly explored by Joan Tough (1976).

Meanwhile, David, naturally oblivious to such consideration, returns to the picture and word exercise he was working on earlier in the morning.

Miss B.:   Come on David, or you'll be miles behind.
Beverley *(to me):* Hello. I like you sitting next to us.
David: When we go somewhere, you go with us, don't you?
Beverley: Are you our group?
R. M.:   Yes, Beverley.
Beverley *(to others):* He's our group.

And here we are, grouped around a table on which are pictures and work cards as shown in Figure 3.11.

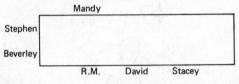

Figure 3.11

David now writes CAR under his picture of a car. He had previously written CAT under it. This done, he finds a picture of an apple and a card with the single word APPLE on it, and settles down to draw the apple. He works slowly, humming to himself. His thought processes may be slow, but he is by no means unintelligent. Mandy and Beverley are moved by the teacher to other activities, but David tries another picture and single word. This time the picture is of a vase and he asks me if he has chosen the correct word; he is aware it begins with *vuh*. At the same moment, Beverley is drawing two boats and writing the number 2 on her paper; Stephen three girls and the number 3; Mandy eight stars with the number 8; Stacey three flowers and the number 3. David asks himself: 'I've finished that, what shall I do next?' Undecided, he turns to Beverley.

David: How many do you have to do on these?
Beverley: Fifty, sixty, seventy.

Then, having advised him extravagantly, she counts out some other cards for him and asks, 'Have you done that one?' David again voices his thoughts aloud: 'I don't know how to do ships. I'll have a try.' He does so. His final page is shown in Figure 3.12.

It is now 2.00 p.m. and twelve children are still working at their tables while the rest are grouped on the floor around the teacher with their 'Janet and John' reading books. After five minutes' work, David takes out his book for marking by Miss Bennett: 'Yes, righto, not bad. It's a pity it's taken you such a long time to do it.' She tests him on one or two items; explains the next piece of work; ensures that he understands; exhorts him to work faster; and back he comes to his desk.

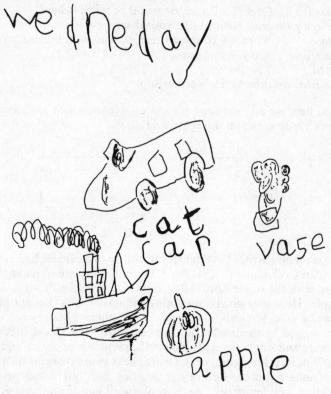

Figure 3.12

He takes an orange card with four trees on it and the word TREES and, as he settles down with this, he decides to tell me that when it was his birthday he was too frightened to go out in assembly, but he says he would not be scared now. Not for the first time today, it is evident that he is a shy, sensitive boy who finds the real world a bit much for him at times. His slowness in work cannot be attributed to laziness; he is, in fact, a hard and painstaking worker. He seems rather to have a personal speed, appropriate for him, which incorporates frequent pauses, flights into fantasy, diversions of attention. To force him to work faster seems rather like making a small car accelerate uphill while pulling a large caravan. Perhaps it can be done, but for what purpose and at what cost? John Holt (1967) writes:

> Timetables! We act as if children were railroad trains running on a schedule...If a child doesn't arrive at one of the intermediate stations when we think he should, we instantly assume that he is

going to be late at the finish. But children are not railroad trains. They don't learn at an even rate. They learn in spurts, and the more interested they are in what they are learning, the faster these spurts are likely to be.

David now has another work book and, letter by letter, copies *Wednesday* from the blackboard, as he did earlier in the morning. Seven minutes later he has completed *Wednesday 29th January*, and is drawing four trees, meticulously colouring the trees in different shades. At this point Miss Bennett asks three children, including David, how many cards they have completed. David has done one and the other two children three each. She tells him he must have completed three by play time. He writes the words *4 trees* under his drawing and the card is complete. It has taken seventeen minutes. Immediately he picks up the card with eight stars on it and begins on that one.

Ever watchful, Beverley looks over my notebook. 'What you writing?' she asks. With the amazement of an observer at a voodoo ceremony she gasps, 'You're writing double'.

Miss Bennett now gives instructions to several children, including David, to bring her their books. She tells him he has two seconds in which to write the word *stars* and he returns to his desk for this purpose with no more urgency than when he set off. He completes the star card in three minutes, apart from the word *stars*, which he again omits, and, when it is marked, receives instructions to do one more. All the other children are now clearing away and lining up by the door for play time. David selects a card with two blue kennels on it and completes this one within three minutes, there being now only David, the teacher and myself left in the room. His work is marked and he is told that, as it is hardly worthwhile for him to go out and join the others, he is to tidy the chairs during break, a task which appears quite agreeable to him. His finished product is shown in Figure 3.13.

At 2.50 p.m. break is over and all the children, now wearing coats and anoraks, are sitting on the floor in front of Miss Bennett, preparing to sing a song.

Children and teacher sing:
> John Brown's baby got a cold upon his chest,
> John Brown's baby got a cold upon his chest,
> John Brown's baby got a cold upon his chest,
> And they rubbed it with camphorated oil.

> Cam-phoram phoram phorated,
> Cam-phoram phoram phorated,
> Cam-phoram phoram phorated,
> And they rubbed it with camphorated oil.

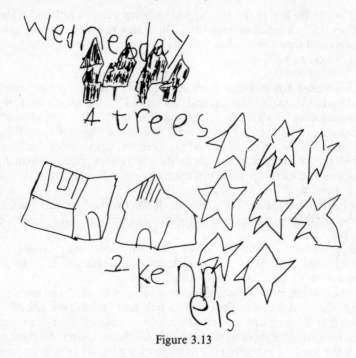

Figure 3.13

Miss B.:   Right. No babies this time.
Children and teacher sing:

> John Brown's b— got a cold upon his chest,
> John Brown's b— *(children laugh)* got a cold upon his chest,
> John Brown's b— *(children laugh)* got a cold upon his chest,
> And they rubbed it with camphorated oil.

The children find it very amusing when one or two of them start to say the word *baby* and laugh each time it happens. They sing the chorus with great gusto:

> Cam-phoram phoram phorated,
> Cam-phoram phoram phorated,

Miss B.:   All right. No baby and no cold this time.
Children and teacher sing:
> John Brown's b— *(children laugh)* got a 'tsch' upon his chest
> John Brown's baby
Miss B.:   No. You aren't thinking.

Children and teacher sing:

> got a 'tsch' upon his chest,
> John Brown's — got a 'tsch' upon his chest,
> And they rubbed it with camphorated oil.
>
> Cam-phoram phoram phorated,
> . . .
>
> John Brown's — got a 'tsch' upon his chest *(children laugh)*
> John Brown's — got a 'tsch' upon his chest *(children laugh)*
> John Brown's — got a 'tsch' upon his chest *(children laugh)*

Miss B.: Well, I really. We'd better start again on that verse. Stephen, I think mummy's come. No, Andrew, not now. Ready? No baby, no cold, and no chest. Let's see if you can be clever. One, two, three . . .

Children and teacher sing:

> John Brown's — got a 'tsch' upon his —
> John Brown's b— *(children laugh)* got a 'tsch' upon his —
> John Brown's b— *(children laugh)* got a 'tsch' upon his chest
>   *(children laugh)*
> And they rubbed it with camphorated oil.
>
> Cam-phoram phoram phorated,
> . . .

Miss B.: Right. Do you remember the song about the crocodile?
Children: Yeeeees. *(with enthusiasm.)*
Miss B.: Well, come on, then. Put your heads crocodile heads up. Oh! the lady thinks she's *very* clever, riding on his back and floating down the river Nile. Right. One . . . two . . . three . . .

Children and teacher sing:

> She sailed away on a lovely summer's day
> On the back of the crocodile.
> You see, said she, he's as tame as tame can be,
> I'll float him down the Nile.
> The croc he winked his eye, as she waved her friends goodbye,
> With a starry smile.
> But at the end of the ride
> The lady was inside,
> And the smile on the crocodile
> Pom! Pom!

Miss B.:   Why was the crocodile so happy?
Several children: Because he wanted to eat her.
Miss B.:   And has he?
Chorus of children: Yeeeees.
Miss B.:   Yes.
Child: Miss, can we have that one about . . .
           (And they next sing a song about a Chinese washerwoman.)

The children obviously enjoy the songs[1] and perhaps the corporate involvement which strengthens their identity as a class. Some sing and do actions; some do actions only; a few merely sit. The group singing is a very different kind of activity from most of those earlier in the day, which tended to be solitary or individual. However, the way in which 'John Brown's Baby' is sung, with varying omission of different elements, demands the same kind of concentration from the children which many of the previous activities also demanded. By contrast, the crocodile and washerwoman songs are much more relaxed and correspondingly fluent. As in assembly this morning, David looks about him, with rather a baffled air, and manages to pick up bits and pieces of appropriate song and action.

The singing lasts ten minutes and there follows a story by Miss Bennett, set in ancient Wales, about a king in a castle, surrounded by mountains and forests. The king and queen owned an enormous dog called Gelert, with huge eyes and a bell around his neck. When the king, who did not know that a dangerous wolf was nearby, had to go away for three days, the dog was left to guard the queen and the baby prince. After three days, the dog rushed out to greet his master on his return, but the king, on seeing blood around the dog's mouth, jumped to conclusions and slew Gelert with his sword. Too late he learned that the dog had, in fact, killed the wolf in a terrible fight in the baby prince's bedroom. After a few days, the king decided to erect a big pillar of stone as a monument to his faithful dog and to put on it the words:

---

[1]Teachers on the lookout for interesting classroom songs may like to dip into any of the following:

Bley, E. S., *The Best Singing Games for Children of All Ages* (New York: Sterling Publishing Co., 1957).
Dobbs, J., Fiske, R., Lane, M., *Ears and Eyes*, Books 1 and 2 (Oxford: OUP, 1974).
Gadsby, D., and Goldby, I., *Merrily to Bethlehem. A Very Unusual Carol Book* (London: A. & C. Black, 1978).
Green, D., *Chorus. The Puffin Colony Song Book* (Harmondsworth: Penguin: Puffin, 1977).
Harrop, B., *Apusskidu* (London: A. & C. Black, 1975).
Harrop, B., *Okki-tokki-unga. Action Songs for Children* (London: A. & C. Black, 1976).
Matterson, E., *This Little Puffin* (Harmondsworth: Penguin, 1969).

HERE LIES GELERT, MY GOOD AND FAITHFUL
DOG, WHO LOOKED AFTER US ALL AND
LOOKED AFTER MY LITTLE BABY SON.

Miss B.:   And if you go to Beddgelert in Wales, you can see that
stone; it's still there to this day.

The story has been well told and the children's attention well held.
Such a tale of danger and savagery would easily translate to 'X' certifi-
cate film and perhaps this is one of its abiding attractions for young
children, rather than its depiction of the quality of fidelity.

'The story' still occupies a powerful place in the primary school
curriculum, and rightly so. It is a means whereby language and
concepts may be developed; multi-cultural and multi-ethnic awareness
extended; fears assuaged; hearts touched; and the world comprehended. To do any or all of these things, the story must be appropriate. It
must be capable of striking some kind of chord in the hearts and minds
of the children who hear or read it and, for this to happen, the teacher
must know well both stories and children. Some tales will be immediately relevant to current experience; others will speak of eternal
hopes, fears, endeavours. As John Sadler (1974) puts it:

Children find the world a rare mixture of mystery and familiarity, of
fearsome dangers and reassuring security . . . Stories must reflect
these feeling experiences and it does not much matter whether they
are about slum children, Greek heroes or spacemen, so long as the
children can identify themselves. The stories that appeal to children
are basically timeless: David and Goliath, Hansel and Gretel, Jason
and the Golden Fleece. Children can tolerate plenty of tension, even
of sadness and tragedy, but they do want a happy ending. Somehow
the ogres, the villains, the figures of harsh authority, must be
worsted or reconciled; otherwise the world is unbearable.

(Sequel I to Chapter 4 offers a list of appropriate fiction across a wide
age and ability range, and I recommend Elaine Moss's article, 'Story-
telling', in C. Richards, 1978.)

As the children button their coats ready for home, their posses-
sions, safely guarded by the teacher, are returned to them – smokey
bacon crisps; biscuits; sweets; two books, including a *Black Beauty*
picture book, which Miss Bennett shows the whole group. It is now
3.15 p.m.

Miss B.:   Good afternoon, Class 4.
Children: Good afternoon, Miss Bennett. Good afternoon everyone.

(Such politenesses, which are also, in their way, assertions of control, are rarely heard at secondary school level.)

Miss B.:   Anybody whose name starts with *duh* go. Come back, Brian. Whose name starts with *sss ... a ... nnn ... wuh ... ruh ... puh ... kuh ... buh ... juh ... mmm ... (and so on).*

David, characteristically, is the last to go and, when he asks for his reading book (in the 'Janet and John' series) he remembers that he has left it at home.

At 3.30 p.m. I am in the hall watching some of the children playing a game with another teacher, when a father comes to collect his child, Roy. He sees him crying and, like the king in the story, presumes the worst. In the belief that another child has hit his lad, he says 'Next time he hits you, kick him in the bloody mouth.'

Sequel I   Learning Theory

How may we describe in more professional, less general, terms the learning which David may have accomplished during his withdrawal remedial lesson? One way is to draw on the views of an American researcher, Robert M. Gagné (1966) and to try to match the very real activities in which David has been engaged with their theoretical categorisations. According to Gagné, these are eight in number, and hierarchical, so that complex learning is based on foundations of more simple learning.

Bearing in mind, then, that children and adults constantly exhibit examples of learning in any or all of the eight categories, what kinds of learning have chiefly occupied David?

(1)   *Signal learning*
This is a 'general, diffuse, emotional response', sometimes merely an immediate involuntary physiological reaction to a signal. An example of this would be the emotion of fear, with its concomitant bodily manifestations, at the sound of an explosion. David will know, as will any school pupil, that the teacher equivalents of the military command 'Attention!' are intended to produce a state of awareness, of preparedness. As such, this would be an indication of signal learning.

(2)   *Stimulus–Response Learning*
This is a rather more considered and deliberate reaction, acquired over a period of time, invariably in the wake of reward or reinforcement of some kind. It is the sort of learning previously seen in Chapter 2, not only in parts of Rashda's E_2L lesson, but also in her word-bingo/flash-card session. David is exposed to it early on in his remedial lesson when he is required to call out the names of cardboard shapes tossed on the floor.

(3)   *Chaining*
Here, two or more previously learnt stimulus–responses may be linked together. An example would be tying shoelaces which, you will remember, David could not do.

(4)   *Verbal–Associate Learning*
This is a form of chaining which involves language. An example of it would be in David's work with the Language Master machine, where a verbal response is required to a situational drawing, of greater sophistication than a mere flashcard.

(5)   *Multiple Discrimination*
To use Gagné's example, this is the kind of learning which enables a boy to name different makes of car by identification of certain distinctive features. He chains together his perception of one kind of tailgate, with a particular kind of bumper, and says, 'Renault 16'. This, in my view, is the sort of learning to which David is most exposed in Mrs Wilder's

lesson. He is called upon to practise visual discrimination of shape and shape sequence; tactile differentiation (as in feeling the pieces of material); auditory discrimination, between different verbal sounds *(dog, den, hen, dad, dig)* and a more sophisticated visual discrimination in selecting from wrongly spelled alternatives *(fuor, foru, four, rouf)*; transference of various multi-coloured shapes to squared paper. In each case, and in a partial ascending order of difficulty, David is required to exercise, and thereby reinforce, a number of discrimination skills.

What, then, of Gagné's four remaining types of learning? These are as follows:

(6) Concept Learning

In this case, discrimination between members of a group is allied to an abstraction of the essence of that group, a generalisation about the major feature which binds all members together. For example, people may be black, pink, yellow; short, tall; fat, thin; interesting, boring; United or City fans, but they are all human, even the City fans. Grasping the concept of being human means being able to appreciate the essential unity in the more immediately apparent diversity. Clearly, this kind of learning is crucial at all stages, including college where, apart from anything else, the concepts of *teacher, school, pupil* will undergo great changes in the course of professional training. David could scarcely avoid such learning, and it is particularly evident in the work he does on the concepts *above*, and *under*. This activity, as we have already observed, is also linked with Verbal–Associate Learning.

(7) Principle (or Rule) Learning

In this instance, a chaining of two or more concepts occurs. For example, if the statement: 'Most citizens aged 18 or over are allowed to vote', is fully understood, as opposed to being merely parroted, then the various concepts of *most, citizens, 18 years of age, vote*, will have been fully comprehended, as will the linking of them together. Clearly, this is a very common and crucial type of learning.

(8) Problem Solving

This is the last, and most complex, of Gagné's sequence, involving, as it does, a combining of old learnt principles into new ones, so as to solve new problems. Such restructuring occurs constantly throughout a day and is seen in such activities as planning the shopping in anticipation of half-day closing; completing homework when the evening has been unexpectedly interrupted; managing financially when the student grant is late arriving; solving a textbook problem. It is the kind of learning which can be verified by requiring the learner to solve other problems of a similar kind, and many examples of it may be found throughout this book.

Such is the nature of Gagné's eight types of learning, let alone the human mind itself, that other interpretations of the kinds of learning David has been involved in may be valid. In any event, linking practice with theory, in the kind of way I have attempted, is always easier in theory than in practice.

Chapter 4

Lucy, Aged 8

We always look at the 'Radio Times' before we go to my nanny's, because she's got a television.

THE SCHOOL

Lucy's junior and infant Roman Catholic school opened with 76 children in 1967. It now has some 250 children on roll (including 14 non-Catholics), with 50 per cent from the predominantly middle-class suburban parish and 50 per cent from outside, which makes for a good social balance. There are seven classes, eight teachers, and a playing field on the attractive site. Each day there is half an hour's specialist remedial attention for the five children in each class who are academically weakest.

THE DAY

It is 9.00 a.m. on a fine, fresh morning. One blast on the whistle in the playground and the children freeze, on account of discipline rather than climate. Another shorter bleep brings them back to life and they line up smartly in class rows. Regular army soldiers could hardly do better and the precision is a sign of classroom orderliness to come.

My 8-year-old subject for the day is Lucy, the youngest in her class, dressed in a turquoise blouse, grey shirt, blue tights and with a multi-coloured hair ribbon tying her fair pony tail. She moves in line with the other 37 children (i.e. 23 girls and 15 boys) to her second-year junior classroom, shown in Figure 4.1.

On the maths wall there are several charts. One shows 'Shapes we see every day', such as a church steeple, a stop sign, a gate, a crane. Another, again produced by the teacher, is about circles and has information by appropriate diagrams: 'All radii and diameters of the same circle are of equal length . . . These are concentric circles. By how much does the diameter decrease each time?'

This is fairly demanding language for 8-year-olds. The military succinctness of the definitions, the pedagogic tone, and the uncompromising use of technical terms foreshadow the language of secondary education. This, as Douglas Barnes (1969, 1976) maintains, is at several removes from children's own, more natural, language and can impose a barrier to real understanding. Certainly, there is both a

The classroom

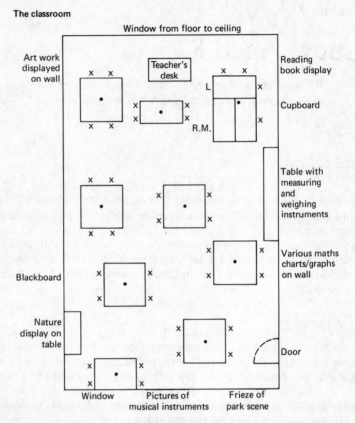

Figure 4.1

subject register[1] and tone, and a school register and tone, that pupils must adjust to; the accommodation is rarely mutual. Perhaps the key point at issue is whether this initially alien language is adequately explained before use, or merely imposed on an uncomprehending multitude. As Richards points out (1978):

> The advantage of a technical vocabulary is that in a particular context each term carries one meaning. In other words, the intention is to convey one concept. A measure of the usefulness of such terms when employed in speech and text books is that they

[1]'The kind or "variety" of English appropriate for a particular purpose in a particular situation (that is, having regard to Subject, Addressee, and Context) is known as a "register" of English.' (A. M. Wilkinson, *The Foundations of Language*, London, Oxford University Press, 1971. For further clarification of this concept see pages 39f. of the same volume.)

contribute to the formation of useful concepts. A good book and a perceptive teacher will present important terms in more than one way, illustrate where possible, discuss central concepts fully without employing large numbers of other terms which are not essential, and never use terms without explaining them.

The classroom observer is at a distinct disadvantage here in his assessment of the situation. Like the theatre critic, he sees the actual production rather than the rehearsals; he can only guess at what has gone before and, in the absence of firm evidence one way or the other, assumes that such wall definitions as are in Lucy's classroom represent statements of existing knowledge, painstakingly taught by the teacher and acquired by the children.

Other visual information on the same wall suggests, in fact, that the definitions are not isolated and ill-digested lumps but, rather, part of a general maths context. There is also, for instance, a bar chart with coloured paper indicating squares (red); circles (fawn); rectangles (brown); triangles (yellow); ovals (green). There are ten identical copies done by the children of the same block graph showing the number of pints (milk?) delivered each day to the school. In addition to this maths material displayed on the walls, there is a variety of maths equipment, work cards and folders in a cupboard.

The reading corner includes many books donated by the Parent–Teacher Association, each with a record card which reads: . . . Borrowed by; . . . Returned; . . . Librarian.' The choice, like the school, is catholic, and includes:

The Wombles by Elizabeth Beresford (London: Benn);
The Family from One End Street by Eve Garnett (London: Muller);
Paddington Takes the Air by Michael Bond (London: Collins);
The Day Jean Pierre Joined the Circus by Paul Gallico (London: Heinemann);
Chitty Chitty Bang Bang by Ian Fleming (London: Cape);
Tales of Magic from Far and Near by Doris Rust (London: Faber);
The Best of Brer Anansi by David Makhanlall (Oxford: Blackie);
The Magic Finger by Roald Dahl (London: Allen & Unwin);
Jackanory Stories (London: BBC).

Fiction material suitable for a variety of ages is offered in the sequel to this chapter.

I ask one small, fair-haired, freckled boy his name and, as he tells me it is Christopher, so he screws a metal ring on his nose. This becomes a reasonably secure fixture, despite subsequent facial contortions. It is the first indication of an interesting repertoire, other parts of which Christopher will reveal as the day goes by.

The headteacher, Mr Gaskell, introduces me to the children and they seem interested and mildly excited. I believe they had been told previously to act normally, just as if I had not been there. They certainly have a brightness and a freshness, like the day, which could not have been specially assumed for the occasion, and are for the most part smartly dressed in their predominantly grey uniforms. They answer their names alertly as the attendance and dinner registers are called. There are thirty staying for dinner. Some children take the opportunity for ten minutes spelling revision before Mass. Others, maybe more confident or less wise, whisper of King Kong and Godzilla as the teacher now collects coach money for a school trip. Miss Trueman is a short, stocky, first-year probationer teacher, who has a firm, no-nonsense manner.

When the bell sounds at 9.10 a.m. she tells the girls first to line up by the door, and then the boys. Soon they are on their way down the corridor to the weekly school Mass to which parents are invited. It is clearly a practice of which the Plowden Report would approve (see para. 108) and, in a denominational school of this kind, can have the effect of strengthening the spiritual bond between children, parents and teachers. In such a setting, there is not the conflict of religious interests that might be found elsewhere, and Dearden's words (1968) may, in this context, be unexpectedly comforting. He writes: 'Prayer and worship are hollow, meaningless activities unless certain beliefs are held about the object to which they are addressed, namely God. One cannot pray or worship ABOUT religion; such activities are logically impossible apart from the presupposition of an actual belief in God.'

The hall is arranged as in Figure 4.2.

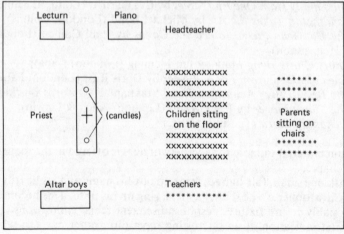

Figure 4.2

With the exception of the two youngest infants' classes, all the children in the school are present as the priest, in green vestments as befits the church season, enters, flanked by two altar boys. The service, which has 'Seeing' is its theme, begins with a hymn.

1   For the beauty of the earth,
For the beauty of the skies,
For the love which from our birth,
Over and around us lies,

Father unto Thee we raise
This our sacrifice of praise.

2   For the beauty of each hour
Of the day and of the night,
Hill and dale and tree and flower,
Sun and moon and stars of light,
Father unto Thee . . .

3   For the joy of human love,
Brother, sister, parent, child,
Friends on earth and friends above,
For all gentle thoughts and mild,
Father unto Thee . . .

4   For each perfect gift of thine
To our race so freely given;
Graces human and divine,
Flowers of earth and buds of heaven,

Father unto Thee . . .

Mr Gaskell conducts the singing, leads the responses and indicates when the children are to sit/stand/kneel. The priest, who is tall, elderly, and crippled, begins by telling the children that in Africa (he does not say which country), where he once worked, the people do not greet each other with 'How do you do', but instead, 'I see you'. That is to be the keynote of today's service.

The priest has an easy relationship with the children but talks rather quickly, and uses such tricky phrases, albeit with explanation, as 'beatific vision'. As he questions the whole school, so individuals respond easily and with confidence. 'How can we see Jesus?' he asks. 'In the Host', replies Lucy, without hesitation.[1] In order to make the point more real, the priest asks a tiny boy to come out to the front and,

---

[1]It is 'the right answer' in terms of Catholic teaching, but one wonders at the level of conceptual awareness involved in such a statement. For further consideration of this kind of difficulty, see Chapter 1, Sequel I on 'Religious Understanding'.

patting him on the head, says, 'If you pull this boy's hair, you hurt Jesus. Whatever you do to him, you do to Jesus.' The idea appears to be appreciated as the bemused infant, now under advertised protection, beams his way back to his place in the ranks of the 250.

The service of mass now takes place and all except the youngest queue up to receive communion. The line includes a number of parents and teachers and the caretaker who, later in the day, will be heard moving about the school singing 'The Mountains of Mourne'.

The service, conducted with dignity and clarity, ends at 10.05 a.m. as the second and last hymn is vigorously sung, with a refrain which reinforces the day's theme of Seeing.

> 1 I know a man who's kind and gentle –
>   To follow him brings peace.
>   I know a man I'm going to love
>   'Till after time shall cease.
>
>   *(Refrain:)*
>   Show me the way to walk towards you,
>   Let your light shine bright.
>   Show me the way and I won't stumble
>   Even though it's night.
>
> 2 I know a man who understands
>   What I can't even say.
>   I know a man who's there to turn to
>   Any time of the day.
>   *(Refrain)*
>
> 3 I know a man whose mother told me,
>   'What he says you do.'
>   I know a man who, dying, gave her
>   To be my mother too.
>   *(Refrain)*
>
> 4 I know a man who died on Calvary
>   To pay for my sin.
>   I know a man and I've decided
>   I'm going to die for him
>   *(Refrain)*
>
> 5 I know a man who said he'd feed me
>   With himself, as bread.
>   I know a man who's living ever –
>   He rose from the dead.
>   *(Refrain)*
>
>   I know a man who gently beckons with his shepherd's rod.
>   I know a man – now listen to me, I know a man who's GOD.

Back in the classroom, the transition from spiritual to temporal is abrupt, being effected by the teacher's words: 'We'll do maths first. That always gets us going, doesn't it?' The children greet this apparent testimony to the corporate laxative power of mathematics with 'Ooooooh!' in a tone of simulated dismay, and take out their exercise books. Lucy is in a group of five (Figure 4.3).

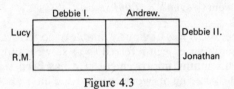

Figure 4.3

Miss T.: Tongues away. The test was four minutes last time and four minutes the time before, so we aim for three and a half today.

Lucy: Why not three and three quarters, Miss?

In absolute silence Miss Trueman now dictates the questions and the children write the answers in their books. Here is the test which does, as Lucy requested, take 3¾ minutes.

(1) 3 times 2	(2) 4 add 4	(3) 6 add 4
(4) 5 add 5	(5) 7 add 3	(6) 8 add 2
(7) 20 take away 10	(8) 15 take away 5	(9) 3 times 3
(10) 4 times 2	(11) 5 times 1	(12) 3 times 4
(13) 100 add 10	(14) 10 take away 7	(15) 6 take away 3
(16) 8 take away 4	(17) 20 take away 20	(18) 10 add 3 add 6 add 1
(19) 10 times 10	(20) 19 take away 9	(21) 2 times 2 add 4
(22) 18 take away 8	(23) 3 times 5	(24) 3 times 4 add 12
(25) 5 times 5 add 25	(26) 30 take away 10	(27) 3 add 2 add 1 add 10
(28) 10 divided by 2	(29) 20 divided by 2	(30) 7 take away 4 add 3

The test, which begins simply, sets out to provide problems involving the four mathematical processes. Seven of the 30 items are straightforward addition, with 2 additions of 4 numbers each; 6 are multiplication; 9 subtraction; 2 division; 4 items involve a combination of processes (i.e. 3 are multiplication and addition; 1 is subtraction and addition).

Confident in the knowledge of her own success, Lucy obtains the teacher's permission to distribute crayons for marking. Either in concert, or individually, children call out the answers under Miss Trueman's direction and mark their own books. In between questions there is strict silence; the whole exercise is treated very seriously indeed.

Lucy: Miss, shall we write how many we've got out of how many?

Miss T.:   Yes. You know what you have to do, don't you?

There appears to be a clearly understood sequence for this regular activity.
  Lucy has 30/30, as have ten to twelve other children.

Miss T.:   Who has got thirty?...twenty-nine?...twenty-eight?...
           twenty-seven?...*(and so on).*

  Christopher, who was obviously unable to concentrate during Mass, and has already twice been referred to as slow, is now praised by the teacher for his maths improvement. He has been standing by Miss Trueman's desk having his work checked and has scored 13/30. *Where* he is going wrong is not clear, since the problems combined a number of different mathematical processes. Moreover, the test itself simply reflects an attainment score. It does not diagnose weaknesses and, without the working by which his answers were arrived at, or, at least, some breakdown of his wrong answers, there is no means of knowing which mathematical processes he can manage and which he cannot.[1] Apart from that, merely asking for the scores in front of the whole class, which is done regularly throughout the land, only serves to confirm the strong in their strength and the weak in their misery, without helping either. Process, rather than answer, is more significant. Perhaps Miss Trueman checks on such process on other occasions.
  With a sergeant major's abruptness, she says: 'Right, now, spelling books out' and, while the children, uninvited but aware of the system, are drawing columns in their books, she writes on the board:

er
ex
ea
ee

  When all are ready, in a matter of seconds, she reads out individual words for a spelling test, arranged in groups with a common element, sometimes giving an example of the word as it might be used in a sentence. The test is as follows:

(1)   *other*   'The other day I went to town.'
(2)   *mother*   'Mother took me to town.'
(3)   *father*
(4)   *brother*

[1]Stephen Jackson's book, *A Teacher's Guide to Tests and Testing* (London: Longman, 1968) provides useful detail on the range of mathematical tests available, both to measure attainment and to diagnose areas of weakness.

(5)	*winter*	
(6)	*summer*	
(7)	*sister*	
(8)	*teas*	(Miss T.: pronounced 'tease'.)
(9)	*weave*	
(10)	*preach*	
(11)	*beneath*	
(12)	*cheap*	
(13)	*seam*	'I am going to sew the seam on my dress.'
(14)	*eager*	'You are all very eager to get them right.'
(15)	*leap*	'I'm going to leap with joy.' (Lucy whispers, 'Miss, that's what you said last time'.)
(16)	*explain*	'Please explain to me what you are doing.'
(17)	*expect*	'I expect all of you to try.'
(18)	*express*	'I caught the express train.'
(19)	*except*	'They all came to my party except Mary.'
(20)	*excitement*	'I was full of excitement at the party.'
(21)	*extinct*	'Dinosaurs are extinct.'
(22)	*extra*	'You have an extra pinta today.'
(23)	*extremely*	'It was extremely cold when we came here.'
(24)	*extend*	'I shall extend my arm in the air.'
(25)	*experiment*	'We have done an experiment.'

Numbers 1 to 7 inclusive have the *-er* sound as their common element; numbers 8 to 15 the *-ea* sound; and numbers 16 to 25 begin with the prefix *-ex*. Such careful selection of phonic items in a spelling test gives it a rationale and makes it, potentially, more of a teaching device than it would otherwise be. In this respect it contrasts with Lorraine's test in the next chapter.

After number 25 Miss Trueman says, 'OK We'll stop there', but relents in the face of the children's cry of dismay, 'Oooooh!' and, saving the best wine until last, offers two more difficult words to finish: 'Right, we'll have some more then.'

(27)	*extravagant*	'Andrew is very extravagant with his money.'
(27)	*expedition*	'Cubs and Scouts went on their expedition.'

Miss T.: We've got to stretch your mind, haven't we, Christopher? We can't have easy ones all the time, can we, Christopher?

It is so simple for a child to be identified as the class dimwit and his inability or laziness can even become the source of innumerable jokes. One teacher I know believes that children with speech impediments should be ridiculed out of them. Some might argue that light-hearted banter in class serves the purpose of goading a pupil into producing better work. Perhaps it could, but which adult likes to be reminded of his weaknesses? After nine lessons of piano learning, I can testify to the power of praise for my poor efforts. Masses of encouragement, laced with gentle criticism, seems a successful diet and, even in mature years, one is absurdly grateful for commendation. Moreover, I have learnt that piano playing *technique* is more important early on than hitting the right notes every time. There seems to be a good educational moral there. Perhaps all teachers should, every now and again, attempt a new skill – let us say swimming, pottery, playing a musical instrument, car driving, typing – in order to be reminded of what life is like as a learner, perhaps even as a remedial pupil.

Moreover, the surroundings in which the learning is attempted are highly significant. Success or failure may quickly become associated with a particular place, and the implications for school are obvious. 'Not only is reward satisfying and punishment annoying', writes Philip Jackson (1968) 'but, after a time, the settings in which one or the other of these conditions is continually experienced begin to engender the associated feeling on its own.'

Context, too, in terms of people is crucial. As I practise my piano pieces – 'The Cuckoo', 'Fairies in the Lawn', 'Scissor Grinders' – to mention but a few well-loved masterpieces, there are only two other people who can hear them. One is my wife, who has said not a word about the ghastliness of the sound produced and, instead, looks forward to Christmas, when we shall be able to sing accompanied carols. No doubt the effect of reading a good deal of Victorian literature. The other is the baby, who actually seems to enjoy the discords.

Children in class are rarely so fortunate. In a highly competitive setting, the weakest come off worst. They either retreat into themselves, or develop some kind of defence mechanism. In Lucy's class, Christopher, showing varying degrees of disturbance, has chosen to be an amiable clown, rather than a nuisance. Willard Waller's comment (1932) is interesting in this respect: 'There is a tendency, he writes, for roles to be carried into the school room ... The clown is still a clown, but his buffoonery must be disguised; it may become covert, or it may adopt a mien of innocence and pose as blundering stupidity.' The headteacher was to tell me later that Christopher, an adopted child, kicked and screamed for four weeks when he first came to school and used to hide under the table.

We now move to the marking of the spelling test. Again the children are quite familiar with the pattern. When asked, each child says the word in full and then spells it out. Christopher is first.

Miss T.:   Christopher, spell 'other'.
Christopher: Other. $u - o - e - r$.

Lucy's hand shoots up like a piston, as it has done and is to do constantly throughout the day, and she whispers urgently and insistently, 'Miss, Miss'. Christopher is corrected, and so on through the list until the last three words. The excitement is now quite remarkable, verging almost on hysteria. Obviously the kudos involved in cracking one of these nuts is considerable. Suddenly it is all over, like the end of the Cup Final and, although evidence of the heightened tension lingers on, normal life may be resumed.[1]

Lucy has 25/27, having failed at these last two hurdles, *exstravagant* [*sic*] and *expidition* [*sic*]. She and the others on her table now discuss their errors. Christopher calls out, 'Miss, I only got seven right'. Lucy, mental arithmetic expert that she is, instantly retorts, 'You got twenty wrong then'. Such a sharp, critical comment may qualify as an example of what the anthropologist Jules Henry dramatised as the 'witch-hunt syndrome'. 'A chief component of this syndrome is the destructive criticism of each other by the students, egged on, as it were, by the teacher' (Philip Jackson, 1968). A little harsh, perhaps, on both Lucy and Miss Trueman, but worth pondering.

It is now 10.40 a.m. and, just before the bell sounds for breaktime, table by table the children take their spelling and maths exercise books out to the teacher. Those who remain in their seats either read their library books or do an exercise from an SRA work book. Lucy's is shown in Figure 4.4. She is working from page 69 of *My Own Book for Listening and Reading* (SRA Laboratory 1c, *Student Record Book for Reading*, by Don H. Parker and Genevieve Scannell).

Lucy reads each riddle very carefully, putting her finger on each word. She then consults the list and chooses the correct ones. Even though she has accounted for two of the three pictures (i.e. parrot and puppy) she takes no chances with the last and again consults the list of words before deciding to write *bridge*, although that is the only picture remaining. Highly able, methodical, convergent girl that she is, she takes no risks.

There is a fifteen-minute break now for all but Miss Trueman, who is on playground duty. I write my notes in an empty classroom, drinking the coffee which the headteacher has sent with one of the girls, Elaine. With the sound of voices and screams vaguely in the distance, one has the curious feeling of being where the action isn't. A journalist two miles from the battle-front.

---

[1]Spelling is considered in more detail in Chapter 5. Here it is sufficient to observe that the cause of good spelling might be better served by a more individualised and natural approach, such as that employed in using *Blackwell's Spelling Workshop* by B. R. Sadler and E. G. Page (Oxford, 1975). This (expensive) box of structurally organised word lists on card enables each child to work individually, at any convenient moment, on a self-administered test, followed by identification of a rule and, where appropriate, discussion with the teacher.

Write the word that answers the riddle. Put the numeral under the picture that shows what the answer is.

3 _____   2 _____   1 _____

1 People talk and so do I!
I can also climb and fly.

I am a ___*parrot*___

2 I have ears like a dog and a tail like a dog.
I bark like a dog, but I'm just a baby.

I am a ___*puppy*___

3 I cross water, but I never move.
I have no arms, but I carry people.

I am a ___*bridge*___

FIND THE WORD HERE		
puppy	carrot	bridge
poppy	parrot	bride
puppet	parent	brick

3 bridge
2 puppy
1 parrot

● Word recognition: choosing among words with similar elements
● Drawing inferences from riddle clues

69

Figure 4.4

Not for long. At 10.55 a.m. the bell sounds again and the children return, Lucy immediately taking up her SRA work book. She now tackles page 55, which is similar to page 69, except that phrases, rather than individual words, are required (Figure 4.5).

Lucy is not working sequentially through the book, page by page, but being more selective, and the children in the group recommend

Complete the verses. Make them rhyme. Make them tell about the picture.

1	2	3
sitting down to dine	staying up too late	playing in the air
winding up some string	eating off a plate	flying towards heaven
perching on a sign	swinging on a gate	staying up till seven
playing with some twine	climbing on a fence	counting to eleven

1. Ten little owls playing with some twine
One was tied up, and then there were nine.

2. Nine little owls Swinging on a gate
One fell off, and then there were eight.

3. Eight little owls Flying towards heaven
One flew too high, and then there were seven.

1 playing with some twine
2 swinging on a gate
3 flying toward heaven

● Concept reinforcement: aural discrimination
● Matching words with pictures

55

Figure 4.5

good pages to each other, which seems an attractive way to proceed. She now confides to the others 'There's a good one on page 78' and then works silently on her own, only looking up occasionally for the odd second. Although the children are sitting in groups, much of their work is isolated and individual.

Debbie II, opposite Lucy, is aware that the answers are printed in small lettering upside down at the bottom of the page. She sees me observe her looking at them and says to Debbie I, 'I wish they wouldn't put the answers in'. A nod in the direction of a clear conscience.

All the children, seated around double desks in groups of four or five, are now very involved, either with SRA work books or SRA work cards. The system in the class is for each child to complete a page or so and then take it to the teacher for approval, as she moves from group to group around the room. Although answers are provided for self-checking, Miss Trueman likes to keep careful track of the work herself.

The chief attraction of such material is that the children enjoy it and are so engaged by it that the class teacher is freed to work with individuals. This is a big credit point in large or small classes and should not be underestimated. Whether the SRA scheme really develops language skills which transfer to other areas of school work and life is to be questioned. Certainly, the ability to do SRA cards will improve with practice, and perhaps the children do get a sense of progress in moving through the graded sequence of cards. However, the English language is not so linear in its development as may appear from the apparently authoritative sequence of the boxes of cards in the scheme. Moreover, work on the cards is entirely unrelated to anything else being done in school, so that a child may be doing maths work on symmetry, a project on dinosaurs, an environmental study based on the local church, but his comprehension card which, in different circumstances, could have been devised to reinforce any of these three areas, is about a bat's system of radar, or frogmen's equipment, or precious stones. Interesting topics, no doubt, but so much more meaningful if related in some way to other school activities.

On one level, SRA is merely the equivalent of a cut-up American textbook, more attractively presented on durable card, in a kind of programme learning device, with amusing but non-relevant word games. On another level, it is a means whereby children may be happily occupied developing a variety of comprehension skills,[1] while the teacher operates on a most desirable one-to-one basis. Perhaps the truth lies somewhere between these extremes.

Undeterred by such considerations, Lucy moves from SRA work book to work card. Sighing a little, she looks up at Debbie and says, 'It's only twenty past eleven'. This is the only indication all day that even stars weary sometimes. She takes the card out to Miss Trueman who asks her to read the comprehension passage entitled, 'Saved By Gum'. Lucy reads it very competently and, at the end, says, 'Ugh! I wouldn't agree with that. Chewing gum!' Dismayed by the very

---

[1]While generally endorsing the value of SRA, when used properly, the Schools Council Project, *The Effective Use of Reading* (1979), points out the lack of evidence for the view that comprehension can be broken down in a series of sub-skills. According to the Project, it appears, rather, to be a global skill.

thought, she exchanges the card for one whose story by Rosalie Koskimaki is entitled, 'How Do Seeds Travel?' (9 Lime. Lab. 1c) but there is no time left.

Miss T.: Let's have one table at a time, the smartest, like this one, lining up by the door.

We all move off to the school hall for a television programme in the series 'Stop, Look and Listen', and on the way two or three children talk about a television film which they enjoyed the previous Saturday – *King Kong and Godzilla*. Our programme today lacks the glamour of such a subject. It is on launderettes and contrasts modern washing machines with English washtubs and dollies of thirty years ago, and river washing in India.

The children watch quite attentively, sitting on the floor of a cold hall, looking at a black and white television set whose screen reflects light in such a way that the picture is difficult to make out. All the children are in relaxed positions except Lucy, who is kneeling up and sitting back on her legs, paying particular attention, like an entranced Muslim. Miss Trueman whispers to me that Lucy does not have a television at home and is therefore all the keener to see it when she can.

After twenty minutes the rather mundane programme ends and the children return to their classroom, where Lucy immediately resumes her SRA work book.

Miss T.: Right. Everything away *(a slight snort of exasperation from Lucy)* apart from your spelling books and pencils. I said 'everything away, apart from spelling books and pencils', and that includes tongues, Caroline.

The class is to have a spelling test the following week, and they now choose ten words from the television programme just seen. As Chapter 2 implied, radio or television programmes need to be integrated into the daily lessons and, to do this properly, requires a good deal of foresight and planning. Without such integration, they become something akin to commercials between lessons, breathers between work sessions. In this instance, the follow-up could have taken the form of a discussion as to whose mothers use the launderette, or what the children's experience of them has been; or perhaps a consideration of various washing styles and habits across time and continent; or even some critical comment on the structure and content and appeal of the television programme itself.

Miss Trueman's form of follow-up is to use the programme to provide ammunition for the next spelling session, and the following words are collected.

- *laundry;*
- *launderette;*
- *spin dryer;*
- *weighing;*
- *scales;*
- *machine;*
- *washed;*
- *scrubbing;*
- *clean;*
- *fresh.*

It will be a thematic spelling test this time, rather than a phonic item test, as before.

Miss T.: Any more?
Debbie: Soap.
Miss T.: How do you spell it, Debbie?
Debbie: *s − o − u − p.*

The children quickly realise that this is not what most people wash with and there is general amusement.

As they call out their suggestions, so the teacher accepts some, such as those just mentioned, and rejects other, including:

- *filthy;*
- *television;*
- *fifteen minutes.*

The criteria for acceptance or rejection is not clear.

There are two minutes left before the bell at 12.00 p.m. to signify the end of a morning school spent largely on what some might call 'basic skills'. It is an unhelpful and ill-considered cliché, implying in theory some clearly defined and universally accepted foundations on which all else is built. In practice, meaning spelling, punctuation, sentence structure and simple computational competence. None of which is to be derided but, equally, not raised above its station either. 'Basic' equipment for a mountaineer means that without which he cannot possibly climb mountains. What is 'basic' equipment for a school pupil? It is certainly not easily determined, but it might include a measure of oral ability; a reasonable store of appropriate words; an ability to comprehend appropriate reading matter; to communicate one's thoughts, ideas and wishes adequately in writing; a general grasp of what numbers do and how they may be manipulated; a degree of socialisation. Technique and technical competence (terms which are preferable to 'basic skills') come later.

Finally, this morning, in response to the teacher's invitation for a song title, Michele suggests, 'I Went to the Animal Fair', and this is what the children sing.

> I went to the animal fair,
> The birds and bees were there;
> By the light of the moon the big baboon
> was combing his golden hair.
>
> The monkey he got drunk,
> Slipped down the elephant's trunk;
> The elephant sneezed and fell on his knees
> And what became of the monkey, monkey, monkey,
> Monkey, monkey, . . .

At this point the song becomes a round, and half the class repeats 'monkey', while the other half sings the verse again. When they try it a third time, it all becomes a bit chaotic, but is obviously enjoyed by the children, who are furiously performing the actions as well as singing.

Miss T.: Erm. Sometimes you sing as though a funeral march was going by, without any gaiety about you so far.

There is a remarkably powerful corporate identity about the class. The children act as one well-disciplined and organised unit, responding to the teacher's commands, rebukes and jokes. The highly competitive spirit appears to please many of the boys and girls. One wonders what its long-term effects will be, on all the children, but particularly the weaker ones such as Christopher.

The bell sounds and the children stand up behind their chairs, some preparing for school dinner, others, like Lucy, to go home to lunch.

Miss T.: If our country depended on you we'd be in a poor way, you don't stand up straight.
Child: Miss, you don't stand up at war.

Miss Trueman acknowledges such logic with good grace.

With that, we move again to the school hall which had previously doubled as a church, and television room, and now serves as a dining space. Outside in the foyer stand four boys, spaced apart from each other like redundant chess pieces, awaiting or enduring punishment. Miscreants on show. Inside all is activity.

The headteacher and I sit with four children, and behind us are the remains of a jumble sale which one class has organised. £10.27p has been raised for a village in Peru devastated by earthquake. By such altruistic work is children's natural generosity harnessed; their moral awareness extended; their concern for others, near and far, developed. Every school has honourable tales to tell of charitable work by teachers and pupils. When we ask the four children on the table what they have bought from the jumble sale, they reply: 'A Yogi Bear book'; 'An Action Man camp bed'; 'Some books'; 'I've still got my money'. The last comment, beloved of chancellors of the exchequer, calls to mind the Parable of the Talents.

Lunch (or 'dinner') as it is called in some parts of the country; 'lunch' being milk, biscuits, crisps in mid-morning) is supervised by ancillary helpers, non-teaching ladies who come into school for an hour or so per day. Today we have potatoes, dumplings, stew, and semolina with currants. The standard of education may vary from school to school, but the quality of food is consistently high.

After the meal there is the Grace. Then, for the children, activities in the playground; for me, note-making in the classroom. While I am so engaged, Lucy and friend walk by the window and give a wave. It is a further sign, if one were needed, of confidence on her part since, up to this point, we have only exchanged a few words.

At 1.27 p.m. the playground whistle sounds and an ancillary lady's desperate scream, 'Will you be quiet', is heard twice. At 1.30 p.m. the school bell rings and the third person to enter the classroom is Lucy, looking fresh and healthy. Another child shows me her jumble sale spoils: a little vase for 3p; a Tweedledee Tweedledum record for 10p; a Donny Osmond photocard for 1p. Treasures indeed.

Miss Trueman now gives instructions for the half-hour period proceding PE. She will see some children individually for maths and the rest may choose between an SRA work book or work card and their reading book. Lucy elects to continue with her SRA card *How Do Seeds Travel?* A boy comes to borrow a crayon.

Boy: Can I have blue, Lucy?
Lucy: Yea. Bring it back.

Debbie II overhears the teacher ask two pupils to ask Class 7 to prepare the apparatus for PE and says, 'Great, we haven't had that for ages'.

Miss Trueman now (i.e. 1.39 p.m.) calls the register, boys' names first, and the children appear easily able to carry on with their work and answer, 'Yes, Miss', at the time their name is called, without any attention being diverted from their tasks. They all work in a very concentrated manner, whispering occasionally.

Lucy now returns the SRA 9 Lime Lab. 1c card to the box on the nature table and, having checked her answers, chooses another card, Lime 11, with a story by Ellen Cafferata entitled, *A Mystery Tower*. She begins work on this immediately and when Andrew, thinking out loud, asks, 'What's the date today?' she instantly replies, without breaking her concentration, 'The twenty-fourth'. She reads through the twenty-two-line story and then tells Andrew, 'I've only got two more to do and then I've finished Lime'. She completes the card apart from the final section, which requires a piece of imaginative writing. When I ask her the reason for this omission, she tells me 'Because Miss says it takes too long'.

This is unfortunate, unless there are other opportunities for the kind of writing that allows children free rein to explore their imaginative and fantasy worlds, as well as their feelings and attitudes, or indeed, for continuous prose writing of any kind. Over the last ten or fifteen years, written work of an incredibly high quality, emanating from children across the ability ranges in primary schools up and down the land, has been published in a variety of anthologies (e.g. the annual Heinemann *Children As Writers* series). Much has been learnt about how to tap this rich vein of experience and skill. The worst excesses of anarchic free expression have virtually disappeared, and been replaced by good, solid, unpretentious practice grounded in accurate observation and honest, disciplined recall. Creber (1965) and Maybury (1967) offer much helpful advice in this respect, and Chapter 6, Sequel II, explores more recent work in the area.

Miss Trueman, seated at her desk, continues to interview individual children, hearing them read; checking their maths books; helping in other matters, until 2.02 p.m.

Miss T.: Right. Put everything away, including tongues, Richard. The quieter we are, the faster we shall go.

Her assertion may now be tested as the children go off to bring PE clothes back to the classroom. She advises me that, as some of the girls are rather shy, she always 'vacates' at this point. I take the hint and disappear for a minute or so while the boys and girls change, speculating on the self-awareness of 8-year-olds.

At 2.10 p.m. all the children enter the hall very quietly and sit in separate spaces on the floor. The PE apparatus has been set out by older boys from Class 7 in readiness: a buck (or horse) and mats; a climbing frame; a sloping ladder with mats; a device resembling a decorator's ladder with planks. The hall is now a gymnasium substitute. It seems wise to make such varied use of such a large space. Necessity becomes a virtue.

The boys and girls are all dressed in shorts and singlets, some of an idiosyncratic kind. Michele's, for example, has 'Remember you're a Womble' emblazoned across it, and Christopher's, with a monkey on the front, proclaims 'Pass the monkey wrench'. Under the teacher's direction the children begin by jumping on the spot sixty times to warm up. It certainly is very cold. They then step on the spot, knees up high, before moving to the gym apparatus, a prospect which excites them all. It is the equivalent of cake after bread and butter.

Lucy, in a group of ten, first tries the sloping bench. She jumps up on the bench, two feet at a time, and then, sitting down, slides from top to bottom. This is different from what everyone else does. Next she moves to the buck and mat, where the activity is more uniform. She jumps up on the buck . . . stops . . . leaps into the air . . . and, after landing on her feet, does a forward roll on the mat. When all the children have tried this, they change to jumping over the buck. Lucy catches her foot initially and is momentarily disconcerted. She moves to the climbing frame, going up high near the ceiling and, a little later, to the decorator's ladder.

She is, in fact, well-coordinated, being tall for her age and quite athletic. The best group academically (including Lucy) is also more assured and proficient at these physical activities. However, to think in terms of groups, instead of individuals, is as dangerous in PE as in other areas of the curriculum and some words of caution from the Department of Education and Science are appropriate.

A wide variation in height, weight, ability and interest is to be found in children of the same age, and different stages of development are represented in a random selection of children of similar age and physique. Achievement depends on the stage of development a child has reached as well as on his innate ability, and it is difficult to forecast the pattern and extent of his future progress. Teaching in physical education, as in other aspects of the curriculum, must therefore be closely related to individual needs and differences, but it is also of value to teachers to know and recognise those characteristics that the majority of children have in common. (1972)

By contrast with Lucy and her group, Christopher is performing very badly, but enjoying himself enormously and trying hard. Different children have differing levels and kinds of satisfaction. At 2.35 p.m. he is sent back to the classroom early for some offence, like a soccer player shown the red card and given his marching orders. He goes without a murmur, but is clearly disappointed.

Ten minutes from time there is a short interlude when individual children demonstrate their skills in front of their peers. Then, after a few more minutes of corporate involvement, it is 2.45 p.m. and playtime. The children return to their classrooms to change, with some of the boys debating whether to play soccer or hot rice in the playground. Ever vigilant, Lucy reminds me that I had planned to have a chat with her and, for the first few minutes of break, we talk about her home and interests and school. What Lucy says, if not its style, reminds me of something I had forgotten – that, despite her poise and confidence, she is still an 8-year-old. Here is part of the conversation.

R. M.: Tell me, Lucy, tell me about your family.

Lucy: Well, my daddy's a solicitor. And my mum she doesn't go out you see. I've got two brothers. Henry and John and Henry is ten, eleven in June, and John's nine, he's ten in June.

R. M.: How do the brothers treat you? Do they treat you well?

Lucy: O.K. I'm glad that I'm having a friend tonight then because John has to sleep in my room for a bit because his room's being decorated.

R. M.: Yes, and you've got a friend staying with you?

Lucy: Yes. She's got to sleep in John's bed. Her name's Stephanie.

R. M.: I see. Mmm. Now tell me, what sort of things are you interested in, Lucy?

Lucy: Swimming and I like to draw and I play with dominoes. I made a zoo out of dominoes yesterday and put zoo animals in them.

R. M.: That sounds very good. I've played dominoes, but I've never made a zoo out of dominoes.

Lucy: And we build dominoes into a set and then knock down end, knock down one piece of dominoes and it all falls down and we tried to use up all the dominoes but what happened was when we were putting the last piece, no not the last, there were about five less, left and it fell down.

R. M.: Fell down before you'd finished it?

Lucy: Yes.

       . . .

R. M.: What about, erm, what about today? You think of the sort of day you've had at school today. Is it a normal kind of day?

Lucy: Yes. Yes.

R. M.: Quite normal?

Lucy: Yes.

R. M.: What sort of things did you like best in it, that have happened so far?

Lucy: The television programme and PE and I liked it when we were doing SRA. When we were doing the activity page at the back.

R. M.: Yes. Why do you like those?

Lucy: Because the code and things like that, they're interesting.

R. M.: You like that, mmm. Why do you like the television?

Lucy: Because it's interesting and it tells you about things.

R. M.: Mmm. Mmm. And I think Miss Trueman said you hadn't got a television at home.

Lucy: No.

R. M.: Is that right? Do you miss it?

Lucy: Not really, because I'm not used to it, except we always look

> at the *Radio Times* before we go to my nanny's because *(R. M. laughs)* she's got a television
>
> R. M.: So you watch it at your nanny's, do you?
>
> Lucy: Yes. And at our friends' houses.
>
> R. M.: . . . And you liked the PE? I thought you did well at PE. You seemed to enjoy that didn't you? Which things did you like best in it?
>
> Lucy: The climbing frame.
>
> R. M.: Yes. I thought you'd probably like that because you went up quite high, didn't you?
>
> Lucy: Went over the top.
>
> R. M.: Over the top. Right near the ceiling.
>
> Lucy: The infants have a ribbon tied on to one of the bars and they're not to go higher than the ribbon.
>
> R. M.: I see. On that same frame?
>
> Lucy: Yes.
>
> R. M.: Well, that's quite a good idea, isn't it?

This is far from a normal conversation. It is more of a gentle interrogation, with Lucy providing the answers. But there is plenty of evidence here of her ability to extend a point and develop a suggestion, drawing on her own experience; of her easy rapport with a relative stranger; of her preparedness to take the initiative in the exchange; of the fact that she knows her own mind and can answer both closed and open questions with precision and clarity and speed.

Lucy is as alert and keen now as at the beginning of the day. Since 9.00 a.m. she has constantly been picking up the smallest detail and, despite being occupied in a variety of tasks, has heard virtually every word her teacher has spoken. This is no special performance for my benefit for the way in which it has been sustained is perfectly natural for her lively personality and sharp mind and, as she said to me in our conversation just now, 'Miss told us to think of it as a normal day as if you weren't there, because just to show how we normally are'. And Lucy is a girl who does as she is told.[1]

---

[1] She is also, by definition, a 'gifted child', and any reader who is particularly interested in this concept may wish to refer to the following sources for further information:
(1) The National Association for Gifted Children, 1 South Audley Street, London W1Y 5DQ.
(2) Director of Education, Education Department, County Hall, Nottingham NG2 7QP, for details of the Curriculum Unit for Gifted Children, set up in 1978.
(3) Schools Council Project Information Centre, 160 Great Portland Street, London W1N 6LL, for details of two projects:
   (a) *Gifted Children in Primary Schools* 1970–1. Age range 5–11. Director, Dr E. Ogilvie.
   (b) *Curriculum Enrichment for Gifted Children* 1974–6. Age range, 7–10. Director, Dr E. Ogilvie.

Listening Skill Builder 5

17

Figure 4.6

She goes outside for the last few minutes of breaktime before 3.00 p.m. when the whole class returns for an activity which is familiar to them, an exercise devised by SRA and intended to develop listening skills. The system is that the children concentrate their attention solely on a picture in front of them while the teacher reads out, in a good clear voice, a story relevant to that picture. Questions follow on the factual

Listening Skill Builder   5   **The Golden Treasure**

HOW WELL DID YOU LISTEN?

Directions: Draw a line under the right ending.

1 a never forgot the poor
  b never felt content
  c was kind and sweet

2 a the storm had forced him into port
  b he wanted to sail one of her ships
  c Both *a* and *b*

3 a told the captain to find his own ship
  b gave the captain an old, worthless ship
  c wanted the most precious thing in the world

4 a go places where no ship had ever gone
  b take her ship to China
  c discover new lands and claim them for her

5 a they might break on the way home
  b there must be something more precious
  c the Proud Lady wouldn't like them

6 a wheat was the most precious thing
  b they should have brought more food
  c diamonds won't fill an empty stomach

7 a gave the wheat to the poor
  b put the wheat in her storeroom for winter
  c was angry that the skipper had brought back wheat

8 a grew and blocked up the harbour
  b sank and was never seen again
  c grew and produced fine grain

9 a blamed the sea captain for her troubles
  b often thought of the wasted wheat
  c tried to remake her fortune

10 a grew old and tired
   b became humble
   c hated everyone around her

Number right

18

Figure 4.7

content of the story and the children underline their answers from a multiple choice set of alternatives. It is, thus, a piece of artificially contrived concentration, which makes use of material of the kind normally written to be read silently, rather than aloud. The picture and Lucy's answers are shown in Figures 4.6 and 4.7.

The fact that Lucy's answers, including the sequence of events of the

DID YOU FOLLOW THE TIME ORDER?

Directions: Write a number in each box to show
the order in which things happened.

4	The skipper and his men were sick and hungry.
3	The ship came to a place where fruits of all kinds grew.
1	The Proud Lady sat in her house as a storm raged outside.
5	The Proud Lady lost all her fortune.
2	The lady gave the skipper her newest, finest ship.

Number right **5**

19

Figure 4.7 continued

narrative, are all correct, leads one to wonder yet again if her mind is
being challenged. Few, if any, of her tasks throughout this day have
been open-ended. Perhaps the proportion of such tasks in school is
small anyway. Creber (1972) recalls that 'When Barnes' team of observers followed a first-year class, in their first term of secondary education, through a whole day's lessons, they found not one example of an
open question which did not require pupils to think aloud, to
construct, or reconstruct from memory, a logically organized
sequence'.

Ten other children also give totally correct responses which, in this instance, is 8/8 since, as Lucy was the first to point out to Miss Trueman, responses three and four involve a misprint and are, therefore, omitted by all children. Instead of blotting such a misprint out of their consciousness, the children could have written to the SRA publishers about it. All kinds of benefits can accrue from such a realistic exercise.

Some boys and girls do not do so well with the test. Our friend Christopher sits at his desk throughout the whole sequence of events, with his head on his arms; no picture in front of him; answering no questions. Is he sulking after the PE rebuke, or tired, or merely feeling uncooperative for no particular reason? Contrast him with Lucy, sitting bolt upright on her chair, hands clasped in her lap, looking fixedly at the picture as if it were a crystal ball with the key to all mysteries. Chance members of the same school class, they are worlds apart in outlook and personality, required to act with the rest of the class in unison.

Certainly, such activities where thirty boys and girls act as one have a value. They emphasise the corporate unity of the class and establish its identity with security. They signify to the teacher the ground which she has attempted to cover with all the pupils in her care. But they have their problems, too. Not least, that an activity which interests or stretches one child may bore or bewilder another, as happens here. Hence the argument for a diversity of tasks at times and for more individualised treatment. Particularly, perhaps, in this context. 'We cannot support the kind of "listening exercise"', says Bullock 'which is applied to a whole class, irrespective of individual capacity and need ... Wherever we saw this being practised ... the able children could have been given more demanding listening experience, and the slow learners suffered from having their inadequacies made public'. (para. 10.21).

Miss Trueman's preference, however, is for the common assignment, so that she and the children know where they stand. She is a strict disciplinarian with a sharp tongue, a firm manner and a sense of humour. The children like her, respond with alacrity, and obey her instructions.

The *Listening Skill Builder* exercise lasts half an hour and, when the marking is complete, the children take out their *Music Time* books (BBC Autumn Term 1970) for singing at the end of the day. The song chosen is ideal for a class activity involving, as it does, a cast of several (if not thousands), mime and drama, and a clear narrative.

Christopher gives me his watch to look after. Does he feel things could get too boisterous for his Timex, as he plays the lead role of Mr Frog goin' a courtin'? Other parts are distributed by the teacher with a firmness (and corresponding compliance) which film producers would envy, and very excited children take up their positions, having pushed back the desks to allow space for movement. The chorus sings the words and the principals, with Lucy as Uncle Rat, mime their parts in a well-understood sequence, culminating in a holocaust reminiscent of Hamlet, as you may now read.

> A frog went a-courting, he did ride,
>   Hum-hum. Hum-hum.
> A frog went a-courting, he did ride,
> Sword and pistol by his side,
>   Hum-hum. Hum-hum.
>
> He rode till he came to Mousie's door,
>   Hum-hum. Hum-hum.
> He rode till he came to Mousie's door
> And in a loud voice he did roar,
>   Hum-hum. Hum-hum.
>
> Mistress Mouse are you within?
>   Hum-hum. Hum-hum.
> Mistress Mouse are you within?
> Yes, dear Frog, I sit and spin,
>   Hum-hum. Hum-hum.
>
> He took Miss Mousie on his knee,
>   Hum-hum. Hum-hum.
> He took Miss Mousie on his knee,
> And said, Miss Mouse, will you marry me?
>   Hum-hum. Hum-hum.
>
> Without my Uncle Rat's consent,
>   Hum-hum. Hum-hum.
> Without my Uncle Rat's consent,
> I wouldn't marry the President,
>   Hum-hum. Hum-hum.
>
> Then Uncle Rat he soon came home,
>   Hum-hum. Hum-hum.
> Then Uncle Rat he soon came home,
> It's two or three years since I've been gone.
>   Hum-hum. Hum-hum.
>
> A pretty little gentleman,
>   Says she. Hum-hum.
> A pretty little gentleman
> Has said he wants to marry me,
>   Hum-hum. Hum-hum.
>
> Uncle Rat laughed till he shook his sides,
>   Hum-hum. Hum-hum.
> Uncle Rat laughed till he shook,
> To think his niece would be a bride,
>   Hum-hum. Hum-hum.

At this point there is opportunity for greater involvement by the children as more of them take the essential but undemanding parts of wedding guests. It is a chance for the less confident although, in fact, everyone in this class seems anxious to participate in any capacity. There is the same attraction to take on a role as was evident in Chapter 1 when currant bun parts were distributed. Such continued acting out of this song, building on the earlier mime of the main characters, gives the words an added impetus and heightens the black humour of the narrative. A catalogue of disasters and odd happenings is about to ensue.

> What will the wedding breakfast be?
>   Hum-hum. Hum-hum.
> What will the wedding breakfast be?
> Two green leaves and a black-eyed bee.
>   Hum-hum. Hum-hum.
>
> The first that came was a big black bug,
>   Hum-hum. Hum-hum.
> The first that came was a big black bug,
> And he fell into the cider jug.
>   Hum-hum. Hum-hum.
>
> The next to come was a rattlesnake,
>   Hum-hum. Hum-hum.
> The next to come was a rattlesnake,
> Who wrapped himself round the wedding cake,
>   Hum-hum. Hum-hum.
>
> The next to come was a bumble bee,
>   Hum-hum. Hum-hum.
> The next to come was a bumble bee,
> Strumming a banjo on his knee,
>   Hum-hum. Hum-hum.
>
> The next to come was a hoppity flea,
>   Hum-hum. Hum-hum.
> The next to come was a hoppity flea,
> Who danced a jig with the bumble bee,
>   Hum-hum. Hum-hum.
>
> The last to come was the old tom cat,
>   Hum-hum. Hum-hum.
> The last to come was the old tom cat,
> Who ate Miss Mouse and Uncle Rat.
>   Hum-hum. Hum-hum.
>
> Mister Frog jumped into the lake,
>   Hum-hum. Hum-hum.
> Mister Frog jumped into the lake,
> And there was swallowed by a big black snake.
>   Hum-hum. Hum-hum.

Miss T.:   Well, considering that we haven't done it since November, that was quite good. Quite good. I still think Mr Jennings *(i.e. Christopher)* thinks that the whole show should be his.

By popular request they repeat the song, with different children taking the character parts.

Miss T.:   This time I expect more singing from the class. Everyone sit down then.
Frog – Geoffrey;
Uncle Rat – Richard;
Big black bug – Jane;
Rattlesnake – Martin;
Bumble bee – Sarah;
Hoppity flea – Alison;
Old tom cat – Louise;
Big black snake – Donald.
Now, if you're not going to do this properly and with more spirit than last time, I think I'll have to stop you. Right. All of us sing. Even the wedding guests. O.K. One, two, three.

Children: A frog went a-courting, he did ride,
Hum-hum. Hum-hum.
(And so on.)

Smiles and grins testify that the first-night performance was just as enjoyable as the dress rehearsal. Lucy sings quite strongly, if off-key occasionally, and is an obvious leader in the singing.

Finally, an appropriate song at the end of the day about sleeping and waking:

Children: Soon as supper's done, Mummy hollers
(Clap. Clap)
Mummy hollers
(Clap. Clap)
Mummy hollers;
Soon as supper's done,
Mummy hollers,
Time to go to bed.

Soon as all our heads touch the pillow
(Clap. Clap)
Touch the pillow
(Clap. Clap)
Touch the pillow;
Soon as all our heads touch the pillow,
Time to go to sleep.

When the rooster crows in the morning
(Clap. Clap)
In the morning
(Clap. Clap)
In the morning;
When the rooster crows in the morning,
Time we all got up.

4.00 p.m. The bell sounds and the children stand and face the classroom crucifix.

Children: Hail, Mary, full of grace,
The Lord is with thee;
Blessed art thou among women,
And blessed is the fruit of thy womb, Jesus.
Holy Mary, Mother of God,
Pray for us sinners
Now and at the hour of our death.
                      Amen.

The grace of our Lord Jesus Christ,
And the love of God,
And the fellowship of the Holy Ghost,
Be with us all, now and for ever. Amen.

Miss T.:   Goodnight, children.
Children: Goodnight, Miss Trueman. Goodnight, Mr Mills.
R. M.:   Goodnight, children. Thank you for having me.
Christopher: I thought you'd say that.

Sequel I Suggested Fiction

The comments offered later in this list on many of the books mentioned may help the reader to decide what might be suitable for a particular boy or girl, taking into account content, interest and readability level. Clearly, teachers must know both children and books well, before they can be reasonably confident of making a good match.

FIRST STORY BOOKS: 2- to 6-years-olds (i.e. for adults to read aloud to the very young)

Berg, L., 1976 *Folk Tales* (London: Pan).
Berg, L., 1970 *Little Pete Stories* (Harmondsworth: Penguin/Puffin).
Chapman, E., 1958) *Marmaduke and His Friends* (and others in the series) (London: Brockhampton).
Coats, A. M., 1970 *The Story of Horace* (London: Faber).
Colwell, E., 1970 *Tell Me a Story* (Harmondsworth: Penguin/Young Puffin).
Corrin, S. and S. 1974 *Stories for Under Fives* (London: Faber).
Craig, C. 1970 *Emmanuel and His Parrot* (Oxford: OUP).
Cresswell, H., 1969 *Rug Is a Bear* (series) (London: Benn).
Gag, W., 1977 *Millions of Cats* (Harmondsworth: Penguin/Pictorial Puffin).
Ireson, B., 1961 *The Story of the Pied Piper* (London: Faber).
Ireson, B., 1963 *The Gingerbread Man* (London: Faber).
Mahy, M., 1969 *The Dragon of an Ordinary Family* (London: Heinemann).
Minarik, E. H., 1965 *Little Bear* (series) (Tadworth, Surrey: World's Work).
Montgomerie, N., 1962 *To Read and to Tell* (London: Bodley Head).
Morgan, H., 1977 *Meet Mary Kate* (Harmondsworth: Penguin/Puffin).
Piers, H., 1966 *Mouse Looks for a Friend* (London: Methuen Educational).
Piers, H., 1971 *Mouse Looks for a House* (London: Methuen Educational).
Potter, B., 1902 *The Tale of Petter Rabbit* (etc.) (London: Warne).
Prøysen, A., 1969 *Little Old Mrs Pepperpot* (etc.) (Harmondsworth: Penguin/ Puffin).
Sedgwick, M., 1970 *The New Adventures of Galldora* (Harmondsworth: Penguin/Puffin).
Tomlinson, J., 1970 *The Bus that Went to Church* (London: Faber).
Trez, D. and A., 1969 *The Butterfly Chase* (London: Faber).
Unnerstad, E., 1968 *Little O* (Harmondsworth: Penguin/Puffin).
Uttley, A., 1965 *Sam Pig Story Book* (London: Faber).
Uttley, A., 1967 *Little Grey Rabbit* (series) (London: Collins).

6 to 8-year-olds

Aiken, J., 1975 *A Necklace of Raindrops* (Harmondsworth: Penguin/Puffin).
Ainsworth, R., 1970 *Ten Tales of Shellover* (Harmondsworth: Penguin/ Puffin).
Bond, M., 1963 *Paddington Bear* (etc.) (London: Collins).
Clark, E., 1974 *Stories to Tell* (London: Brockhampton).

Colwell, E., 1963 *A Storyteller's Choice* (London: Bodley Head).

Corrin, S. and S., 1976 *Stories for 6 Year Olds and Other Young Readers* (Harmondsworth: Penguin/Puffin).

Cresswell, H., 1968 *The Barge Children* (London: Brockhampton).

Cresswell, H., 1971 *A Gift from Winklesea* (Harmondsworth: Penguin/Puffin).

Cresswell, H., 1976 *The Piemakers* (Harmondsworth: Penguin/Puffin).

Doongaji, D., 1970 *The Cave that Talked* (New Delhi, India: Children's Book Trust).

Doongaji, D., 1970 *Three Fish* (New Delhi, India: Children's Book Trust).

Edwards, D., 1970 *My Naughty Little Sister* (etc.) (Harmondsworth: Penguin/ Puffin).

Fisher, M., 1965 *Open the Door: A Collection of Stories* (London: Brockhampton).

Keats, E. J., 1969 *A Letter to Amy* (London: Bodley Head).

Keats, E. J., 1972 *Goggles* (Harmondsworth: Penguin/Puffin).

Keats, E. J., 1972 *Pet Show* (London: Hamish Hamilton).

Kidd, M., 1970 *Shobhana* (New Delhi, India: Children's Book Trust).

Kidd, M., 1970 *Ashok's Kite* (New Delhi, India: Children's Book Trust).

Lindgren, A., 1976 *Pippi Longstocking* (Harmondsworth: Penguin/Puffin).

Lindgren, A., 1977 *Pippi Goes Abroad* (Oxford: OUP).

Lofting, H., 1966 *Dr. Doolittle* (series) (Harmondsworth: Penguin/Puffin).

'Savitri', 1970 *Two Little Chicks* (New Delhi, India: Children's Book Trust).

Storr, C., 1967 *Clever Polly and the Stupid Wolf* (Harmondsworth: Penguin/ Puffin).

Storr, C., 1970 *Polly and the Wolf Again* (Harmondsworth: Penguin/Puffin).

Thomson, D., 1971 *Danny Fox* (series) (Harmondsworth: Penguin/Puffin).

Tomlinson, J., 1973 *The Owl Who Was Afraid of the Dark* (Harmondsworth: Penguin/Puffin).

Uttley, A., 1969 *Magic in My Pocket* (Harmondsworth: Penguin/ Puffin).

Uttley, A., 1970 *Little Red Fox* (Harmondsworth: Penguin/ Puffin).

Wilder, L. I., 1969 *Little House in the Big Woods* (Harmondsworth: Penguin/ Puffin).

Wilder, L. I., 1969 *Little House on the Prairie* (Harmondsworth: Penguin/ Puffin).

Williams, U. M., 1969 *Gobbolino: The Witch's Cat* (Harmondsworth: Penguin/Puffin).

Williams, U. M., 1970 *Adventures of the Little Wooden Horse* (Harmondsworth: Penguin/Puffin).

8- to 11-year-olds

Allen, E., 1974 *The Latch-Key Children* (Oxford: OUP).
When a group of children find that their London playground is to be destroyed by planners, they decide to wage battle against authority.

Barry, M. S., 1974 *Tommy Mac* (Harmondsworth: Penguin/Puffin).
A realistic account of the escapades of a Liverpool junior schoolboy.

Bawden, N., 1970 *A Handful of Thieves* (Harmondsworth: Penguin/Puffin).
A gang of children pursues a small-time criminal.

Berna, P., 1967 *Flood Warning* (London: Heinemann/New Windmill Series).
Children hold out during severe floods until rescue arrives, and the experience brings the best out of them.

Berna, P., 1970 *A Hundred Million Francs* (Harmondsworth: Penguin/Puffin).
A gang of children tracks down some crooks who have stolen 100 million francs from the Paris Express.

Boston, L., 1975 *The Children of Green Knowe* (Harmondsworth: Penguin/Puffin).
This is the story of Tolly, a small boy staying with his great-grandmother at her home Green Knowe; the past history of the old house and the stories of her ancestors.

Brand, C., 1975 *Nurse Matilda Goes to Town* (London: Brockhampton).
The fearsome Nurse Matilda arrives wherever there are naughty children. As they improve, so does she. Full of humour and practical jokes, which appeal to younger children.

Brown, R., 1973 *The Viaduct* (London: Hutchinson Educational).
A detective-type story in which boys follow clues leading to the discovery of an interred steam engine.

Brown, F., 1963 *Granny's Wonderful Chair* (London: Dent).
A collection of short stories from many different countries and sources.

Cooper, S., 1974 *Dawn of Fear* (Harmondsworth: Penguin/Puffin).
A gang of boys faces the reality of war when their friend's house is bombed.

Cresswell, H., 1976 *The Night Watchmen* (Harmondsworth: Penguin/Puffin).
Original fantasies, full of whimsy and humour.

Dejong, M., 1973 *Journey from Peppermint Street* (London: Collins).
This author's books have a strong emotional appeal, and portray vividly the thoughts and feelings of a child, especially when faced with new and often frightening experiences.

Dickinson, P., 1970 *The Weathermonger* (Harmondsworth: Penguin/Puffin).

Dickinson, P., 1971 *Heartsease* (Harmondsworth: Penguin/Puffin).

Dickinson, P., 1972 *The Devil's Children* (Harmondsworth: Penguin/Puffin).
Dickinson's trilogy, serialised as *The Changes* on television, presents a picture of England in revolt against the internal combustion engine.

Farjeon, E., *The Little Bookroom* (Harmondsworth: Penguin).
A collection of short stories.

Fuller, L. H., 1970 *Swarup Returns* (New Delhi, India: Children's Book Trust).
Story set in village India of a woman who earns her living by selling cloth. Insight into the life style of Swarup and her neighbours, with the moral: Honesty is the best policy

Garnett, E., 1971 *The Family From One End Street* (Harmondsworth: Penguin/Puffin).
The dated, but still very popular, story of an ordinary family and their adventures.

Hughes, T., 1971 *The Iron Man* (London: Faber).
The strange and powerful story of the giant mechanical man who first terrorises, then saves, mankind. Written in vivid prose that lends itself to reading aloud.

Kastner, E., 1971 *Emil and the Detectives* (Harmondsworth: Penguin/Puffin).
  Written over forty years ago, but still fresh. Emil travels to Berlin, where his
  money is stolen. Helped by a gang of boys, he manages to track down the thief.
King, C., 1970 *Stig of the Dump* (Harmondsworth: Penguin/Puffin).
  Ben is a lonely boy, who finds a friend in Stig, the caveman living in a hut
  made from pieces of junk in a Kent chalk pit.
Lewis, C. Day, 1970 *The Otterbury Incident* (Harmondsworth: Penguin/
  Puffin).
  A fast-moving narrative, full of incident, interesting observations of
  children, lively dialogue and good descriptions of gang fights.
Lewis, C. S., 1970 *The Lion, the Witch and the Wardrobe* (Harmondsworth:
  Penguin/Puffin).
  One of seven famous stories in which children enter the land of Narnia
  through the back of the wardrobe.
Lively, P., 1975 *The Ghost of Thomas Kempe* (London: Piccolo).
  A book which is deeply rooted in the Oxfordshire countryside and its tradi-
  tions, and is the story of Thomas Kempe, a seventeenth-century sorcerer.
Norton, M., 1964 *The Borrowers* (London: Dent).
Norton, M., 1975 *The Borrowers Afloat* (London: Dent).
  Stories of the mysterious little people who live in the nooks and crannies
  under the floor boards and are responsible for the disappearance of those
  small things you lose: pins, matches, etc.
Pearce, P., 1970 *A Dog So Small* (Harmondsworth: Penguin/Puffin).
  Story of the fortunes of Ben Blewitt and his longing for a dog of his own.
Sherry, S., 1973 *A Pair of Jesus-Boots* (Harmondsworth: Penguin/Puffin).
  A small boy comes to realise the truth about his crooked elder brother whom
  he idolises.
Shivkumar, K., 1970 *Four Brothers* (New Delhi, India: Children's Book
  Trust).
  The story of Indian brothers who, by their different jobs, keep the family
  lands together. The moral: Unity is Strength.
Shivkumar, K., 1970 *The King's Choice* (New Delhi, India: Children's Book
  Trust).
  Folktale of Aesop variety, illustrating the notion of being hoist with one's
  own petard.
Southall, I., 1972 *Let the Balloon Go* (Harmondsworth: Penguin/Puffin).
  A day in the life of a handicapped child who climbs a tree.
Storr, C., 1968 *Marianne Dreams* (Harmondsworth: Penguin/Puffin).
  Recovering from an illness, Marianne draws a house, and everything she
  sketches comes to life in her dream world.
Tolkien, J. R., 1966 *The Hobbit* (London: Allen & Unwin).
  Famous fairy tale. Ideal for reading extracts aloud.
Townsend, J. R., 1970 *Gumble's Yard* (Harmondsworth: Penguin/Puffin).
  Children, deserted by their step parents, fend for themselves and help solve a
  crime.
Travers, P. L., 1971 *Mary Poppins* (London: Collins).
Travers, P. L., 1973 *Mary Poppins Comes Back* (London: Collins).
  Stories about an elusive and superior nanny, who turns up out of nowhere
  and leaves when she's ready.

INFORMATION ABOUT BOOKS

Children's books are constantly rolling off the presses and there are several periodicals which help teachers and librarians to keep some track of them. They include the following:

Children's Literature in Education (APS Publications Inc.). Quarterly. Personal subscriptions (UK only) to Mrs B. E. M. Collinge, 2 Sunwine Place, Exmouth, Devon.

Growing Points. Six issues per annum. Published by Margery Fisher, Ashton Manor, Northampton NN7 2JL.

Books for Your Children. Edited by Anne Wood and Jean Russell. Quarterly. Library circulation rates from Mr Lang Dewey, 21 Larchwood Road, Woking, Surrey GU21 1XB.

The Junior Bookshelf. Six issues per annum. Information available from The Publisher, Marsh Hall, Thurstonland, Huddersfield HD4 6XB.

Chapter 5

Lorraine, Aged 9

We had a bird, but it died on Friday

THE SCHOOL

There are 474 other junior children in Lorraine's school, along with a headteacher; fourteen full-time staff; one part-time remedial teacher; and no less than four part-time needlework teachers. A rather curious phenomenon, which means that craft activities must be sex-orientated. A separate infants school of some 200 children is on the same site and serves the entirely suburban, owner-occupier, catchment area. The junior school, which has been academically very successful for many years, is unstreamed by design. In other words, all children are tested after their first year and then grouped according to age, sex and ability, to produce a balance within each class. In addition, certain children are extracted in small groups each day for a quarter of an hour's remedial reading, and each is heard individually. All buildings and grounds are modern, attractive and well cared for.

THE DAY

It is a bright, sunny yet cold-ish Friday at the end of November, and the focus of attention for today is Lorraine, who is quite smartly dressed in the blue and grey school uniform, blue and yellow tie, white shirt, blue cardigan, white knee-length socks and brown shoes. She is of medium height for her age, with long, brown, untidy hair, brown eyes, and a quiet, possibly shy, manner. Later in the day she is to tell me of her two brothers, Peter aged 7 and James aged 4, her mum and dad and rabbit and fish. One of her favourite games is to play 'mummies and daddies' with her dolls and best friends Dawn, Susan, Tracey and Alison. At school she says she liked handwriting and tables and spellings. In other words, fairly straightforward, clear-cut tasks which make few imaginative demands.

All children enter the attractively decorated hall to the music of Grieg's *Peer Gynt* suite and settle down to enjoy the school assembly, conducted by first-year Class 3, whose spokesgirl is Tracey.

Tracey: Good morning, children.
Children: Good morning, Tracey.

After this greeting, there follows Hymn number 78 from *The Junior Hymn Book*, edited by Geoffrey Clinton (London: Hamish Hamilton, 1964):

1 O Jesus, I have promised
  To serve Thee to the end;
  Be Thou for ever near me,
  My master and my friend;
  I shall not fear the battle
  If Thou art by my side,
  Nor wander from the pathway
  If Thou wilt be my guide.

2 O Jesus, Thou has promised
  To all who follow Thee,
  That where Thou art in glory
  There shall Thy servant be;
  And, Jesus, I have promised
  To serve Thee to the end;
  O give me grace to follow
  My master and my friend.

3 O let me see Thy foot-marks
  And in them plant mine own;
  My hope to follow duly
  Is in Thy strength alone;
  O guide me, call me, draw me,
  Uphold me to the end;
  And then in heaven receive me,
  My Saviour and my Friend.

The hymn is by John Ernest Bode, 1816–74, and number 577 in *The English Hymnal*, where two more verses are printed. These have presumably been omitted by Clifton on account of their relative unintelligibility to primary school children. However, how comprehensible these remaining verses, and the other hymns quoted in this book, are to the children who sing them is impossible to say. Certainly, no prose or poetry half so difficult would be used in the normal English lesson. In fact, Colin Harrison, of the Schools Council's *Effective Use of Reading* Project (1979) has commented orally: 'The most intense and continuous reading practice in junior schools' (i.e. intensive scrutiny of the text) 'was to be found in assembly – for example, "Onward Christian Soldiers", – particularly if played by a Grade Three pianist.'

Yet, because of tradition, such hymns are sung each day by companies of children spanning vast age and ability ranges and 'Christians should be grateful', says Blackie (1967), 'to the teachers who take such pains to make it genuinely devout'. The significance lies not in precise understanding, but in overall impact of the ritual as has been indicated in previous pages in relation to other rituals. The matter is discussed further in Sequel I at the end of this chapter.

When the hymn has been sung, Tracey politely requests: 'Please sit down for our story.' This turns out, surprisingly, to be a tale of Cowboys and Indians. Not immediately applicable to a Christian school assembly, you might think, but wait a while, and remember that Annie Oakley had a special skill which she made good use of. Not, as you might have suspected, to bump off the Indians, but rather to provide food and entertainment. In other words, Annie Oakley used her special skill for the benefit of others, and that is the theme of this morning's assembly.

The story is acted out to prove the point. Annie raises her gun in the air three times; says 'BANG!'; and each time down falls a Colonel Sanders-type stage-prop chicken. And that is without even aiming. Hence, the rashness of the three gun slingers from Class 3 who, complete with ten-gallon hats and mid-western accents, challenge Annie to a shooting competition, with various remarks of a male chauvinist nature. They are, at least, magnanimous in defeat and their leader, the ousted champion, observes: 'Young girl, you are the finest shot I've ever met.' Perhaps this is a Women's Lib tale also.

It has certainly been very carefully prepared and well acted, and has held the attention of all children and staff. The assembly is neatly rounded off, and the moral reinforced, with a prayer about the use of all gifts, and then hymn number 85 from the *Junior Hymn Book*.

O Lord Jesus, to whom the Wise Men brought their gifts, we bring
Thee our gifts of praise and thanksgiving.
We offer Thee the work we can do best, as well as things that
are harder for us. Help us to do them all gladly for Thy sake.

Amen.

1 The wise may bring their learning,
  The rich may bring their wealth;
  And some may bring their greatness,
  And some bring strength and health.
  We, too, would bring our treasures
  To offer to the King;
  We have no wealth or learning,
  What shall we children bring?

2 We'll bring Him hearts that love Him,
  We'll bring Him thankful praise,
  And young souls meekly striving
  To walk in holy ways.
  And these shall be the treasures
  We offer to the King;
  And these are gifts that even
  The poorest child may bring.

3 We'll bring to Him the duties
  We have to do each day;
  We'll try our best to please Him
  At home, at school, at play;
  And better are these treasures
  To offer to our King,
  Than richest gifts without them;
  Yet these a child may bring.

                    (Anonymous)

The headteacher, Mr Durham, now rises to his feet to thank the participants for their assembly efforts which were so successful. He has three further points to make. First, there is no chess report that day. Secondly, children are to be well behaved for the forthcoming Lord Mayor's visit; they are not to use the foyer doors, nor interfere with the Christmas decorations. Thirdly, they should have their collection money ready during the day for the fund to assist those recently injured in the city centre explosion.

With that, the children are dismissed and leave the hall in an orderly manner, bound for their classrooms. Lorraine's 9-year-old contemporaries, thirty-eight in all, including twenty-one girls and seventeen boys, are very well dressed and materially well cared for. They have liveliness and confidence, and some of the boys, as will be noticeable throughout the day, can hardly curb their precocity.

Their classroom is light and attractive. It is of fairly lengthy oblong shape, with one side consisting completely of windows which look on to the playground. The back wall is dominated by a big frieze of the surrounding area as it was sixty years earlier, and below this are tables of materials to delight an historian interested in primary and secondary sources: horse brasses, an old telephone, an old clock, plate, coins, old newspapers, books and pamphlets, photographs. The wall opposite the windows is largely devoted to festive decorations and has a Christmas tree, Halloween pictures and writing, as well as book reviews which, like certain hotels, indicate the appropriate star rating. At the front of the class, in addition to the traditional blackboard, are four desks with odd boxes and books on them; notices concerning the panoply of mathematical signs; lists of days of the week, months of the year, numbers, monitors, etc., and a box of reading cards, one for each child. The school puts considerable stress on reading ability, and the deputy head monitors teachers' work in this area, with the intention that all children achieve as high a reading standard as possible by the time they leave. The desks in this classroom are placed neither in small groups, nor serried ranks, but in four major blocks, with about ten pupils randomly allocated to each block. So much for the physical setting.

With the exception of those in the choir, who have yet to arrive, Class

9 are now engaged in preliminary maths and reading activities as they answer in French numerals to the register called by the teacher: '*un . . . deux . . . trois . . . quatre . . .*' It is a small indication that French is taught in the school.[1] Mr Weston, the teacher, is a man in his late 20s with beard and long hair, fashionable trousers and a blue polo neck sweater with the sleeves rolled up. He has a strong voice, cheerful manner and a pleasant, lively tone.

Lorraine is working from a maths book entitled *8 A Day*, by A. L. Griffiths (London: Oliver & Boyd, 1970). It is one of a series of maths books by Griffiths based on the system of introducing some mathematical idea (rather than concept) with an explanatory example, followed by an unvarying number of test items (e.g. *4 A Day; 5 A Day; 6 A Day*, and so on), designed to consolidate the original maths notion. The reprints of the series from 1970 onwards indicate extensive sales and certainly this is an approach which one commonly finds in junior schools, although the logic of it is questionable. Why 6 a day? Why not 2, if you understand what you are doing? There may be virtue in practice and consolidation, but surely medicine should be dispensed individually on the basis of a professional diagnosis?[2]

Undeterred by such considerations, Lorraine seems to have evolved a rather idiosyncratic method of multiplication. Witness her answers, only two of which are correct:

(1)	$5 \times 2 \times 6$	=	69
(2)	$7 \times 2 \times 5$	=	70
(3)	$3 \times 4 \times 5$	=	60
(4)	$6 \times 2 \times 50$	=	59
(5)	$19 \times 5 \times 2$	=	202
(6)	$2 \times 17 \times 5$	=	38
(7)	$6 \times 3 \times 5 \times 2$	=	16
(8)	$3 \times 2 \times 5 \times 3$	=	13

This is quite disturbing. No pattern to these errors is discernible, except some possible confusion with addition. The answers seem quite arbitrary, as though Lorraine has virtually no grasp of the multiplication process. Although Mr Weston has been moving round the class from individual to individual, he has missed the stages by which Lorraine arrived at her answers. Hardly surprising in a class of thirty-eight. I missed it, too, which is more reprehensible since I am sitting next to her, as Figure 5.1 will show.

---

[1] For some consideration of foreign-language teaching at this level see: *French in the Primary School: Attitudes and Achievement*, by Clare Burstall (NFER, 1970).

[2] For further comment on mathematics, see Sequel II at the end of this chapter, and, for an historical survey of varying kinds of maths teaching, see ch. 1 of *Approach to Mathematics*, by L. G. Marsh (London: A. & C. Black, 1970).

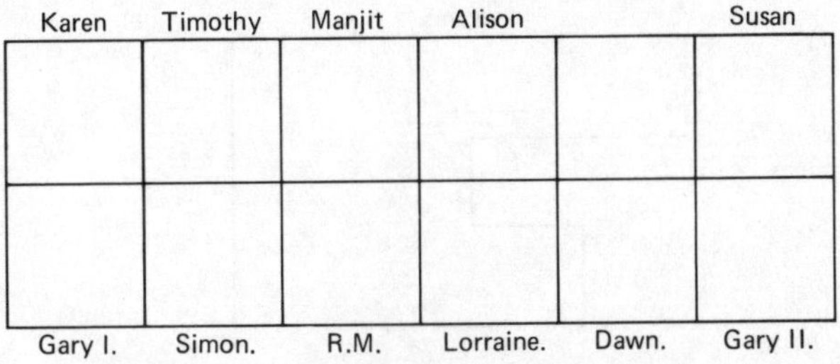

Karen	Timothy	Manjit	Alison		Susan
Gary I.	Simon.	R.M.	Lorraine.	Dawn.	Gary II.

Figure 5.1

Lorraine has seemingly treated her '8 A Day' almost like prescribed tablets, the important thing being merely to take them, irrespective of the effect they might have. She is, in fact, in a mental fog, of which she is only dimly aware, and there is to be more evidence of this as the morning proceeds. She appears unable to profit from any practical concrete experience of number she might have had in earlier years. Leonard Marsh writes (1970b) that 'Children working with materials reveal that time and time again they return to simple experiences as a preliminary to extending their scheme for tackling a problem', but Lorraine appears to be bereft of appropriate strategies for solving these abstract number problems now. She stumbles like a stranger at night over a ploughed field.

Having spent seventeen minutes on the exercise, she moves to area work and the sums on the board, clearly drawn, but with no attempt at scale (Figure 5.2).

Her attempt at number 5, which shows understanding of the method, is given in Figure 5.3. The centimetre-squared paper is clearly of great help.

There is a fairly sustained level of conversation as work proceeds. Lorraine rarely speaks, working steadily and silently. Others are not so inhibited.

Manjit: (to anyone who will listen): Did you see Sykes when they were sitting on the roof? Mr Brown was laughing his head off . . . *(He does a little more maths)* . . . I'm going to get Evil Knievel *(presumably he means as a Christmas gift)*.

Research, using neck microphones to monitor children's language throughout a school day, could yield fascinating results.

Mr Weston goes out with a few children to clean out the fish tank in the school foyer. The remainder continue with their work and chat, as they were doing before he left the room.

Gary I *(to me)*: How long are you going to be here?

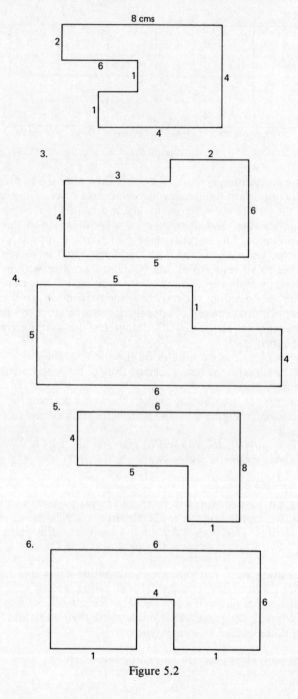

Figure 5.2

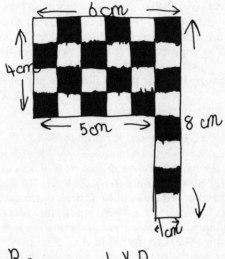

$$A\,Rea = L \times B$$
$$A\,Rea = 8cm \times 1cm$$
$$A\,Rea = 8cm^2$$

$$A\,Rea = L \times B$$
$$A\,Rea = 4\,cm \times 5cm$$
$$A\,Rea = 20\,cm^2$$

Figure 5.3

R. M.:   Just for the day

He pulls a face, presumably to indicate that he is quite happy for me to stay. It is a kind of hospitable gesture to indicate his friendliness. He remarks that, the year before, a student had taken him for maths in a small group and that he had enjoyed it.

After six minutes the teacher returns and explains to the fish tank group that they must leave the guppies as live food for the other fish. Momentarily horrified by such impending cannibalism, the children return to the less emotive world of mathematics, but, when the choir members come in at 10.00 a.m., Alison shows that nothing has been forgotten and, using a powerful Old Testament word, tells them: 'Two little fishes are going to be sacrificed.' Simon reinforces her comment with, 'Poor innocent little guppies. He goes and kills them', but, when questioned by Gary, 'What about your goldfish?' he laughs in such a way as to indicate that his own hands are far from clean.

From this moment on, my thoughts constantly return during the day to the fate of the guppies, as if to some friends awaiting execution. Are the children similarly concerned? Perhaps they are made of sterner stuff. Or perhaps show-biz personalities are paramount:

Manjit: What's Jerry Lewis going to turn into?

Gary mumbles an answer which is lost forever.

Meanwhile, Mr Weston sporadically addresses the whole class, either about the work they are doing or, less often since there is less need, about the need to reduce the noise level. He marks the '8 A Day' sums on the blackboard and children correct their own work. Lorraine thinks she has three correct answers but, in fact, she only has two, and those, as explained earlier, appear to be attributable to pure luck or perhaps copying. She is terribly confused. She cannot find the original exercise in the book; does not ask the teacher, is baffled by the whole process, but shows few outward signs of incomprehension. Physically present, but mentally anywhere, she goes through the motions almost in a stage of amnesia. Many children, in classrooms throughout the land, must similarly disguise utter bewilderment and, in classes of near forty, may remain undetected. If they are shy and lacking in confidence, as Lorraine appears to be, their plight is worse, for they rarely ask questions.

At 10.15 a.m. a cardboard box of assorted crisps is brought in and the children descend on them as if they were gifts from the New World.

Gary I: Did you see 'Monty Python' with all the pillar boxes?
Timothy: My dad went to Margate and brought some limestone.
Simon: You're mad.
Gary (to Manjit): You cheat in everything.
Manjit (laughing): I don't cheat in chess.

At 10.20 a.m. the class is told to put the work away.

Simon: I wonder if those two little fishes have died yet.

Another teacher, Mr Swan, comes in to talk rather movingly about the appeal mentioned in assembly by the headteacher. Mr Swan speaks of one person he knows, an apprentice, who, having spent seven years in training, had a leg blown off in the explosion: 'One class has collected ninety-six pence. Can any class beat this? What sacrifice can you make? What about your biscuit money?

Simon: My dad brought me a piece of shrapnel from the post box.

For the first time this morning Lorraine speaks, very briefly, to someone else. Her best friend, Dawn, tells me: 'My dad has knocked down a wall in our house and made one room out of two. My mum wants a porch.' Dawn's concerns appear to be domestic; those of the boys relate mainly to television. Diana now approaches Lorraine: 'If you're my friend, I'm your friend.' Such emotional blackmail, implicit in the friendship equation, seems to be a popular ploy by human beings of all ages. The same phrase is used by 4-year-olds, and its adult equivalent, in negative form, seems to be: 'If you do that, Mummy won't love you any more.' Diana's overture is accepted by Lorraine with a smile and off they go for a quarter of an hour's break, after which they return to maths.

This time, they are working from what Mr Weston calls their 'ordinary maths book' (i.e. *Basic Mathematics*, by A. L. Griffiths, Book 3, London: Oliver & Boyd, 1972) and he moves around the class checking the work of individuals. Such movement could be compared with the slowed-down track of the ball-bearing in a pin-ball machine. Some coils it strikes are briefly illuminated; others, struck or not, show no illumination and add nothing to the total score. The ball bearing's movement is haphazard and arbitrary; the teacher has a design and strategy. As Kant puts it in *Critique of Judgment:* the movement of the one is 'purposive', the other 'purpose-ful'. Mr Weston aims for those he missed last time round, including some who rarely show any spark. However, possibly on account of my proximity, he omits Lorraine, who appears just as bewildered as earlier.

This time she is faced with another of those cold peremptory commands often found in textbooks, which distance pupil from task: 'Find the products':

$$6 \times 4 \times 3$$
$$6 \times 4 \times 3$$
$$6 \times 4 \times 3$$

and asks me for help. I check the procedure with Dawn, just to be sure. Each horizontal line of figures is computed (i.e. total 72); the vertical line of answers is then added together (i.e. 72 + 72 + 72). Answer: 216. I explain the method to Lorraine and she manages the next one by herself:

$$9 \times 2 \times 4$$
$$9 \times 2 \times 4$$
$$9 \times 2 \times 4$$

Then, with more help from me, the next two:

$$8 \times 3 \times 5$$
$$8 \times 3 \times 5$$
$$8 \times 3 \times 5$$

$6 \times 2 \times 10 \times 5$	$6 \times 2 \times 10 \times 5$	$6 \times 2 \times 10 \times 5$
$6 \times 2 \times 10 \times 5$	$6 \times 2 \times 10 \times 5$	$6 \times 2 \times 10 \times 5$

Lorraine's success with these problems suggests that, had the class been smaller, she might have been able to receive the individual help she needed and could then have coped with her '8 A Day' before break.

Dawn now tries to involve me in her work, and so does Gary, with the result that I am forced to change an observational for a teaching role. It is certainly more satisfying, but it also means that the normal situation is being altered more than is inevitable anyway merely by my passive presence. It is interesting to note what is said in the NFER survey, *The Teacher's Day* by S. Hilsum and B. S. Cane (1971) about the problem of an observer's presence altering the situation under observation. It is clearly a danger which the project team anticipated and, at the end of each day's monitoring, teachers were questioned regarding the extent to which they or their pupils had been affected.

> There was no day at all when a teacher thought the observer had substantially affected the classroom situation. There were only 10 days out of the 188 when the teachers reported that they themselves were disturbed; and on these days the teacher was either conscious of the observer's presence for a short while at the start of the day only, or experienced a slight feeling of constraint at odd times during the day. The consensus of opinion regarding the effect on pupils was similar: on the vast majority of days (163 out of 188) the observer's presence did not, according to the teacher, affect their pupils in any way.

In so far as I am able to estimate the effect of my own presence, I would guess that the interference level was generally insignificant. Only in Lorraine's case does involvement loom rather larger in becoming morally inescapable. She needs individual attention from anyone on hand to give it. As for one's effect on the teacher, again this would seem largely negligible. No one can radically alter their teaching style, or the children's learning and behaviour patterns, consistently throughout a whole day. It is rather like leaving a tape recorder running; after a while you forget it is there.

The boys, meanwhile, continue their half-hearted work and whole-hearted chat: 'My brother's a sixth former' . . . 'My brother goes to college' . . . 'He doesn't, he doesn't'.

Timothy: My dad's going to be the referee.

Manjit: Oh God, so he has the day off.
Gary II: We're going to win. Christmas can't come. He goes to his
            granny's on Sunday.

The majority of primary school teachers appear now to permit such conversation while work is in progress. At its worst, it is aimless gossip which replaces or inhibits anything remotely taxing. At its best, it is a sociable activity which helps to strengthen the bonds of personal relationship and actually may enhance the quality of schoolwork. Each teacher must judge for himself when that fine dividing line is crossed.

At 11.25 a.m. Mr Weston leaves the room to help prepare the fish tank for the Lord Mayor's visit. Prehaps they are to be presented to the First Citizen. Two boys, with hands on their heads, take advantage of the teacher's one-minute absence to lift their desks with their knees, as if by magic.

Upon Mr Weston's return, the children are instructed to put away their maths work and take out their local history books. All third- and fourth-year pupils are involved in a substantial project on the surrounding area which incorporates visits by and to local citizens; studies of local church and archive records, tombstones, photographs, maps, architecture; model-making; ancient craft simulation; interviews with historians, professional and amateur.

Environmental studies is capable of many different emphases – artistic, scientific, linguistic, sociological. The particular emphasis here is historical, and it is worth reminding ourselves at this stage of the potential value of an historical perspective. John Jennings (1977) summarises seven claims which may be made. He writes:

1   History is an important subject. It is essential to the creation of a politically articulate electorate in that it deals with the acquisition, use, abuse, and loss of power and, uniquely, shows the long-term effects of political and economic action.

2   Secondly, through its study of remote periods and of world history, it demands the active understanding of societies with radically different assumptions from ours.

3   Thirdly, it teaches children how to evaluate evidence, to argue from incomplete evidence.

4   Fourthly, it helps to develop children's understanding of causes and effects and of chronology.

5   Fifthy, it is the source of a wealth of true stories – of adventure, romance, tragedy, mystery, comedy – that no child should be denied.

6   Sixthly, it is an important element in leisure pursuits.

7   Finally, it promotes the development of skills in narrative, description, analysis and constructive argument.

Whereas the stress on oral history in the school project would generate a wealth of material in category five, the chief justification for it
would, no doubt, be found in Jennings's categories three, four and
seven. I revisited the school several weeks after my one-day's observation, in order to see the final exhibition of materials from this two-term
local history/environmental studies team teaching enterprise. Very
impressive and original it was, too, involving work by 200 pupils and 6
teachers.[1]

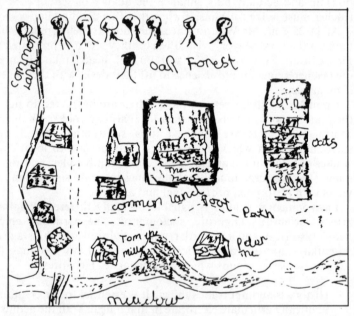

Figure 5.4

However, perhaps at this stage it is difficult for those in the ranks to
appreciate what the final outcome might be, although Gary tells me
that he is enjoying the project and he proceeds to explain his own book.
Lorraine has taken out hers and is labelling and colouring her
bird's-eye drawing of the land. It is shown in Figure 5.4 and her
account of a villeinous life is given in Figure 5.5. When Mr Weston
approaches and asks if she has written anything, her nod is rewarded

[1]For any teacher or student who wishes to develop or extend an environmental studies
interest, the following books are recommended: (1) Bainbridge, J., *Land Marks* (series)
(Oxford: Blackwell, 1976). (2) Lines, C. J. and Bolwell, L. H., *Teaching Environmental
Studies in the Primary and Middle School* (London: Ginn, 1971). (3) Perry, G. A., Jones,
E. and Hammersley, D. A., *The Teacher's Handbook for Environmental Studies*
(London: Blandford Press, 1968). (4) *Science 5–13* (London: Macdonald Educational,
1972). The twenty books in this Schools Council Project are a *must* for any teacher.

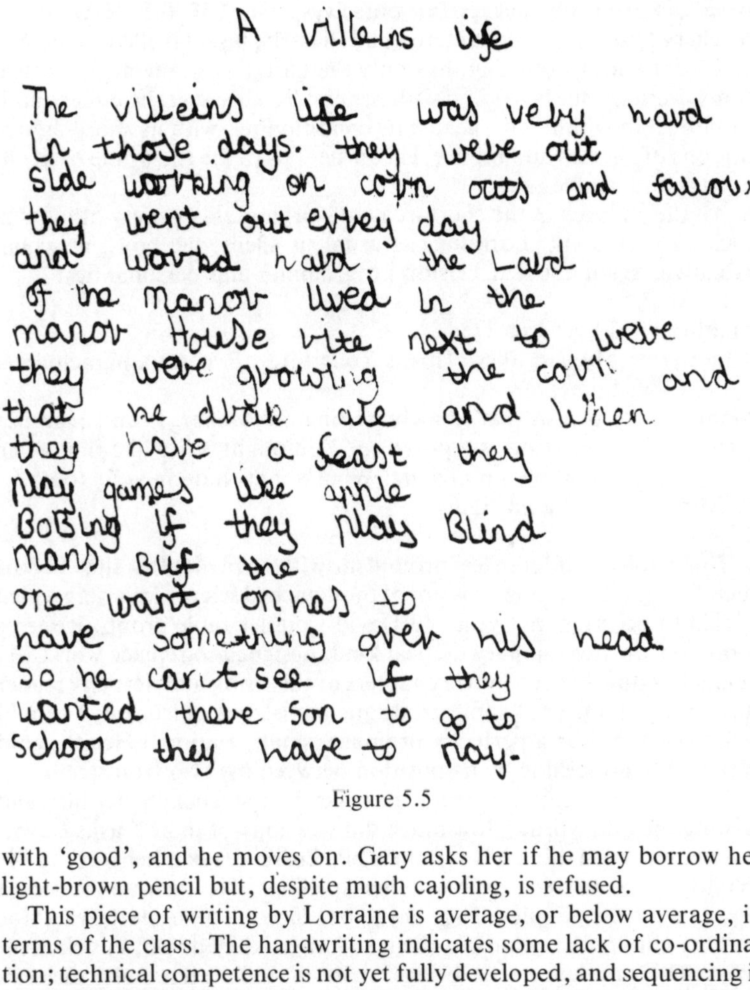

A villens life

The villeins life was very hard
in those days. they were out
side working on corn oats and fallow,
they went out evrey day
and worked hard. the Lard
of the manor lived in the
manor House rite next to were
they were growing the cobn and
that he drak ate and When
they have a feast they
play games like apple
Bobbing if they play Blind
Mans Buf the
one want on has to
have something over his head
So he can't see if they
wanted there son to go to
school they have to pay.

Figure 5.5

with 'good', and he moves on. Gary asks her if he may borrow her light-brown pencil but, despite much cajoling, is refused.

This piece of writing by Lorraine is average, or below average, in terms of the class. The handwriting indicates some lack of co-ordination; technical competence is not yet fully developed, and sequencing is questionable. However, she has clearly been at pains to include as much information as she can, and she is able to record several facts she has learnt, either from the teacher or from reference books. In terms of James Britton's categories, which are considered in Chapter 6, Sequel II, the piece is transactional.

Anxious, I think, that I should see good work, Mr Weston hands me one of the best topic books, having, earlier in the day, given me 'a good maths book' to inspect. It is a natural reaction. Most of us, as teachers, have a vested interest in those who are academically successful. Perhaps because we feel they will reflect creditably upon us. Or perhaps because they are the only ones we really understand, having been academically successful ourselves. One of the best infants teachers I have ever encountered had, herself, been labelled 'remedial' at school and, to this day, has only the barest of academic qualifications. Perhaps she is so good with her children because she understands failure from within. Our academic conditioning, with its short-sighted notions of success and failure, encourages us to see the whole of life as a perpetual hurdle race.

All the children in the class are now working on a variety of tasks in their project book. Lorraine, as usual, is silent; the boys, as usual, talkative, again about television programmes and personalities.

Manjit: I hate Ken Dodd.
Timothy: My dad likes 'This is Your Life'. I've got a parachute at home.
Manjit: Look at that scrawly writing *(i.e. mine)*. I can't read it.
Gary: You're not supposed to. You might write like that when you grow up. *To me*: What's that thing in your tooth?
R. M.:   It's a gold filling.

Three or four children leer around me with open mouths, showing me their fillings. Their interest is not of the detached scientific variety which I tried to describe in 7-year-old David's dinner-table group. It seems more like the diversionary tactical kind, designed to replace work. My filling has now figured in two chapters of this book and, lest any reader has a mental image of some grotesque monstrous obtrusion, I should point out that it is a perfectly ordinary, small, National Health, gold piece, only noticeable by its position between my two front teeth.

For several minutes, Lorraine has been sitting, sucking her biro and writing the odd word. 'How much did you copy of mine?' asks Dawn. No answer, but I think it was quite a bit. Lorraine takes her work to Mr Weston, who corrects some of her spellings. He then announces a reprieve for the guppies. They are to be placed in a jar on the radiator and the children may look at them so long as they do not knock them over. The announcement brings sighs of relief that only such an eleventh-hour pardon could provoke. Lorraine looks up and listens to the news, but her thoughts remain hidden.

It is 11.55 a.m. and the boys and girls are told to clear away their books and wait for the bell. As they sit with arms folded, Mr Weston takes advantage of the spare time for some mental arithmetic.

Mr W.:   Eight fours, Andrew.
Andrew: Thirty-two.
Mr W.:   Stand by the door. Marilyn, seven sixes.
Marilyn: Forty-two.
Mr W.:   Stand by the door.

Children who answer correctly are allowed to line up; others wait in their seats. Early escape is the reward for a right response, rather like remission of sentence for good conduct.

At 12.10 p.m. three children only are left in the classroom. Simon is washing out in the sink the gravel from the fish tank; Shirley has earache and remains in to keep warm; Lorraine has just tape recorded a short conversation with me. She felt that she had had 'quite a good morning', and had enjoyed doing the area shapes from the blackboard, as well as the reading, writing and tables. In the afternoon she was anticipating 'craft or anything'. Her speech is quiet and hesitant and its content thin. When asked what she watched on television, she replied, 'Cartoons. Comedies. I can't remember anything else'. Manjit, Gary, Timothy and Co. would have been garrulous, if not eloquent, on such a subject. Undoubtedly, Lorraine is quite talkative with her girl-friends when they are playing together. To be tape recorded by a comparative stranger must be a fairly taxing experience for her.

In the absence of specific details about our school dinner, since I forgot to record them in my notebook, let me present you some statistics to digest, which will show the enormous scope of the Schools Meals Service and indicate one of the unique features of British educational provision. The immense value in terms of health and socialisation would be reckoned by many teachers to be an adequate pay-off for the tremendous administrative burden imposed on clerical and teaching staff. On a selected day in autumn 1974–5, the number of pupils in maintained schools taking dinners on payment was 5,023,000. The number of free dinners was 750,000, making a total of 5,773,000. The total taking dinners, as a percentage of pupils present, was 70·1 per cent and, of these, 13·1 per cent were served free of charge. The proportion of free meals served in any one school is, incidentally, a useful, quick, if crude, indicator of social, as well as food, intake (see *Education Committees Year Book* for 1977–8). Many a portly head-teacher has been overheard to observe at meetings: 'I have seventeen free dinners.'

Afternoon school begins at 1.30 p.m. but, twenty minutes before this, a number of boys and girls are in the classroom, preparing it for craft by putting coverings over the desks, and paint brushes and water in strategic spots. David asks me: 'You're a script writer, aren't you?' and, possibly echoing Manjit's earlier words, Lorraine adds, 'A scribble writer', and laughs. Her confidence appears to be increasing.

When the bell sounds the rest of the children return in ones and twos. Manjit enters singing a pop song: 'The Girls grab the boys and they go wild, wild, wild'. Mr Weston is, significantly, not far behind.

Mr W.: Quickly sit down, please . . . Can we have everyone sitting down, boys, please? . . . Right, erm. Can we have everyone

> sitting down then? Right, erm. Register then ... I'm still
> waiting ...

It is a small comment rich in what have been called teachers' *focus*
words (i.e. *right* ... *erm* ... *please* ... *then* ...). Notice, too, the pedagogic pseudo-questions, designed to promote classroom order, and the
reliance on shared assumptions between teacher and pupils. All of
which, and more, is tentatively explored in the first half of a book by
John Sinclair and Malcolm Coulthard (1975).

Soon there is silence.

Mr W.: Can you clear this mess up that you made this morning? ...
   Right ... erm ... Girls?
Girls: *Un ... deux ... trois ... quatre ...*

There is a periodic investigation of the whereabouts of those whose
French numbers are not called out, during which time Lorraine is
involved in cleaning out parts of the sink, a job she obviously enjoys.

Mr W.: Boys?
Boys: *Un ... deux ... trois ... quatre ...*
   (Once again, *onze* comes out as *awze*)
Mr W.: Right. Hands on your head, everyone.

Immediate silence enables Mr Weston to give further instructions.
Children will be involved in activities relating to Christmas. Choice and
variety are now permitted, whereas neither was allowed during the
morning session. Some will finish their Christmas cards, either
working singly or in pairs. Some will be working on large pieces of card
to produce a Biblical scene, which will ultimately decorate the
windows. Its subject will either be the stable scene; the three kings; the
shepherds and the angel; or those following the star.

Susan: Who was following the star?
Manjit: The three kings, stupid.

This leads into a question and answer session between teacher and
children regarding the details of the Biblical birth narratives. Lorraine
sits quietly, staring down at the table, and then, looking around at
those children who answer, she whispers one response to herself – 'the
lambs' – and puts up her hand to answer, but is not asked.

The discussion over, most children settle to their various tasks.
Lorraine is not clear what to do and goes out to ask for guidance. Mr
Weston offers her a piece of paper but she rejects it and elects to work
with Dawn and another girl on their Christmas card. The three girls

stand around this picture of a colourful and attractive, if lop-sided, rabbit, about 60 by 45 centimetres, each painting a part of it, before moving on to produce multi-coloured patches around the rabbit by dabbing with small sponges. There is a little conversation between the other two girls, but Lorraine is generally quiet, although fully accepted as a member of the trio.

All the children in the class are now actively involved on different tasks, either working alone or in pairs or small groups. Some are producing a nativity scene motif for the window decoration. Others are engaged in elaborating on single letters from the word CHRISTMAS (e.g. a Father Christmas with a 60 centimetre high 'S' around him). Others are carefully designing cards.

As they are thus engaged, so they adopt a variety of comfortable positions in which to work. Some paint standing up; others sitting down; a few, lying on the floor. Some can concentrate for long periods of time. Manjit, for example, who did little work of a non-oral variety this morning, is absolutely silent for half an hour, completely absorbed in his own nativity scene.

Lorraine, on the other hand, is not so involved and moves regularly from painting to sink, now sponging paint from her skirt, now cleaning out her saucer and fish-paste jar. When she paints it seems that she invariably goes over parts already covered, or touches up parts here and there, rather than risk anything new. More often, she leaves her little group and moves around the room, or into the corridor to look at the decorations, telling me *en route* that she does not want to do any more on the rabbit. She shows particular interest in a painting of 'MERRY CHRISTMAS' in glistening letters (made by sprinkling glitter particles over newly painted letters and then shaking off the loose bits). Then she hovers in the doorway, sometimes sucking her thumb, sometimes hopping from one foot to another, looking like an attractive little waif. Such free-wheeling sessions seem to be important to some children and cannot always be contained within normal break periods. Conversely, optimum learning and concentration periods come not to order. Like telephone calls, they are unanticipated and of varying duration.

All this time, Mr Weston has been a peripatetic adviser, going round giving help; distributing paint and paper; relaying information regarding the whereabouts of other materials; asking why so many children are round the sink; holding up a painting to establish its ownership.

At 2.34 p.m. he announces, 'Time to pack up', and begins to distribute clearing-up jobs. Children move in all directions, like a snooker formation struck by the cue ball, collecting paintings to hang up for drying, washing out brushes and pots, replacing scissors and pencils. Such regular tidying up is a constant feature of classroom life and it needs to be done efficiently and smoothly, as it is here. Lorraine is asked to pick up some pieces of paper from the floor and this she does, slowly and meticulously, chasing minute scraps with brush and pan. Nine children are flushed out of the stockroom; two or three settle down with reading books; Dawn tells me that her dog always jumps on her bed in the morning to wake her up for school. It is an odd, irrelevant, inconsequential comment and therefore, perhaps, worth recording.

At 2.45 p.m., when the bell sounds, girls and boys line up in separate rows by the door. It must be second nature for many teachers to distinguish between their pupils in this way but, administrative convenience aside, one wonders if there is much to be said for it. Emphasising sexual identity, as is done many times within the ritual of many a school day, does not seem to have much point.

Lorraine, however, is in neither line. Instead, she is concentrating on hunting for bits of rubbish. Like many pupils, she clearly enjoys tidying up. She steps in the bin to stamp down for more space, gets her foot stuck and falls over. It is almost the classic clown ploy here performed artlessly. Only after two exhortations from the teacher is Lorraine persuaded to leave her job and follow her peers into the playground.

After a quarter of an hour's break, all have returned and, on hearing Mr Weston's words, 'Pencils out, please', the word goes round in a whisper, 'Spelling . . . Spelling'. It is, indeed, and the test commences. As is customary in this kind of game, single-word test items are generally put within the context of a simple sentence, or a brief discussion. In some cases, the isolated word gives rise to a short language lesson. Unlike Lucy's spelling test in Chapter 4, the words here have either been selected quite arbitrarily, or to reflect children's individual errors in the past few days. Here are the items:

(1) *mountain* (Mr W.: Give me a sentence with the word 'mountain' in it.
                    Pupil: The mountain is very tall.
                    Mr W.:   High, not tall. What's the name of the tallest mountain?)

(2) *newspaper* *(A short discussion ensues about local and national newspapers.)*

(3) *middle* (Timothy: Johnny threw a dart in the middle of the board.)

(4) *curtain* (Mr. W.: For every curtain in this room, the girls made a press-stud button.)

(5) *playmate* (Julie: My playmate always makes friends with me.)

(6) *settle*

(7) *extra* (Mr W.: The newsman shouted, 'Extra, Extra! Read all about it!'

In the discussion which follows, the link with number two is developed.)

(8) *meddle*   (Mr W.:   'Don't meddle in anyone else's affairs', said the wise old man.)

(9) *fountain*   (Jacqueline achieves rhythm, if not sense, with: 'There was a fountain on top of the mountain *(the children laugh)*.

(10) *paddle*   (Mr W.:   A canoe has one paddle.

Andrew: The steamer had a big paddle.)

(11) *platform*   (Mr W.:   The train is about to enter at platform six.

Alison: Mr and Mrs Brown met Paddington on Paddington Station's platform.)

(12) *honest*   (Pupil: My sister isn't very honest.)

Lorraine has all the words correct except the first, which she wrote as *moutain*. The children mark their own spellings, as is the custom, and then hand in their books for later rechecking by the teacher.

Lorraine's spelling test did not generate the same degree of heightened emotion as occurred in Lucy's class, where the atmosphere was almost hysterical. Yet it was conducted as a serious activity, and in such a context that the children knew that something important was happening. It was, in military terms, the equivalent of a major kit inspection, rather than routine checking of equipment and, because of that, it carried with it the associated feelings of unnaturalness and tension. Without minimising the significance of the importance of spelling (and without over-emphasising it either), it does seem that a better standard might be obtained by a more natural approach, placing it within the context of normal on-going work and investigation. It could become, to use Bullock's words, 'part of the fabric of normal classroom experience, neither dominating nor neglected' (para. 11.14).

In this respect, I find the list of 'handy hints' produced by Mike Torbe (1977) very helpful and, with his kind permission, would like to quote them now. He makes ten points.

1   Teaching from spelling lists, on the basis of study followed by tests, does not help the child to become an efficient speller in his writing.

2   Slightly better is to use the test followed by study of the words spelled incorrectly; but this causes only a marginal improvement.

3   Spelling rules are of little help, because if they are thorough enough to explain a pattern, they're likely to be incomprehensible to the children.

4   Children who have a good general understanding of sound—symbol relationship, even if they do not spell well at the moment,

are, as Margaret Peters says, 'well on their way' to becoming good spellers.

5 Teachers who have an enthusiasm and enjoyment for spoken and written language, and a care for it, have pupils who are likely to be good spellers.

6 An interest in words, their meanings, shapes, history and sound, generates improved spelling.

7 The more interested pupils are in what they write, the more attention they are prepared to give to its appearance, including spelling.

8 When children recognise that their writing is for a real public audience, not just the teacher but other people, they are more likely to be concerned with their spelling.

9 Good spelling habits are:
  − The habit of checking guesses by looking the word up, or asking.
  − The habit of proof-reading.
  − The habit of spelling analysis: How is it pronounced? Is the spelling phonetic? How can I remember the difficult bits?

10 Spelling is changing all the time, but slowly. What one generation finds appalling, the next generation accepts ...
  ... Be careful, therefore, about condemning words too quickly
  ... Give your time not to outraged attacks on what offends you, but on the more urgent and useful task of teaching pupils how to spell by considering the recurring patterns of English spelling.

Perhaps such an approach, designed to take the heat and unnaturalness out of teaching spelling, while probably rendering it more effective also, should be welcomed. But old habits, like old soldiers, die hard.

The test done, Lorraine and her classmates now read their fiction books for a few moments, anticipating a singing lesson. However, when Mr Weston returns from his fruitless search for a tape recorder, he informs them that they will finish the day with reading. It is 3.30 p.m. on a Friday and the children are restless.

Gary informs me that his book has got bare pictures in it, and so it has, showing young children having a shower and a bath. The boys and girls nearby laugh at Gary's words and I imagine his book is quite popular, if only for its visual element. The word *bare* seems to be a particularly rude one for young children.

I ask Lorraine about her library book (*A Dog and Two Red Heads*, by Jan Macdonald, London: Harrap, 1959) and she tells me, 'It's all right'. The jacket blurb informs us that the book is about an orphan from Glasgow who goes to live with his grandparents in Morayshire. Lorraine has the book open in front of her but is not interested in it. There is more attraction in the jokes and comments of those about her.

Manjit: Are you a C. M?
Simon: Why?
Manjit: If you were, you'd be a sex maniac.
Simon: Did you hear that joke about the Irish mastermind? He was asked, 'What's your name?' . . . 'Pass'.
Gary: Why did the Irish road sweeper break his leg when sweeping leaves? . . . He fell off the tree.

It is the season of mists and Irish jokes, and even Debbie is emboldened to ask me a riddle, albeit not an Irish one: 'What did the big chimney say to the little chimney?' I feign ignorance, but her answer is not what I expect or understand: 'You're too young to ring'.

At 3.45 p.m. Mr Weston calls all children to order and they prepare to listen to him read a story from *It Must Be Magic* by Miriam Huber and Frank Salisbury (Herts: Nisbet, 1962). It is, in fact, a Grimm fairy tale of a mouse, a donkey and a bear, to which the class pays reasonable attention. Lorraine concentrates particularly hard, following the narrative closely in her copy of the book. After five minutes the errant tape recorder is brought in but rejected at this late stage in the day.

A minute before 4.00 p.m. the children are instructed to line up by the door in their separate ranks. The teacher says: 'It's definitely the girls' (i.e. the boys are moving) . . . 'Now it's the boys' (i.e. the girls are moving). When the bell sounds, the girls are allowed off first, to a small cheer.

Sequel I   School Assembly

We have seen in earlier chapters that the school assembly, often the first and only corporate experience of the day for all children, can have considerable power. In Rashda's case (Chapter 2), the stress fell on reinforcement of the school as a caring community. This was true also of David's assembly (Chapter 3) which, in addition, highlighted the significance of the individual within the group, via the impressive birthday-boy ritual. Lucy's Roman Catholic school (Chapter 4) could assume a reasonable degree of acceptance of one particular Christian stance, and therefore could hold a full-scale mass for pupils, teachers and parents. In this instance, there was a community of faith in which worship was not inappropriate.

However, in a pluralist society, and in a school where education should 'scrutinise' rather than 'assume' belief (Hull, 1975), the school assembly, mandatory since the 1944 Education Act, becomes highly questionable unless it can be justified on social and/or curriculum grounds.

In this respect, I want to draw heavily on an article by Miss Susan Tomkins (1976), primary schools RE adviser for the Christian Education Movement. She attempts to view the school assembly in curriculum terms by evaluating it against the views of P. H. Phoenix (1964), an American educationist, who identified a series of six patterns of human understanding. Briefly, these are as follows:

(1) *Symbolics*
   This is the most fundamental in that it comprises language, mathematics and para-linguistic features such as gesture, to communicate meaning. The language of the large assembly differs from that of the class or small group and it could be argued that children should experience this kind of language which, in Douglas Barnes's terms (1976), often smacks of 'performance' rather than 'exploration'.

(2) *Empirics*
   This places stress on factual information such as that offered by the physical and biological sciences, psychology and social science. 'An assembly which is well presented and the culmination of interesting work, helps to fix the facts in the pupils' minds because they have the cue of the performance to remind them when they wish to recall the facts later' (Tomkins, 1976).

(3) *Aesthetics*
   This realm of meaning involves drama, music, literature and the visual arts. Clearly, the Annie Oakley assembly which Lorraine experiences is largely in this category, although it features in others also. Singing hymns or songs together; watching a play; looking at pictures; listening to music; hearing a story, are all aesthetic experiences which have occurred in the assemblies described in this book.

(4) *Synnoetics*
   Phoenix gives this name to that pattern of human understanding which is

concerned with knowledge of oneself in relation to others. Can an individual learn something of himself when confronted by, or involved in, a large gathering? Can he develop his self-identity when part of a larger unit, learning how to sit quietly, respond appropriately, and participate when required?

There will be occasions in later life (e.g. social clubs, political meetings, church or resident associations) when such expertise will be needed, but that is not sufficient justification. The here and now is crucial David (Chapter 3), it seems to me, was in precisely this process of coming to terms with himself amongst a large number of other people. You will recall his tentative participation and the fact that he was anticipating a time when he would be able to take on the star role of 'birthday boy'. In David's case, mental preparation was preceding the event, and was a vital part of the process.

(5) *Ethics*
Involving the realm of moral judgements, this area is clearly one which many teachers and pupils would associate with the school assembly. The fact that the assembled children will be at different stages of moral development does not seem to assume the significance that it should. Perhaps the unifying factor at primary school level is that all children will be at the stage of depending on others for their own code of right conduct (i.e. heteronomy), rather than being able to rely on internalised moral principles (i.e. autonomy). The need for conformity, which can easily degenerate into an expression of authoritarianism, may neutralise any direct and intended moral education. However, as Peter McPhail indicates (1972), we learn not only from direct instruction but by observation, by ethos and attitude, by the way in which we are treated. Thus, the actual conduct of the assembly, from the ways in which children are ordered about, to the places where they sit or stand, will have its moral impact. We all learn from example as well as instruction.

(6) *Synoptics*
Here the other realms of meaning are integrated and a coherent understanding emerges. Although such an all-embracing realm is basically beyond the understanding of most primary school children, maybe there are occasions when children can store away the essence of an experience, such as that conveyed in an abstract act of worship, so as to draw upon it later in the development of their understanding of themselves and their world.

Thus, while it is difficult to tolerate state school assemblies which purport solely and constantly to be acts of worship by a believing community, it may be possible to justify them on certain curriculum grounds. Few would dispute that they have some sort of place. The problems start when one tries to define precisely what that place is. To close this section, as I began, with Miss Tomkins: 'If the assembly dies out because an act of worship is considered inappropriate, and there is nothing to replace it, this may well be a great loss to the British primary schools.'

REFERENCES

Barnes, D. (1976). *From Communication to Curriculum* (Harmondsworth: Penguin).
Hull, J. (1975). *School Worship: An Obituary* (London: SCM).
McPhail, P. (1972). *Moral Education in the Secondary School* (London: Longman).
Phoenix, P. H. (1964). *Realms of Meaning* (New York: McGraw-Hill).
Tomkins, S. (1976). 'From worship to curriculum', *Learning for Living* (Summer), vol. 15, no. 4, pp. 149–53.

Sequel II Maths Teaching Comment

It was fairly evident in Chapter 5 that Lorraine's grip on certain mathematical processes and concepts was quite tenuous. When given individual help she could achieve some success, but, left to her own devices, she floundered. The vast majority of primary schools, according to the HMI report of 1978, spend a good deal of time on maths teaching, but what actually occurs during that time is clearly of greater significance. Lorna Ridgway (1976) outlines her criteria for good maths teaching and good maths learning and, with her kind permission, I should like to quote the nine points she makes.

1   Since the ultimate capacity to think abstractly does not originate in abstract teaching but depends upon the learner's own interaction with the external world in thought-provoking situations, the teacher's responsibility is to provide for the appropriate mathematical activity in breadth and in depth.

2   Children proceed along a broad front; a variety of numerical and mathematical ideas at approximately the same level is provided.

3   All pupils need not necessarily go through all processes in the same order.

4   The programme is so arranged that the learner returns frequently to the same aspect of mathematics to renew his grasp and deepen his understanding.

5   Recording of number and mathematical experience often takes forms other than the numerical. Young children grasp and use number ideas expressed in pictures, diagrams, charts, graphs, histograms, mapping and three-dimensional structures and use them more effectively than they did the former purely computational 'sums'.

6   Apparatus, text-books and task assignments are used flexibly as learning aids; at any level their use may be modified, dispensed with or prolonged as necessary.

7   Mechanical mastery dependent upon rote-learning has a very limited place: it is not usually undertaken unless the process it represents is fully understood: but the terms required to express mathematical ideas are memorized through constant use and this memorization may occasionally be tested.

8   Individual interest is highly valued: children may prolong their work in an area that interests them even if other aspects or subjects are temporarily neglected.

9   Much help is available to the teacher. Commercially produced equipment abounds, from beads and bricks to the structural materials of Cuisenaire rods, Stern or Dienes blocks, Logiblocs, metrication kits, Poleidoblocs and calculators. The literature is rich, ranging from theoretical studies . . . to practical guidance.

　　. . . There are well designed schemes such as the Kent and the Croydon Mathematics Projects, worked out by teachers themselves. Commercial assignment-card kits make individual work comparatively easy, although there is often need to use them selectively.

Such a programme and approach would surely be endorsed by most experienced primary school teachers, yet the ideal is always difficult to match in reality. Somehow, Lorraine's struggles seem far removed from these statements, and yet those very struggles highlight the continuing need for some such plan of campaign as that outlined here.

Chapter 6

Peter, Aged 10

I do some more Reading Lab if I get the chance

THE SCHOOL

Peter's school opened in 1974 and is likely to remain fairly small with some 160 children, three classes of infants on the ground floor and four of juniors upstairs. Serving an area of small mid-1930s owner-occupier semi-detached houses and new council town houses, the school, which is tucked away at the end of a cul-de-sac, initially took in a disproportionate number of children with behavioural problems. Some were from the nearby children's home, and others had either been advised or required to leave the schools they had previously been attending. Perhaps any new school, like a New Year's resolution, offers promise to those who have previously failed, or been unhappy, or been declared redundant.

Near the attractive building is a brook, a small bank with mature trees, a sunken wall, a pond which was previously a rubbish dump, and a scrap metal yard. In other words, sources of considerable interest to any school keen on environmental studies, as this one is.

There are seven full-time teachers including the head, who spends most of his day around the school in classrooms or working with individual children, two part-timers for needlework and remedial attention, and a nursery assistant. Parents often come in to help with practical activities, particularly cooking.

THE DAY

It is 9.00 a.m. on Monday morning, a dull day with rain on the wind. Sixteen or so children are grouped like molecules in small clusters of three or four in an open-plan-style classroom. All appear to be healthy and well cared for and quite smartly dressed in colourful clothes. There is an element of vertical grouping as the class, numbering some thirty-two, contains 9 to 11-year-olds. This includes thirteen boys, one of whom is, reportedly, a kleptomaniac receiving psychiatric attention. Some of the girls showing signs of fashion consciousness are wearing modern-style shoes and have the remains of nail varnish on their fingers.

Peter is in one of the groups, a tallish boy with fairly long curly hair, spectacles, and a brace on his teeth. Brace apart, he is rather like the stereotype of the scientist in embryo. There is no school uniform and he is dressed in tweed trousers, a purple shirt, a dark-red baggy jumper and brown shoes.

The classroom is as attractive and colourful as a miniature department store at Christmas. Different parts are set aside for different activities, although dividing lines are by no means hard and fast. The practical area has a functional appearance, with tiled floor, sink, work surfaces, pottery wheel, clay, paints. The reading corner offers another image, with a carpeted area, easy chairs and cushions, a switched-on bedside table lamp, and displayed books of all kinds. Elsewhere, two caged gerbils[1] run about in sight of a model of the Golden Gate Bridge, San Francisco. Mobile and plastic shapes hang from the ceiling girders. The walls and windows are covered with evidence of what the children have recently been working on. There are paintings, collages and pieces of writing about fire. Graphs indicate that the three most popular daily newspapers for parents are the *Sun, Mirror*, and the local evening paper. (One teacher whom I know, from another school, is astute enough to verify such results as these, obtained from the children, by records of sales from every local newsagent within his catchment area.) The most popular children's comic is *The Beano*, and the least popular, *Jinty*.

In addition to the graphs, there are colour prints which show scenes from the school youth hostel trip to Ludlow. An ordinance survey map pinpoints the school in its surroundings. There are twigs, branches, pottery, embroidery, prints, paintings, trays, boxes, fabric, an old boot, as well as charts, posters and more conventional classroom paraphernalia. (See Sequel I at the end of this chapter for a list of the school stock.)

This classroom is a treasure house whose message is the same as Howard Carter's to Lord Carnarvon on discovering Tutenkhamen's tomb. When asked, 'Can you see anything?' he replied stammeringly, 'Yes, wonderful things'. Every boy and girl can find something of interest in this room. Even so, few teachers would entirely support the assertion of John Dewey (1966), tantalising as it is: 'The only way in which adults can consciously control the kind of education which the immature can get, is by controlling the environment in which they act, and hence think and feel.' As Dearden questions (1968): 'Which environment is THE environment or the one that is to be stimulating, or structured? Can one literally PROVIDE experiences?' Perhaps not, but few children, I imagine, would happily exchange this room for one with completely bare walls and bleak brown desks. The difference is

---

[1]See an article by Roger Harris, 'Locusts, gerbils and barley: keeping living things in primary schools', in C. Richards (1978).

that between a personalised, attractive bedroom, and a solitary confinement cell.

The boys and girls, by now up to their full complement, are standing or sitting, waiting for their teacher, who is also deputy head, delayed with a parent. (In fact, this turned out to be Peter's father, who had come to discuss the secondary school his son should move to at the beginning of the next academic year, and who was the first parent to broach the matter at this stage.)

Mr Barnes, the teacher, enters. He is a tallish, bearded man in his early 30s, dressed in a brown suit, purple shirt and yellowish tie. He is quietly spoken, with a gentle but firm manner. It is not without significance that he taught these children the previous year also. Straight away he is surrounded by a group of them who appear to have brought him cellophane bags containing small black sponges. These are, in fact, coals for the eventual launching of their hot-air balloon. Almost by way of reciprocation for their gifts, Mr Barnes hands out individual white folders to each child. Peter's, with his name on it, contains material from the SRA scheme which we have encountered in previous chapters. Amongst other papers, he has a green Power Builder Progress Chart and a pink Rate Builder Progress Chart. Who could fail to be impressed by the promise of such dynamism and energy, even if they are only comprehension exercises?

Peter elects not to work in his own classroom and goes next door to the tiny library, a room lined with shelves and containing a television, a spirit duplicator, a Polaroid camera, a slide projector, and other pieces of audio-visual equipment, all within easy reach of any child. The school trusts its older pupils not only to work on their own, but to do so near valuable equipment, if they wish. This is something which Peter particularly appreciates, as he will indicate later.

There are four chairs around the table in the library and a few cushions on the floor, to suit all sedentary tastes. Two other children are reading in the library as Peter collects his SRA card from the box and immediately settles down to work on the short prose piece, *Junks of the Yangtze*, by Anne Terry White (2 Purple, Lab. 11a) (Figure 6.1).

The story is written in a dramatic tradition, designed to appeal to juniors with a taste for adventure and proximity, through literature, to danger. Notice the use of the present tense, with regular elisions ('isn't', 'it's', 'that's'); the numerous exclamation marks and question marks; the short sharp sentences; and the rhetorical flourishes ('He was born on a junk'; 'He will die on a junk'). Multiple-choice questions are so designed as to check a child's reading of the lines, between the lines and beyond the lines. Items in the vocabulary section are based on words in the prose story, and thus there is something of a marriage between the piece of fictional/factual reading and the grammar exercises.

Junks of the Yangtze

By ANNE TERRY WHITE

1 Probably there isn't a more dangerous river-voyage anywhere on earth than the 350-mile stretch between the cities of Ichang and Chungking. On that short trip up the Yangtze there isn't a junk that hasn't had at least one hairbreadth escape. One junk out of ten is badly damaged. One out of twenty is wrecked. How many lives are lost is unknown.

2 Under the best conditions, a struggling little junk will make the trip from Ichang to Chungking in twenty-five days, travelling between dawn and sunset.

3 The junk isn't pretty to look at. It is a freight ship, and nothing is expected of it except that it gets where it's going. Low, square-nosed, with a high stern, it is about

120 feet long by a dozen feet wide. Besides cargo, it carries the skipper and his family, who live in the junk, and about a hundred men. Some seventy or eighty of the crew are trackers. These fellows walk along the river-bank and tow the ship. Imagine them on a perilous path cut in the face of a cliff.

4 The men are nearly naked. Their bodies are bent, every muscle taut. Each tracker has a short piece of bamboo rope round his body, and this rope is fastened by a slip-knot to the bamboo tow-rope. The men are in single file, one on one side of the rope, the next man on the other. They are chanting a singsong phrase to keep in step.

5 Three gangers see to it that the trackers

Figure 6.1

After three minutes of work, Peter is called back to the classroom to pay his dinner money, a traditional Monday morning ritual, and sits chatting with two of his friends. Others are doing the same while they await their turn. Some chat about television programmes. Some read their books, amongst them the following:

Friday and Robinson by Michel Tournier (London: Aldus, 1972)
Jack Frost by Ruth Ainsworth (London: Heinemann, 1966);
The Dribblesome Teapot by Norman Hunter (Harmondsworth: Penguin, 1971).

keep moving once they have started. Otherwise the ship may slip into the strong current and drag them all into the water, perhaps to their death. The gangers shout and bring their bamboo sticks down on the backs of the slackers – the gangers can tell who is pulling and who isn't. But all the time the three men strain to hear the sound of a drum. The drum sends up instructions – when to move, when to halt. For sometimes the trackers must stop.

6 Away in the rear three men are spread out at a distance from one another. Their eyes are on the 1,200-foot tow-line, which is constantly catching on boulders and pieces of rock that stick out. The business of these men is to keep the line clear. It is dangerous work climbing along ragged rocks to push off the rope before it gets torn to pieces by the heavy boat tugging at its lower end.

But much more dangerous is the work of the naked men perched on the rocks far out in the swift-running river. Their business is to wade or swim behind the tow-line and throw it clear of the rocks. Every hour of the day these strong swimmers risk their lives. Many a time they have swum out with a cord round their bodies to rescue a drifting junk whose tow-rope has broken. They have the deep respect of the crew.

8 In the water, the junk is inching along. She is trying to round the point of a great reef that goes half-way across the river. The pilot, standing on the foredeck, is rapping out orders to the fifteen or sixteen men beside him who are frantically working the great bow-sweep that helps guide the craft.

9 The drummer is beating a tattoo with a couple of sticks. It is the signal to the trackers that all's well. Should the tow-line get caught or anything else go amiss, he will instantly change the rhythm.

10 The helmsman is grasping the fourteen-foot tiller. He is a practical expert, this pilot. He knows nothing of instruments: he knows only the Yangtze. He has been up and down this river so many times that he knows every rock and whirlpool in it.

11 And where is the skipper? He is perched on top of the deckhouse, anxiously watching everything that's going on. At the moment his eyes are glued to the reef. His heart is in his mouth as the junk starts to round the point. The water is low and the rocks jut out of it like so many dragons. Will the pilot make allowance enough? Will the tow-rope hold? If it breaks now, destruction is certain: for there, just astern, is another reef waiting to smash his drifting vessel.

12 And those whirlpools! If his ship gets caught in one of those, it's all over with it – it could never pull out.

13 Rapids! There are twenty major rapids between Ichang and Chungking. No two are alike. Each has to be tackled in a different way. The skipper knows he has the best pilot on the river – but still . . . The last rapids just before Chungking make a brave man's heart leap to his throat. Three men are lost at that place every day in the year, they say.

14 The junk is approaching a bend in the river where a signal station is located. The station is signalling: "Steamer coming down!"

15 The steamer has the right of way. Already the pilot is guiding the junk to the side. More delay. A nasty lot, those steamers. But the skipper envies them, too. They have so much easier a time of it in the gorges than the junks. A steamer can do the 350 miles in three days. Three days! Think of it!

16 The future, he knows, belongs to the steamboats; but the future is far away, the skipper thinks. He will go up and down many times before the future sweeps the junks from the river. He is stirred by the awesome Yangtze, which calls for everything man and vessel can do. He is proud of his ugly, hard-working, all-enduring ship – he wouldn't trade it for a steamer. No! He was born on a junk. He will die on a junk.

Figure 6.1 contd

Since the headteacher is out of school collecting equipment, Mr Barnes has additional duties and is again occupied with a parent for ten minutes. On his return he walks round with his register, collecting the dinner dues; the children do not queue up at his desk. Whether he is absent or present, there is no perceptible change in the children's behaviour as they read, chat, write. All are actively and sensibly engaged. It is a pattern which will remain constant throughout the day until PE and the story. Such is the organisation, as will be made clear shortly, that the teacher is freed to become a peripatetic adviser, working with

6. According to this story, the most dangerous of the jobs described is
   A) towing the ship
   B) climbing ragged rocks to free the tow-rope
   C) swimming behind the tow-line to throw it clear of rocks in the river

7. The work of the gangers is
   A) to see that the men towing the boat keep moving
   B) to see that the gang of workers is fed
   C) to give the trackers signals on drums

HOW WELL DID YOU READ?

Can you see the writer's purpose?

1. The author wrote this story to
   A) compare the work of Chinese junkmen with that of steamship operators
   B) describe the Yangtze River
   C) tell the story of the hard-working Chinese junkmen and the perils of the Yangtze River

Did you note the details?

2. The trip from Ichang to Chungking takes a junk
   A) 25 days
   B) 3 days
   C) from dawn to sunset

3. Power to move the junk along the river is supplied by
   A) electricity
   B) steam
   C) man's strength

4. Trackers are men who
   A) swim behind the tow-line to keep it free of the rocks
   B) walk along the bank of the river, pulling the boat
   C) give the signal if anything goes wrong

5. The most important qualification for a helmsman is
   A) to know how to use the ship's instruments
   B) to know everything about the river
   C) to know how to handle the men

How well do you organize?

8. In an outline of the information given in this story, one main heading might be "Dangers the junkmen face". Which would not be a suitable subtopic under this heading?
   A) Whirlpools
   B) Rocks jutting out of the water
   C) Trouble with the ship's engine

Can you form the right conclusion?

9. From the facts and feelings expressed in this story we can conclude that
   A) junks are superior to steamers on the Yangtze
   B) steamers may replace junks sooner than the skipper thinks
   C) junkmen would rather operate steamers

10. The junk in this story
    A) still performs a useful service
    B) was practically useless at the time this story was written
    C) had a crew of men who had never made the Yangtze River trip before

LEARN ABOUT WORDS

A. Often you can tell the meaning of a word from other words round it. We call this "getting meaning from the **context**".

Figure 6.1 contd

individual children, rather than remaining the dominant focal point of the room.

Mr Barnes now speaks very, very quietly and asks all children to close their books and listen to what he has to say. He wishes to see Group 1 first in the English corner, with their English and maths books. Group 3 will find their week's work detailed in the maths corner. Group 2 have finished their graphs and all have been handed in except Veronica's and that is now ready. They will try another graph this week, different from those of last

Directions: Find words in the story that mean:

1. little Chinese ship *(1)*
2. singing *(4)*
3. shirkers: people who don't take responsibility *(5)*
4. standing: waiting watchfully *(7)*
5. save from danger or harm *(7)*
6. moving inch by inch, slowly *(8)*
7. wrong *(9)*

B. Often a word has more than one meaning, depending on how it is used.

Directions: Choose the meaning of each **bold-face** word as it is used in the story; write its letter.

8. **stretch** *(1)*

   A) distance; space
   B) spread out
   C) make tense

9. **file** *(4)*

   A) row of persons, one behind another
   B) tool with small ridges or teeth
   C) place for keeping records, papers

10. **slip** *(5)*

    A) narrow strip of paper
    B) small twig cut from a plant
    C) slide suddenly

11. **current** *(5)*

    A) flow of water
    B) of the present time
    C) flow of electricity through a wire

12. **sound** *(5)*

    A) healthy
    B) noise: something that can be heard
    C) body of water

13. **round** *(8)*

    A) circular: in the shape of a circle
    B) pass round: navigate past
    C) kind of song

14. **craft** *(8)*

    A) boat
    B) trade requiring skilled work
    C) skill in deceiving others: slyness

15. **do** *(15)*

    A) act: behave
    B) be satisfactory
    C) travel

C. instruct   teach

Words with similar meanings are called **synonyms**.

Directions: Column II gives the synonyms for the words in Column I. Choose and write the synonym for each word in Column I, using the words in Column II.

I	II
16. important	guiding
17. journey	vessel
18. pulling	major
19. steering	voyage
20. boat	helmsman
21. pilot	dawn
22. ruin	tugging
23. sunrise	destruction

D. re + call = recall = to call **back** or to call **again**

When the letters **re-** are added to the beginning of a word, they are called a **prefix**. The prefix **re-** often means "back" or "again". When you add a prefix, you make a new word. Sometimes **re** is not a prefix but is part of the word. **Red** is an example.

Directions: Each word below starts with the letters **re**. Only one word in each pair begins with the prefix **re-** meaning "back" or "again". Write that word.

24. reappear, reader	29. reed, refund
25. real, remake	30. regal, refill
26. reason, refresh	31. recount, reach
27. replace, reckon	32. reawaken, reign
28. rewrite, redwood	33. render, renew

Figure 6.1 contd

week and perhaps involving surveys on spending money or bed times.

The issue of grouping for learning is one which every school and class teacher must come to terms with. Age and/or ability are the most common criteria used. Age groupings would be either CHRONO-LOGICAL (i.e. complete classes of more or less the same age) or VERTICAL (i.e. children of varying ages within the same class). Ability groupings would be formed either by STREAMING (i.e. children of similar attainment in the same class) or by UNSTREAM-ING (i.e. mixed-ability classes, either by design or arrived at in a random manner) or, in a large school, by BANDING (i.e. a hierarchy of two or three bands, say A, B, C, with children of varying ability within each band. In theory, all Band A children would have an academic attainment higher than all Band B, and so on). In addition to these methods of grouping, there is also TEAM TEACHING, which may cut across any of the groupings just mentioned. In this instance, a team of two or more teachers is responsible for two or more classes.

Whatever the overall system of school grouping, each teacher needs to decide the most appropriate way in which to organise his children within the classroom. Sometimes the class will be taught as a unit, and this is appropriate where a body of information is to be conveyed or a process explained. Sometimes there will be individual or pair work. Often there will be group work, as in Peter's class at this moment. The advantages of such a group approach are clear. Facilities and materials, often in short supply, may be more economically used; the problems of classroom management may be eased; a measure of choice, either of content and/or sequence, may be permitted; social interaction can occur and a natural working relationship develop; the talents of a number of children may be enlisted and combined. It all depends on the task in hand. The ideal is to ring the changes on these different methods of grouping, choosing whatever is appropriate for whatever activity, so that children may experience the social, linguistic and academic demands and benefits of each.

Mr Barnes reminds his class of a check list of activities which he has written on the blackboard and which need to be covered by everyone at some time during the week. The time-tabling of the work is left to the children. This might be termed by some an example of the 'integrated' or 'undifferentiated day'.[1] Strictly speaking, it is neither. 'Flexible week' might be a better term, since the sequencing of the work is a matter for the children, provided that all tasks are completed by Friday.

These tasks include, as the blackboard indicates, SRA; mathematics; *Sound Sense* (i.e. a book of language exercises by A. E. Tansley); word games; handwriting; reading; Batik tie and dye; science; new books. The teacher has also provided a clip board with a list of names on it of boys and girls he wishes to hear read, either that day or the day after. When they have read to him they can cross their names off the

---

[1] In fact, it fits precisely into the second type of integrated day described by K. Rintoul and K. Thorne (*Open Plan Organisation in the Primary School*, London: Ward Lock Educational, 1975). They draw upon an article by P. E. Moran 'The integrated day' (in *Educational Research*, vol. 14, no. 1, 1971) and state that in this mode of organisation: 'Tasks, assignments or jobs are given to the children who are allowed to decide for themselves when, and in what order, they are tackled. The assignments may be given by work cards, or verbally, or listed on the blackboard. The time allowed for the completion of the assignment varies from one, two or three days, to a week or even a fortnight . . . Recording children's work, and maintaining a balance between the various areas of knowledge causes some concern – the system demands a teacher's organizational expertise.'

list. The tie and dye group needs to try again since the dye did not take too well previously. Equipment for the science experiments is in the practical work area.

Clearly, such a flexible mode of organisation requires considerable planning by the teacher before school starts. The structure may be unobtrusive but there is no doubt of its existence. Just such a point was made by Bennett (1976) in his research into the relationship between 'teaching styles and pupil progress'. His results indicated quite unequivocally that formal methods of teaching (which he carefully defined) were linked with a greater measure of progress in the basic skills (also defined). However, there was one case observed of a 'High Gain Informal Classroom' and, about this, he wrote as follows:

> The teacher was a woman in her middle thirties with ten years' teaching experience. The school was situated in a new town and the class, according to the teacher, comprised pupils with the full range of abilities . . . The curriculum emphasis was placed on the cognitive rather than the affective/aesthetic. Standards were set by the head . . . The teacher had her own system of records, mainly of attainment, including records of group and individual work, and also of social behaviour. She had also built up a large stock of teaching materials over the years. With reference to incentives, she stated that she was the main incentive . . . In the context of open-plan primary schools it has been said by practitioners and advisers alike that successful implementation requires good organisation and a clear structure. This would seem to be exemplified in this classroom. Although the classroom was evidently orientated towards informal practices, the content of the curriculum was clearly organised and well structured.

The same could be said of Mr Barnes's classroom and curriculum.

At 9.40 a.m. he calls for Group 1 which moves, as do the others, to action stations. Peter returns to the small library room and immediately settles down to his SRA work alongside six or seven other children, including five from his own class. He works steadily and thoroughly, occasionally speaking to his friend Kevin (for example, about sharpening his pencil) or listening to him (for example, about a query on his work card). In other words, comments related to the work in hand.

A social scientist in the making comes in to ask about pocket money. 'What pocket money do you have on school days?' she says. One of the boys claims to receive 50p a day, but this is hotly disputed by his friends (or creditors). Peter answers, 'Thirty-five. No. Forty-five', and the statistic is duly recorded for the graph which Veronica is producing. Do they really receive so much money?

The construction of graphs based on real, up-to-date information, has more than intrinsic interest. It gives children an opportunity to exercise certain social skills in the acquiring of information – i.e. they often work together, interviewing both friends and strangers. It gives them the opportunity first to record information in a relevant context and then to evaluate it – i.e. to develop powers of discrimination. It allows them to exercise mathematical and language skills – i.e. in the presentation of their findings. Above all, since a visual medium is often more accessible to more people, the graph is a modern means of conveying information and one which children will meet constantly in later life.

Kevin now checks his SRA answers and is loudly accused by Peter of copying them from the answer card. Claims and counter claims are heard. The two boys discuss their answers as another teacher comes in to work with one of her children. Such one-to-one correspondence is frequent in this semi-open-plan setting, with children engaged in a variety of tasks and having the freedom not only to choose the sequence of those tasks and, in many cases, the tasks themselves, but also their place of working. All the classroom doors along the corridor are open and one can hear the subdued sounds of talking, walking (i.e. some of the children are measuring the corridor), and moving of chairs. Boys and girls are constantly coming into the library for a variety of purposes; many to use the reference books; some to take off the hook a rubber with a large tab attached which proclaims: I AM AN ENGLISH RUBBER.

This tab performs the same function as those enormous plastic slabs attached to hotel keys; it makes them more difficult to lose or over-look. As such, it is a small reminder of the organisational skills needed in any classroom, but particularly one where children are encouraged to move around a good deal. Lorna Ridgway (1976) offers a useful list of 'aids to good housekeeping in the classroom'. Most of these nine points are observed by Mr Barnes and his colleagues.

1   A clear indication of the location of task-areas and their appropriate material.
2   Labels on the outside of boxes, packages and tins.
3   Notices on cupboards and shelves stating the contents.
4   Colour-coding on the backs of jigsaws and similar equipment.
5   Grading systems by colour or number indicating levels of difficulty in task-cards, text-books and apparatus.
6   Plenty of hooks within the children's reach for aprons, brushes and cloths, wall pockets and bags.
7   Printed statements of simple job-analysis (e.g. the best way to clean out the guinea-pig cage).
8   Indexing of books, at first in the book-corner by colour code or

other simple classification, then, in the main library by the selected school system.

9 Indexing of the resource centre.

It is now 10.02 a.m. and Peter is still working quietly and steadily. One minute later he goes in search of the SRA check card saying, 'Out the way!' to one of the nearby girls. Within context the command is less rude and less brusque than it might seem in print.

Peter has all but one of his thirty-two answers correct; Kevin has seven wrong. For a moment or so the two boys discuss who is the brainier as they compare their scores on the gold, purple and orange cards. The school itself appears neither to promote nor discourage academic competition and its neutral stance has the effect of focusing attention on the task. But, individually, children compare themselves with each other and, with such a highly structured hierarchical scheme as SRA, could scarcely avoid doing so.

Dearden (1976) does a great deal to clarify thinking on the old chestnut of competition versus co-operation, while acknowledging that such a polarisation of attitudes is misleading. Invariably, in classroom as in later life, elements of the two will be juxtaposed. What Dearden does, while retaining a philosopher's objectivity himself, is to state the morality argument in deeper terms than one normally encounters. This is what he says:

> There are strong moral objections concerned with the effects of competition on interpersonal relationships...Hobbes in the *Leviathan* placed its first amongst the three principal causes of quarrel among men. Competition, it will be said, excludes many opportunities for co-operation. It stifles sympathies and erodes the sense of fraternity with our fellows. Seeing them as rivals, we see the price of their success as being our own self-esteem, we are relieved by others' defeat, and even find ourselves glorying in others' failures. Emotions and attitudes towards others are engendered and released which are little, if at all, removed from malice, for others' loss may be our gain. And wanting to triumph over others can itself become functionally autonomous. In a predominantly competitive school regime, some must be unsuccessful and be consequently threatened by a general loss of self-esteem. To protect this, they will, if they do not despair, withdraw their concern from success in learning and locate it elsewhere.

This is what happened with Christopher in Chapter 4. Peter, however, is one of society's more successful participants.

When he has completed two more purple cards, he will move on to rose. He visits his classroom for a moment before returning to register his success on his record card. Meanwhile, Kevin reads aloud from his new card a passage entitled, *The Methodical Composer* (Gold 2, Lab. IIa), about a man's meticulous habits of eating daily fifty strands of spaghetti, each thirty centimetres in length. Peter chuckles at the story but then says, 'Can you read in your mind?' For a moment or so Kevin proves he can, but soon returns to his preference for reading aloud.

Peter now delves into the SRA box, as a secretary might into a filing cabinet. 'You're mad if you can't do orange', he says to the girl nearby and produces for himself a purple card (Purple 10, Lab. IIa) with a prose piece called, *Treasure Trove* by Bill Beatty. Unlike Kevin, who is still declaiming to anyone within hearing distance, he reads his card silently. Then, for a moment, a small group of children discuss the colour-coding system, showing every awareness of its subtlety and hierarchy, as children in a streamed school do of their classes, however cunningly devised the nomenclature. Their minimum ration per week is two cards, but they can do as many as they like. One glorious week Peter completed ten. When corrected by a friend for using the word 'sliva' for 'silver', he says, 'Yeah, that's my word for it'.

At 10.20 a.m. Mr Barnes enters with a cardboard box.

Mr B.: Peter, do you want biscuits?
Peter: No, thank you, sir.

It is a kind of preliminary before break time at 10.30 a.m. when most of the junior boys play football, most of the girls play ball games or wander around in pairs, arm in arm, and straying infants, untrained for such encounters, feel as if they are stumbling across a battle-ground.

As I write my notes in the classroom, two girls enter to practise their recorders and vehemently discuss which note is E and which G. I escape such controversy and elect to talk in the staffroom over coffee with a researcher from the National Foundation for Educational Research (NFER), who is monitoring teacher language and classroom control techniques, using chest microphones and his own observations to record the data. This reminds me that I have yet to hear any teacher utter any rebuke or to see any children criminally engaged. All of them, so far, appear to have been usefully and lawfully occupied.

After break the classroom fills up again and Peter and Kevin enter discussing their game of football, one side apparently having scored twenty-two goals. If only England were so adventurous!

Peter collects a sheet of paper from a tray in order to copy out the results of a science experiment he undertook the previous week. His final version, which is analysed in Sequel II at the end of this chapter, is shown in Figure 6.2. The word omitted from the penultimate line is 'room'.

my experiment

1. Air does weigh Something because me and Robert Cheadle did an experiment to see if air did weigh anything, and it did. We weighed an empty balloon, and an empty margarine carton on a balance beam until they were equal by putting plasticene on the empty balloon end. So when it was equal we blew the balloon up and tied the end up with string. And when we let it go the balloon was the heaviest so we put Sand in the margarine carton to balance the beam. So when they were even there was about one gramme of Sand in the margarine carton So the air in the balloon weighed about one gramme.

2. The air in an ordinary weighs about the Same as a bag of coal.

Figure 6.2

Various activities are going on around the room. Sixteen children are grouped around Mr Barnes, looking at a graph; two children in a corner are doing maths work; one girl is using washer discs as an aid in her maths corrections; two boys are working on a science experiment. From time to time children discuss their tasks with each other: 'What do we have to do?' ... 'How many have you got wrong?' ... 'Is this one easy or hard?' ... Learning is a participatory affair, a social, rather than a lonely, pursuit. 'Anyone can cheat at this', says one girl. 'I know', says another, 'but Sir said he'd trust us.'

Peter continues to write slowly and carefully. Two children near him are discussing Christmas presents. One is having an electric guitar and the other an organ. Peter tells them that his mum and dad would never be able to afford those as they had just bought a carpet. There is no sense of loss or envy in his voice; it is merely a statement of fact.

The copying exercise takes sixteen minutes in all and the completed sheet is put in a wire basket for the teacher's attention later. Such a system permits more flexibility than an exercise book, but each child collects together his best monthly piece of work in a cumulative folder which stays with him throughout his school career. He takes it with him when he moves on to secondary school.

Mr Barnes is now called out by a colleague experiencing tape-recorder problems. 'These interruptions', write Hilsum and Cane (1971) somewhat naively, 'sometimes short, sometimes long, sometimes stemming from inside the classroom, sometimes from outside – occur on most days, so that each teaching day contains an element of unpredictability.' That is, presumably, to discount any unpredictability inherent in teaching itself. However, the children continue to work in their teacher's absence. A moment later he is back to carry on with studying the graph.

Peter wanders about for a minute or so, contemplating his next task, almost like a managing director thinking about his next piece of dictation. 'How do you distinguish between daydreaming and feverish mental activity?' asks the *Times Educational Supplement* for 8 September 1978, commenting on the Schools Council Open Plan Schools inquiry. No doubt, it is often difficult to assess when time is being wasted or well spent. There is no problem on this occasion, however, such is Peter's air of involved, yet not intense, preoccupation. He watches the teacher for a moment and then is off to the library in search of his previous SRA card on the treasure trove. Perhaps such choice is an easy option for him.

He chuckles to himself as he rereads the card and appreciates a point in the story and before long has completed it. He is clearly able to work in a concentrated manner, whatever potential distraction is nearby. He takes the answer card but says to himself: 'I don't need it anyway. It's obvious what these are.' He marks his answers, scoring 8/10 and 32/33.

At 11.35 a.m. he returns the card to the box in the library and kneels on the floor colouring in his record sheet, reminiscent of a salesman marking up his successes, albeit on the floor. Again, he discusses the merits of different cards with one of the girls.

Peter: En I on silver twelve, Joanne?
Joanne: Yeah.
Jackie: Oh, bloody hell *(as she struggles with her card)*.

Then he chats with Tina who, he learns, does two or three cards per week and is on rose. If he can do five or six per week he will catch up with her. He questions Karen:

Peter: What's the most you've done in a week?
Karen: Three.

Another little statistic to tuck away.

Peter now picks out his third card of the day, the last of the purple SRA cards (Purple 3, Lab. IIa). This has a prose passage called, *Lawrence, Friend of the Arabs*, by R. J. Unstead, a very popular writer of history and religious education textbooks. Peter settles down to work on it.

Susan utters her thoughts out loud: 'How many threes in 121? Both flesh and spirit are weak. 'Oh, my God', she laments with the Psalmist, and inspiration comes through her mumbles. 'Oh, that's a good idea', she says to herself, and puts pencil to paper.

A handbell signals lunch time at twelve o'clock and no one stirs. Then, one by one, like actors at the end of a play, they pack away and go out to dine in family-type groups on faggots, peas and potatoes, plums and custard.

I chat with Peter for a while and he talks easily about his mum and dad, his brother aged 6 and sister 8, about football, cricket, quiz books and television. His Sunday schedule, with perhaps the 8.00 p.m. item omitted, would be many a schoolboy's dream. Here it is.

10.30 a.m.	Get up.
11.00	Breakfast.
11.15	Playing 'up the park'.
1.30 p.m.	Lunch.
2.00	Television (i.e. soccer; a film; cartoons; a detective series).
5.30	Out again for football.
7.00	Tea.
7.30	Television.
8.00	Bath.
8.30	Television.
9.30	Bed.

Peter's eyes positively shine when we discuss his SRA Reading Laboratory activities. These are quite normal, he tells me, for a Monday morning and if he gets the chance later in the week he will return to them.

R. M.: You seem to like the Reading Lab, Peter *(laughs)*.
Peter: Yeah, I do.
R. M.: You're doing as many cards as you can, are you?
Peter: Yeah.
R. M.: Why are you doing that?
Peter: I don't know. I just want to finish first and I like doing it anyway.
(He is a satisfied customer in other respects, too, as his comments on the school indicate.)

R. M.:	Now, Peter, tell me a bit about the school. What do you think of it?
Peter:	Very good.
R. M.:	Yes. Why do you think it's very good?
Peter:	We.., they take you for trips and everything. They don't lock the cameras away and they don't lock the tape recorders away. The televisions, they just keep them out for your use, like some of the schools they just lock them away.
R. M.:	Mmm. Have you had any experience of that in a school?
Peter:	Yeah. At me old school they just locked everything away. I didn't see the things. I hardly saw the things, but I knew we had some. But they just locked them away.
R. M.:	I see . . . Peter, tell me about your day at the old school. How was it different from this kind of day?
Peter:	Well, we used to sit in the rows every day and we used to sit in the same old desks. Er . . . we had stories all the time. Couldn't do the work we liked. Er . . . nothing else really. They didn't let you wander around either like you can do here. That's it really.
R. M.:	You think it's a good thing to be able to wander around?
Peter:	Yeah.
R. M.:	Why?
Peter:	Well, I dunno . . . it's wander . . . wander around and see what you want to do. At our old school you had to wait and see what you had to do.
R. M.:	Yes. You don't think that people waste time here?
Peter:	Oh, a couple of 'em do. But, more or less, most of 'em don't. They get on with their work.
R. M.:	Do you work harder here than you did at your old school?
Peter:	Yeah.
R. M.:	That's interesting, isn't it? You work harder even though you've got more freedom. Why is that then?
Peter:	Because I want to go to a good senior school and er . . . anyway I just like . . . it's better work here altogether. They had a sort of Reading Lab but that was absolutely easy. It wasn't as hard as this and I like hard work.
R. M.:	Yes. I got that impression of you working today. It's one of the things I've been interested in. You seem to be able settle down to your work and concentrate on it . . .
Peter:	Yeah.
R. M.:	Even though there are a lot of other people about, all talking about different things. That doesn't seem to worry you at all.
Peter:	No. Not really. I only leave that till play time.

Clearly, then, Peter is a serious-minded lad with an independent viewpoint, with some degree of self-analysis, and with strong motivation to succeed. At the same time, he is a balanced person, able to get on very well with his peers. He talks easily and with the confidence of someone who knows his own mind and is prepared to say what he thinks with firmness, but without arrogance. He is able to be objective about his own situation and to compare present with past experience. The school's credit points which he identifies would not all be every 10-year-old's choice: outside visits; accessibility of interesting equipment; choice of seating place and work; freedom to move about and act on your own initiative; use of a demanding reading laboratory.

Although it is lunch time now, a number of children are in the classroom, engaged in a variety of lawful pursuits. The margin between work time and play time, like the horizon on a hazy day, is not sharp. Two girls are playing the recorder; one calculating on an adding machine; a boy is smoothing a clay pot; three girls are doing maths; one girl is reading. Mr Barnes, too, has dispensed with his lunch break and is working in the classroom.

Then, at 1.30 p.m. scheduled schooling begins again. Peter enters and, after having regained his SRA card, as a miser might his money box, he spends ten minutes crouching in the corridor with Kevin measuring with a metre rod distances children jump from stationary positions. Peter manages to win a ½p bet during this activity. A little group gathers around participants as the results are plotted. Peter settles down to his work card, sitting this time in the corridor at a table near the jumpers. Occasionally, he gets up to inspect jumping results. Lorna, a tall girl of West Indian origin, makes a giant leap, much to the admiration of the onlookers and the gratification of the graph-makers.

One of the many interesting features about this class is how children occupy different seats throughout the day. They do not appear to be possessive over their territory (which provoked comment in Chapter 2) and I have yet to hear that evangelical call: 'Save us me seat!' Instead, they move to different places as the mood or activity takes them.

By 2.02 p.m. Peter has checked his card and achieved 9/10 on one part and 31/33 on another. Such marks might indicate that he is not being challenged, as I felt could be the case with 8-year-old Lucy. Alternatively, he could be consolidating his position and gaining in confidence thereby. Certainly, we know from his remarks just recorded, that he feels he is working hard, and he is not a boy who likes to free-wheel. He is proud of his achievements and makes them clear to Mr Barnes, who checks through the work, explaining, as he does so, a point about suffixes.

The notion that school pupils must *constantly* be pushed to their limits would, if relentlessly pursued in an unthinking manner, breed a nation of neurotics. The cause of excellence, to which we all subscribe by virtue of our profession, may be better served by variations in pace, which allow time for thinking and for renewal. 'We have got to make sure we are stretching all the children all the time', says the author of a *Times Educational Supplement* article of 11 October 1974, on mixed-ability grouping, as though children were permanent victims on the rack. But this is not how we work as adults. Our effort, like our heart-beat, changes according to circumstance, to meet different demands. The heart should not pound all the time, but be in such good condition that it can respond to any reasonable call made upon it.

Having conquered the purple cards, Peter moves on to rose and a short piece by the science fiction writer, Arthur C. Clarke, *In Search of a Killer* (Rose 9, Lab. IIa). However, he is diverted for a while and asked by one of his friends to participate in a science experiment. This involves being timed while running around the playground, with pre- and post-measurements of pulse rate. Four boys are working together on this project; Andrew has the stop watch. Peter duly performs on this now sunny but very cold day and is recorded as follows:

Pre-run pulse rate:	69
Post-run pulse rate:	79
Time taken for the run:	40 seconds

He is puffing heavily. Other children are recorded, including Lorna, who needs a re-run because the first measurement appeared to show a slower pulse rate *after* the run. They measure again. Peter races with her to begin with but, fifteen metres behind after sixty, retires from the unequal struggle. Lorna knocks three seconds off the record and registers a pulse rate of 98 (pre-run 87).

The boys discuss the results, continue with their measurements for a while, and then return upstairs to present their findings. Mr Barnes questions them:

Mr B.:   Did you use a stethoscope?
Pupil: No. Just by hand.
Mr B.:   What does it mean when your pulse rate increases?
          (Discussion follows.)
Pupil: I haven't got a pulse.

Mr Barnes shows the boys a stethoscope and explains how it works. They all discuss this and the significance of their pulse-rate findings.

This kind of approach to learning was indicated earlier in this chapter with the report of Peter's science experiment. Here it is seen at its most overt as 'learning by discovery'. At its best this is, paradoxically, a precise and disciplined activity. It has more in common with the thorough work of a detective, using reliable techniques to sift evidence and weigh information, rather than the haphazard and hopeful metal detector searching of a beach boy who dreams of finding buried treasure just below the surface. The stress is on the techniques of inquiry as much as their results; process as well as product.

The Plowden Report (1967) defines the concept and practice of discovery learning in clear terms:

> In a number of ways it resembles the best modern university practice. Initial curiosity, often stimulated by the environment the teacher provides, leads to questions and to a consideration of what questions it is sensible to ask and how to find the answers. This involves a great exercise of judgement on the part of the teacher . . . Essential elements are enquiry, exploration and first-hand experience . . . If, as children become older, they jump to generalisations too readily from the results of a single experiment, the teacher should see that they repeat their experiments. By this means children's understanding of precision, reliability and the nature of evidence can be increased. Some enquiries will certainly lead children to books, and information picked up from books or from television will also provide starting points for enquiry. But if primary school science is confined to knowledge taken from books, the whole purpose of the study of this area of the curriculum will be lost. (para. 669)

Clearly, Peter and his contemporaries are engaged in this kind of learning.[1]

Compare this approach with what David Ausubel (1969) calls, 'reception learning', where the material comes to the learner in final packaged form, often by exposition from the teacher. At the extremes, discovery and reception learning may be poles apart but, more often, they are each to be found at some stage along a continuum, so that at the middle point the term 'guided discovery' could be embraced by both sides. Ausubel himself refers to the 'unwarranted belief that reception learning is invariably by rote and that discovery learning is invariably meaningful'. He goes on: 'Actually, each distinction constitutes an entirely independent dimension of learning. Hence, both reception and discovery learning can each be rote or meaningful, depending on the conditions under which learning occurs.'

When 'rote learning' takes place, the new knowledge is not related to existing cognitive structure in a fundamental manner. In meaningful learning, the new knowledge arises logically and rationally from the old. If we take the analogy of a piece of furniture, we might say that rote learning is the equivalent of a veneer, grafted on to the finished article, meaningful learning is the grain within the natural wood.

---

[1] For suggestions as to how to develop children's interests in pulse and breathing rates, see *Ourselves*, Schools Council 'Science 5–13' Project (London: Macdonald Educational, 1973) Stages 1 and 2, pp. 50–1.

Perhaps, finally, a diagram may clinch the matter, and I find that by Rae and McPhillimy (1976) particularly helpful in explaining the relationship between the dimensions of learning just discussed. It is reproduced as Figure 6.3 with points A, B, C, D, representing the four extreme possibilities:

A   Rote reception learning.
B   Meaningful reception learning.
C   Rote discovery learning.
D   Meaningful discovery learning.

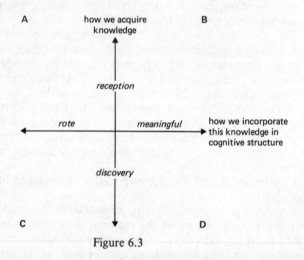

Figure 6.3

So much for the style of Peter's present learning. But he has been learning in other ways too. He has had experience so far today of working on his own; as one of a pair; as a member of a small group. He will shortly be a member of a class and, at the end of the afternoon, he will be in a competitive team structure during PE. In this way he is experiencing a variety of demands and learning how to conduct himself in a variety of contexts.

The class now prepares for the story, an activity which takes place daily, as a corporate involvement for all the children. The story is by Joan Aiken, *A Harp of Fishbones*. Having first asked the children what a harp is, what it looks like and how you play it, Mr Barnes goes on: 'You can have a very large harp, where you have to sit and you have to stand the harp on the floor. But some harps are small enough to hold in your hand and play in your hand. I think this story is about the sort of harp that you could hold in your hand.'

In fact, the story is of an orphan girl, Nerryn, who is often punished by her employers for day-dreaming. She lives near a forest and works primarily for an old man, a would-be drunkard if he could afford it, called Timorash. Gradually, she collects information from a strange old woman, Saroon, about her dead father who had once played a harp of gold but had never returned from the strange kingdom beyond the forest. Nerryn determines to follow in her father's steps and she constructs a harp from the bones of large carp which she catches bodily while she is swimming in the mill pond. She journeys through the forest, charming the dangerous vultures *en route* with her playing. On arrival in the strange kingdom she releases from thrall all the frost-bound statuesque inhabitants who had been cursed by the goddess for their inordinate love of gold. 'I shall not come among you again until I am summoned by notes from a harp that is not made of gold, nor of silver, nor any precious metal, a harp that has never touched the earth but came from deep water, a harp that no man has ever played.' Nerryn has fulfilled the requirements of this curse and made possible the return of the goddess. There is singing and dancing in the kingdom as the little girl is welcomed by her grandfather, none other than the king. She makes a brief visit to the village in triumph and humility before returning to the kingdom, realising that the old woman, Saroon, who had given her such useful advice and information, was, in reality, the incarnation of the spirit and music of the water.

Physically passive, but mentally active, Peter followed the narrative very carefully, smiling and laughing quietly at the parts he found amusing. There were two interruptions during the reading. One by the head-teacher, who had come to collect some materials and who apologised for his intrusion. One by a parent who had come to collect her child's reading book (in the 'Nippers' series).

Despite these two interruptions, which were both unobtrusive and quiet, by people sensitive to the situation, the children remained silent, held by the narrative and concentrating on it. Like the lovers of gold in the story, these children, too, were held in thrall. Of a rather less rigid variety, certainly, but, nevertheless, powerful.

Grouped informally, sitting on the floor around Mr Barnes's armchair, they followed the tale. One girl absent-mindedly plaited the hair of the girl in front of her; one boy handled a large fish jawbone. The fact that such an object was in the classroom at all is no coincidence. Like the stethoscope, it is here to relate to work in hand, to extend experience and make it more immediate, more vivid. It is further evidence, if that were needed, of Mr Barnes's planning, his imaginative awareness and professional involvement.

At 3.30 p.m. the story finished and the children were reluctantly released from the fantasy which had gripped them and returned to the real world. In this instance, the world of PE. Normally, these two activities of story and PE would be reversed in sequence but, on this occasion, the hall had been earlier occupied.

Six or seven boys and girls have forgotten their kit. Peter borrows a pair of blue shorts from Mr Barnes's cupboard and all go off to their cloakrooms to change.

Five minutes later the whole class has reassembled in the dining hall which doubles as a gym. It contains a piano, rostrum blocks, climbing frames, benches, buck, balls, hoops, a hot-air balloon (awaiting a good day for launching), an overhead projector, a record player, a needle-work exhibition. There is no need, however, to thread one's way through this equipment, since the hall is large and light and has ample space in the middle for movement.

The children run round clockwise, then anti-clockwise. They jump up high, then crawl low. They hop high, then, like hiccuping crabs, nearer the floor. They leap over high (imaginary) fences; they burrow through earthbound (imaginary) tunnels. They move; freeze; move again. All seem to enjoy the contrasts and variety of these preliminary warm-up exercises. Peter, certainly, is fully involved and reasonably co-ordinated.

Next comes team work. Four teams are self-chosen, very quickly indeed, and each stands in line preparing to pass a ball from front to back, alternately over heads and under legs. Peter is situated half-way back in his team of eight, enjoying the activity and relating well to the other team members. This game over, the balls are dispensed with and, beginning with the front member of each team, each boy or girl moves down the line, climbing over and under each alternate child. Confusion reigns. Teacher explains. Confusion again. Peter's team resorts to cheating, the last refuge of the bewildered.

Finally, four teams again, with footballs to be tossed by each facing team leader to each boy and girl in turn and rolled by them back under the tunnel of legs of those in front to the team leader. Each member of the team acts as leader at some point.

At 4.00 p.m. the bell sounds with the teams still busy. Six minutes later they finish and prepare to go home, a good time had by all. The lack of a clear demarcation line here at the end is curiously appropriate. There is no sense of occasion as school day ends and home life begins. The two worlds, in Peter's experience, have never been very far apart anyway.

Sequel I School Stock List

Every school has a certain amount of money to spend each year on equipment. This is called a 'capitation allowance' since it is based, per capita, on the number of pupils in the school. How that money is spent gives some insight into the educational philosophy being worked out.

Here is a stock list for Peter's school, kindly supplied by the headteacher. Such a list is outdated as soon as printed, for obvious reasons, but it will give some idea of the range of materials and aids available in one small junior and infant school. Titles of specific books in the library are not included.

Audio-Visual and Reprographic

Automatic projector
screen
daylight screen (for group work)
portable tape recorder
radio/tape recorder
stereo tape recorder
micro projector
overhead projector
3Ms stencil cutter
thermal copier

instamatic camera
polaroid camera
stand TV
portable TV
headphone set (7 piece)
stereo microscope
8 × 30 binoculars
record player
ink duplicator
spirit duplicator

Maths

Main scheme – 'Maths for Schools' by Harold Fletcher (Addison-Wesley)
All the usual measuring apparatus: weight, length, capacity, time, area and number, geometry, algebra, textbooks and work cards.

PE and Games

6 hockey sticks
2 sets wickets
10 skipping ropes
padder tennis net
4 netball posts
2 softball bats
1 bounce back

16 assorted bats
3 cricket bats
balls: 8 large, 6 medium, 2 rugby,
  6 aerflow, 20 rubber, 12 tennis
5-a-side posts
4 rounders posts
jumping stands
4 skittles
1 box shuttles

Gymnastics

2 large trestles   1 small trestle   1 curved and 1 straight ladder
1 agility mattress   3 mats   1-2 section box   3 padded benches
2 balance bars   1 bench   2 planks   (1 with detachable trestle)

Music

Hymn books, song books, percussion instruments (glockenspiel, xylophone, drums, tambourines, cymbals, triangles, wood blocks, etc.)

Main reading schemes
'Breakthrough to Literacy' (London: Longman), 'Ladybird' (London: Ladybird Books), 'Sparks' (London: Blackie), 'Nippers' (London: Macmillan Education), 'Racing to Read' (London: E. J. Arnold), 'Pirates' (London: E. J. Arnold), 'Language in Action' (London: Macmillan Education)
Reading games and pre-reading material of all sorts

Environmental studies
Magnifiers, collecting apparatus, nets, traps, containers, etc.
soil auger, geology hammer, weather station apparatus
aquaria, animal cages, greenhouse and equipment
maps of the area, photographs

Science
Batteries, bulbs, magnets, pulleys, lenses, butane heater and a variety of scrap materials useful for primary science, steam engine

Craft/Art
Paint, crayons, charcoal, chalk, fixative, drawing inks, printing ink, fabric inks, rollers, lino cutters, lino scraperboard, dyes, PVA adhesive, paste, clay, woodwork tools, soldering iron, electric kiln, glazes, fabric scraps, sewing machines, natural fleece, carders, spindles, spinning wheel.
A variety of source materials, natural and mechanical forms

Animals kept in school
Mice, rabbits, guinea pigs, hamsters, gerbils, tropical fish, aquaria, stick insects, terrapins, Xenopus

Cooking
Belling stove, aprons, utensils, scales, etc.

Library of reference books
Some slides and visual aids

Construction sets
Large plastic bricks, meccano, lego, sticklebricks

Play
Wendy House, water bath, sand tray, puppet theatre and glove and string puppets

Sequel II Children's Writing

Peter's account of the science experiment he did with Robert Cheedle is probably in direct line with traditional primary school writing about practical work and processes. There are no set headings, as there will be later in many a secondary school, such as: Experiment; Method; Apparatus; Description; Results: Conclusions. There is no elimination of the personal element by use of the passive voice, and no avoidance of first-person narrative. Instead, there is a clear, straightforward, detailed narrative account of what the boys actually did, with their conclusions arising from that experiment. Only the last sentence gives information which they have clearly derived from some other source and, if true, it is an interesting fact which neatly rounds off the piece.

During the last decade or so, much attention has been paid to why children write, who they write for, and the relationship between the language they use and the learning they achieve. Professor M. A. K. Halliday in 1969 ('Relevant models of language', *The State of Language*, Birmingham University *Educational Review*, vol. 22, no. 1) identified seven functions of language:

1 *Instrumental:*   to get things done.
2 *Regulatory:*   to get other people to do what one wants.
3 *Interactional:*   to maintain relationships between people.
4 *Personal:*   to express one's own feelings, beliefs, attitudes.
5 *Heuristic:*   to find things out.
6 *Imaginative:*   to pretend or fantasise.
7 *Representational:* to impart information.

A teacher who wished to make practical use of such categories would be able to monitor deficiencies in his pupils in a particular area and also would be able to decide whether his own assignments allowed children to operate across the full range of these categories. It would also inevitably make the teacher more sensitive to language in use. Peter's piece would fall clearly into category 7, although there are elements, too, of category 4.

Another system of language categorisation, this time of spoken language in young children, is that devised by Joan Tough, referred to elsewhere in this book. Further detals may be found in *Listening to Children Talking* (London: Ward Lock Educational, 1976) but some immediate overlap with Halliday will be evident from the category headings of:

1 Self-maintaining.
2 Directing.
3 Reporting.
4 Towards logical reasoning.
5 Predicting.
6 Projecting.
7 Imagining.

Perhaps the most appropriate language categorisation for present purposes is that by James Britton (1970, 1971). He identifies three main strands in children's written work as:

(1) *Transactional:* i.e. the language of information receiving and conveying, and for negotiating the many *transactions* of daily life such as writing for a ticket, booking a holiday, requesting factual detail. This is clearly akin to Halliday's category 7.

(2) *Expressive:* i.e. the language of hopes, thoughts, feelings; of personal expression, revealing oneself as an individual. Halliday's category 4 comes to mind.

(3) *Poetic:* i.e. language which is shaped and designed so that the form may itself carry something of the meaning (such as in a poem, a well-constructed narrative, joke or anecdote).

Britton makes the point that none of these modes is superior to the others; they each have their value and children should be helped to operate in all three, with much practice in the expressive mode forming the foundation for the transactional and poetic. The reason for this is that the expressive mode tells us most about the writer himself; it touches him most closely. He is encouraged to draw upon his own real direct experience and to record what he sees and feels as accurately, as honestly, and as unpretentiously as he can. With such a grounding in genuine observation, he will be in a strong position to operate then in any mode.

Britton's theory is clearly reflected in the Bullock Report, especially in the notion of 'Language Across the Curriculum', which seeks to identify a single unifying force in education around which all teachers may unite. That force is language, understood not as the medium in which learning is ultimately expressed in written or spoken form, but the means *through* which that learning occurs. In other words, language is an integral part of the process of learning, as well as the expression of the final product of that learning. It is not merely the destination, but the journey as well. When we try to grapple with the inchoate thoughts darting around inside our heads, like so many sparks shooting off into nothingness, we endeavour to turn those thoughts into words and thus encapsulate the experience. We get a better grip on our world by employing language in the process, and, thus, language and learning itself are inextricably linked. As the Russian poet Osip Mandelstam puts it (and this is quoted in Bullock): 'I have forgotten the words I intended to say, and my thoughts, unembodied, return to the realm of the shadows.'

To put this a different way, and to quote from a second publication which bears Lord Bullock's name (i.e. *Hitler* Harmondsworth: Penguin, 1952): 'Words build bridges into unexplored regions.' That was said by the dictator himself, who spent much of his time exploring other country's regions.

So the message for every teacher of every age range and subject is clear. Let the children explore their world through their own language, spoken and written, in an active and involved manner, rather than as passive recipients. This is not a recipe for chaos in the basic skills. Constraints there must be at some stage – of spelling, punctuation, technical terms, form, and so on. Good writing is a matter of considerable discipline; wild gibberish has little to recommend it. But the disciplining should be subtly done, by sensitive teachers aware of the effects of their checks and balances, and it should not be done too rigorously, too early.

Every teacher is a teacher *in* and *of* language, and this was a key idea behind the Schools Council Project, *Writing across the Curriculum* (1976) which, like the Bullock Report, drew on Britton's categories for its theoretical base. Details of publications from this project are given at the end of this sequel in the further reading section.

It should be observed that any theory should be under sceptical but respectful scrutiny from students, teachers and researchers alike. Gordon Wells, for example, has recently provided a critique of Tough's categorisation (See 'Language use and educational success: an empirical response to Joan Tough's "The Development of Meaning",' *Research in Education*, no. 18, November 1977.) The first shot, too, has recently been fired across Britton's bows, and this could mark the beginning of a period during which his threefold categorisation comes increasingly under critical analysis.

The critique is by Jeanette Williams in *Learning to Write, or Writing to Learn?* (Windsor: NFER, 1977). In this small book some eleven criticisms are made of the project and its theoretical basis, and include condemnation of its methodology and statistical evidence; of its lack of objectivity and rigour according to linguistic criteria; of its epistemological standpoint; of its lack of practical applicability. Fire enough shots and some of them may remain embedded, never to be dug out later.[1] One feels that Britton's theory cannot be quite the same again but, for the moment, it remains as one of the few categorisations of language which teachers may use by which to become more sensitive to what is being said and what is being written. We should all, in Halliday's phrase, 'learn to listen to language'.

BOOKS FOR FURTHER REFERENCE

Adams, A. and Pearce, J. (1974). *Every English Teacher* (Oxford: OUP), ch. 6.

Barnes, D. *et al.* (1969). *Language, the Learner and the School* (Harmondsworth: Penguin).

Burgess, C. *et al.* (1973). *Understanding Children Writing* (Harmondsworth: Penguin).

Clegg A. B. (1965). *The Excitement of Writing* (London: Chatto & Windus).

Daily Mirror (annual). *Children's Literary Competition*, an annual anthology, now published by Heinemann under the title *Children as Writers*.

Jones, A. and Mulford, J. (1971). *Children Using Language* (Oxford: OUP).

Martin, N. *et al.* (1976). *Writing and Learning across the Curriculum* (London: Ward Lock Educational).

Rosen, C. and H. (1973). *The Language of Primary School Children* (Harmondsworth: Penguin).

[1] See Britton's reply, however, in Andrew Wilkinson and Graham Hammond, (eds), *Language for Learning*, Exeter University, vol. 1, no. 1 (1979).

Chapter 7

Teacher Training: Pre-service and In-service discussion Points and Tasks

Each of the foregoing chapters lends itself to discussion by students in teacher training and practising teachers. In each case, four key questions spring to mind:

(1) What sort of day did the main figure have?
(2) What different experiences did he/she undergo?
(3) What and how did he or she appear to learn?
(4) How would one describe the relationship between children and teachers?

Apart from these obvious matters of interest, there are more individual issues which affect the boys and girls and I should like to indicate some of these for each of the six chapters.

CHAPTER 1. MIKE

(1) As a lively and interesting extrovert, Mike is potentially disruptive. How does Mrs Hilton contain and harness his energies? Are her methods, your methods?
(2) At one point in the morning, the children in Mike's group who have plastic objects for maths work use them in a game of Cowboys and Indians. Would you allow this in your class? Why or why not?
(3) What opportunities do the children in the class have to talk about their own experience? How can such opportunities be valuable to them?
(4) There are well over a hundred professional systems of interaction analysis and language categorisation, and a useful commentary on some of them is to be found in the Open University 1976 unit, Block 11, entitled *Classroom Interaction*, part of course E 201. Interested readers are referred to the following books as being the most helpful for present purposes:

Flanders, N. A., *Analysing Teaching Behaviour* (Reading, Mass.: Addison-Wesley, 1970).

Sinclair, J. McH. and Coulthard, R. M., *Towards an Analysis of Discourse* (Oxford: OUP 1975).

Tough, J., *Listening to Children Talking* (London: Ward Lock Educational, 1976).

Tough, J., *Focus on Meaning* (London: Allen & Unwin, 1973).

The exchanges between Mrs Hilton and her class, recorded in this chapter, could be subjected to analysis of the kind suggested by the writers just mentioned. Equally, they lend themselves to searching, but less systematic, scrutiny by small groups of students in training or experienced teachers. If you are so involved, look particularly at:

(a)   The approximate proportions of teacher/pupil talk.
(b)   The specific language style (i.e. idiolect) of Mrs Hilton, in so far as this can be determined from a transcript.
(c)   The kinds of question asked and the ways in which they are asked.
(d)   The variety of purposes for which language is used.
(e)   The roles of teacher and pupils involved.

(5)   How much religious and moral influence does there appear to be during this day?
How much social class influence, and of what kind is it?

(6)   One can group the main elements of moral education into six categories (according to J. Wilson *et al.*, *Introduction to Moral Education*, Harmondsworth: Penguin, 1967), namely, the ability to:

(a)   Treat others with consideration.
(b)   Understand and identify with the feelings of others.
(c)   Master the facts relevant to the making of moral decisions.
(d)   Formulate social rules in relation to society.
(e)   Make rules for one's personal conduct,
                              and
(f)   the skill to put these into practice.

Clearly, these will be achieved, if at all, at different stages and ages. In what practical ways could each of them be appreciated by infants, and by juniors?

How may the infant, and junior, school, by organisation and network of relationships, contribute to this moral development of the individual? (Some ideas are suggested in the NFER booklet in which the foregoing six points are recorded: H. Blackham (ed.) (Windsor: NFER 1976), *Moral and Religious Education in County Primary Schools*.

(7) The children hear, or sing, a number of rhymes and songs throughout the day. What is the value of this? Which rhymes and songs are popular with children you have encountered? Why do you think these are particularly popular?

(8) If you were Mike's teacher, what areas of work would you feel you needed to concentrate on with him?

(9) In writing of the cultural ingredients in the educational process, Bernstein draws a distinction between the 'instrumental' and the 'expressive'. Instrumental refers to the acquisition of specific skills and expressive relates to the transmission of models of 'conduct, character and manner' (Bernstein, B. B. *et al.*, 'Ritual in Education', in Cosin, B. R. *et al.* (eds), *School and Society*, London: Routledge & Kegan Paul, 1971).

Try to distinguish between these two elements of cultural transmission in the description of Mike's day (or of any of the other 'days' in the book). At what points, if any, do they appear to overlap?

(10) According to Ronald King (2nd edn, 1978), 'It is possible to distinguish a number of important elements that comprise the infant teacher's child-centred ideology. These are: developmentalism, individualism, play as learning, and childhood innocence.'

What evidence for the existence of these four elements do you find in Chapter 1?

CHAPTER 2. RASHDA

(1) Do you share my views on the possible values of Rashda's school assembly? How might the 'hidden curriculum' be operating in the second hymn? Have you any reservations about assemblies in this kind of context? (See Chapter 5, Sequel I.)

(2) What strategies are used throughout the day for getting the children's attention?

What methods do you use?

In what circumstances is it very difficult to be successful, no matter what your methods are?

(3) Does the classroom environment and equipment appear to you to be adequate? What do you consider an ideal classroom environment? Why?

(4) Discuss and/or produce materials and ideas for any of the following, and stimuli for encouraging and developing spoken language with young children.

(a) Various displays: objects worthy of close examination; objects differing in colour, texture, smell, sound; natural phenomena (portable); objects related to a particular theme, such as Earth, Air, Fire, Water.

(b) Children's own collections: match-boxes; stamps; autographs; pop-star pictures; fashion photos; football programmes; coins; precious objects; soldiers; dinky toys; models.

(c) Dolls and puppets.

(d) Hobbies and sports.

(e) Telephone.

(f) Clothes box.

(g) Shops and shopping.

(h) Sounds effects.

(i) Photographs, pictures, posters, drawings, cartoon strips.

(j) Pets.

(k) Wendy houses.

(l) Cooking.

(m) Objects from home which have a story.

(n) Books.

(o) Television, radio, films, tape recorder.

(p) Visitors into school.

(q) Outside visits.

(r) Local people in the community and members of the family.

(5) Discuss the lesson of English as a second language (E_2L). Is this the kind of provision you would make for your pupils who have such needs?

(6) Map out a lesson plan for Rashda's next E_2L session, making use of Sequel I at the end of Chapter 2.

(7) What do you feel about the 'magic carpet' ritual?
Describe other rituals you have encountered.

(8) Discuss the apparent strengths and weaknesses of the remedial reading lesson.
(Information about reading materials may be obtained from the Centre for the Teaching of Reading, University of Reading School of Education, 29 Eastern Avenue, Reading RG1 5RU, Berkshire. Tel.: Reading 62662.)

(9) Devise an adequate record card by which to monitor Rashda's progress in reading.
What other kinds of record are valuable, and why?
Refer to the Schools Council Project, *Record Keeping in Primary Schools* (London: 1979) and consider the development of a pupil's reading profile, possibly based on information in the section, 'The assessment of reading' in *Language Performance*

(Assessment of Performance Unit, 1978) available from DES, Room 1/27, Elizabeth House, York Road, London SE1 7PH.

(10) Look at the document which now follows, entitled, 'Hearing Children Read'. It is intended for use with students in teacher training.

Which parts, if any, do you disagree with?

In what ways does it match the various reading activities of Rashda's day?

Hearing Children Read

Suggested technique (to be varied as appropriate for the age range and occasion and as is consistent with time).

(1) With infants, let us assume regular and thorough reading practice. With juniors and secondary school pupils, regular and thorough practice still, but perhaps more selective, according to need.

(2) Teacher moves round the class from individual to individual, hearing each one read aloud (but quietly) and/or questioning him on what he has just read silently (i.e. in order to check comprehension).

(3) Teacher might ask pupil to recap on what he has read and/or to speculate on what might happen next, and to give reasons for such speculation.

(4) Teacher might ask pupil about characters, plot, incidents, illustrations.

(5) Teacher might ask about the meaning of individual words, phrases; give explanations; try to develop language and ideas.

(6) Teacher might occasionally read aloud (but quietly) a sentence or paragraph, in order to indicate normal speech rhythms.

(7) Teacher keeps mental and written record of diagnosis of strengths and weaknesses of each pupil, and of material being read.

Remember that you can learn more from an error than from a correct response.

When you hear weak or beginner readers, do they appear to:

(1) Just guess the word without looking for clues?

(2) Look at the illustration, if there is one, then guess?

(3) Make use of the sound of the initial symbol, either spontaneously, or if given by you?

(4) Sound out the symbols and attempt to blend them into a word?
   – e.g. $j - a - m$ jam.

(5) Sound out letters which should be silent?

(6) Get help in recall from being directed to patterns in symbols? — e.g. *oo* as in 'look' or *tt* as in 'little'.
(7) Use capital letters as a clue?
(8) Go back to the beginning of a phrase and reread?
(9) Read on, past the unknown word, to get the meaning?
(10) Look at you and just wait to be told the word?

Whatever the approach of the weak or beginner reader, you will be able to plan your course of action, based on picking up clues from this kind of assessment.

NB: Remember that the whole reading activity should be a pleasurable one for the children and for you, with the stress on enjoyment rather than inadequacy and failure.

Note
Chapter 3 of Gloyn and Frobisher (1975) deals in a most practical way with the teaching of reading to infants and is strongly recommended. This chapter, along with the Schools Council *Breakthrough to Literacy* manual by D. Mackay, B. Thompson and P. Schaub (London: Longman, 1970) should give any student confidence to tackle the crucial job of teaching young children to read.

There is, too, a very helpful booklet, which is regularly revised, called *Hearing Children Read*. This is by Dr E. J. Goodacre and available from the Centre for the Teaching of Reading, University of Reading School of Education.

CHAPTER 3. DAVID

(1) Notice the assembly ritual for the 'birthday boy'.
Describe other birthday ceremonies you have encountered in school. What are the uses and dangers of such rituals?
(2) Is the classroom lay-out as you would want it?
In what ways can lay-out affect learning experiences?
(3) What kinds of teaching style does David meet in his day?
What do you regard as an ideal style, and why?
(4) What, in your view, is David's most urgent need?
How would you propose to try to satisfy it?
(5) Is he slow or lazy?
How do you distinguish between these characteristics in children you teach or have taught?
What different kinds of provision do you make for those thought to be slow, and those described as lazy?
(6) After scrutiny of the stock list in Chapter 6, Sequel I, decide what should be bought with the next available £50 capitation allowance, assuming supplies of basic materials are adequate.

(7)   Write an alternative sequel to this chapter, based on some learn-ing theory other than Gagné's, and relating it, where you can, to David's experience.

(8)   Look at the document which now follows, entitled 'Remedial Work (particularly in reading)'. It is a fairly general statement of some Dos and Don'ts for students in training.
In what ways do David's teachers appear to conform to the docu-ment's recommendations?
In what way do they appear to take a different line?

Remedial Work (particularly in reading)

(1)   Remedial help is required at all ages and stages. Each of us is defi-cient in some skill area. It may not be reading, but what of swimming, pottery, drama? In other words, we need to develop a wide and all-embracing concept of what the work is all about. All teachers are remedial teachers, but the term 'remedial' is a dangerous, if convenient, label.

(2)   With regard to the organisation for remedial work, there are basically two methods. One is to stream according to ability, and thus group most of your remedial children in the bottom class. The other method, which is more common in junior schools, is to operate in mixed-ability classes, with withdrawal groups for those children who need special help. At present, we generally withdraw children only for special help in maths and English (i.e. reading; writing; speech). In an ideal world, we might withdraw children from across the ability range for extra tuition in all kinds of activities.

(3)   In order to know the specific attainment of individual pupils, and precisely *where* each pupil is failing, you must devise means of being able to check *individually* on the *process* of working, for example calculating a sum; reading a sentence; working out a problem. The actual answers to the problem may be relatively unimportant; the process by which they were arrived at is highly significant. One method for the teacher is to operate in such a way that, when the whole class is occupied in some activity, you can go round and work with individuals on a one-to-one basis. Remember that you are not so much teaching a class as thirty-five or so individual children, each with differing backgrounds and experiences; with different motivation and interests; with differ-ent speeds of working and different levels of attainment.

(4)   When you first encounter a so-called 'remedial child', try to discover his present state of health, his medical history and the family medical history. (I am stating the ideal.) Where there is doubt, the child should have a full medical examination, which would involve audiometric, opthalmic, neurological tests. Many

errors in reading and writing are caused by a child's poor pronunciation, or by positive speech defects. Remember, too, that the child may be emotionally disturbed; may come from a broken home; may have been to seven schools; may be a member of a family of ten children. This knowledge may not help you to solve his problems, but it could help you to understand them. More often than not, there will be about four or five possible causes of any trouble.

(5) Think, too, of personality and temperamental factors. If a child cannot answer a question which you ask him, it may be because he is shy or embarrassed; or dislikes you; or is having an off day; or did not hear what you said; or did not understand it; or was shouted at the last time he ventured to answer a question. It may also be because he does not know the answer! Your own speech should, of course, be clear, including those at the back and those in sunlight.

(6) Try constantly to monitor in your head the language you are using with the children. Tape record yourself occasionally, so that, later in the evening, you may hear again those honeyed words of wisdom which your children were privileged to hear, such as 'Presumably, one tends to feel on certain occasions that ...blah...blah...blah...' (Learn to avoid the tone of this sixth point, and remember that sarcasm can be a terrible weapon.) Do not do too much talking; children are not necessarily learning anything merely because you are talking to them. Do not waste time talking to the whole class when only a small group of children needs the particular help you are trying to give them.

(7) Bear in mind the content of your lesson or of the activity the class is engaged in. Is it sensible? Is it worth doing? Does it relate to the children's own lives? Can they understand what you are on about? What are you trying to achieve?

(8) Make use, where you can, of diagnostic tests and of any information you may have from the educational psychologist. Treat such 'evidence' respectfully, but also sceptically, keeping an open mind. Maintaining individual records is most valuable, providing they are informative and diagnostic. See Donald Moyle's book, *The Teaching of Reading* (London: Ward Lock Educational, 1968) for examples of records which give specific information about the reading work a child is doing; where he appears to be failing; the course of remedial action proposed.

(9) Before systematic phonic work is possible, certain abilities appear to be necessary. A. E. Tansley and R. Gulliford (*The Education of Slow-Learning Children*, London: Routledge & Kegan Paul, 1960) state these as:

(a) To be able to give the more usual sounds for the common letters.

(b) To discriminate between letter sounds, for example in such exercises as:

   (i)   Which of these words is out of place? – *man, mill, met, cap*?

   (ii) Which of these words is out of place? – *cat, hat, foot, fire*?

   (iii) Listen to these words – *baby, boat, boy, box.* Which of these do they start with? – *c, p, b, t*?

   (iv) Tell me a word which begins with *t, d, c* ?

(c) To detect rhymes, for example to select the non-rhyming word in a set of rhyming words, or to give a word, either spontaneously or from a given choice of words, which rhymes with another word or group of words.

(d) To blend sounds, i.e. letters, phonograms, syllables.

For some possible exercises on which structured remedial programmes could be based, see A. E. Tansley, *Reading and Remedial Reading* (London: Routledge & Kegan Paul, 1967).

(10) In reading, concentrate on words the child gets wrong. Look for common patterns emerging (for example particular phonic sounds he cannot manage; first letters he does not recognise). Combine 'Phonic' and 'Look and Say' approaches to reading. Drill weaknesses, but do it sensitively. Give success; be patient; structure the learning in simple stages; offer variety; do not humiliate; make the learning experience pleasant. Above all, be convinced that you and the child are going to SUCCEED. TEACHER ATTITUDE IS CRUCIAL.

CHAPTER 4.   LUCY

(1) Discuss the ways in which Lucy's school assembly is different, having first read Chapter 5, Sequel I.

(2) What evidence is there that Lucy is intelligent?
How do you distinguish between intelligence and conformity to teacher's demands?

(3) The need to provide stimulating work for the more able child was particularly highlighted in the HMI Survey, *Primary Education in England* (HMSO, 1978).
Is Lucy intellectually challenged during the day, or merely going through the motions, or perhaps consolidating her knowledge?

(4) How do you account for the atmosphere in her class?
What are its chief characteristics?
What kind of atmosphere do you try to promote in your class?

(5) What do you understand by the term 'basic skills'?
To what extent is it a helpful and a misleading concept?

(6) What are the traditional and more modern aspects of Lucy's day? Does she seem to spend proportionately the same amount of time during the day on each activity and in each grouping as junior school pupils are reckoned to spend? (i.e. by Michael Bassey, *Nine Hundred Primary School Teachers*, Windsor, NFER, 1978). Bassey gives the breakdown for a 27½ hour week (Table 7.1):

Activity			*Grouping*	
Maths	5		Classwork	9
Language	7		Groupwork in one subject	6
Thematic Studies	4	22	Group work in more than one subject	4
Art and Craft	2		Self-organised individual work on assignments	3
Music	1			
PE	3			
Assembly	2			
Administration	1			
Play time	2½			
Total:	27½ hours per week.			

Table 7.1

(7) How do you cope with the Lucys and Christophers together in *your* class?

(8) Drawing on your own experience of stories which have been well received by children, add half a dozen titles to the list of suggested fiction in the sequel to this chapter.

(9) A Schools Council Research Project set out to determine what teachers felt their most important aims to be. The results, as recorded in *The Aims of Primary Education: A Study of Teachers' Opinions* by Pat Ashton *et al.* (London: Macmillan, 1975) were as follows:

(a) Children should be happy, cheerful and well balanced.
(b) They should enjoy school work and find satisfaction in their achievements.
(c) Individuals should be encouraged to develop in their own ways.
(d) Moral values should be taught as a basis of behaviour.

   (e)   Children should be taught to respect property.
   (f)   They should be taught courtesy and good manners.
   (g)   They should be taught to read fluently and accurately.
   (h)   They should read appropriate material with understanding.

Commenting upon these aims, Dearden (1976) writes: 'No reference to maths, science, the arts, P.E., or languages in the eight most important aims. With the exception of reading and moral education, there is a total concentration on attitudes, to the exclusion of content.'

How do these aims seem to match the experiences recorded in Lucy's day, or in any of the other days in this book?

Explain, with your reasons, how you would rank these eight aims.

What do you feel about Dearden's comment?

CHAPTER 5. LORRAINE

(1)   Describe the last school assembly you witnessed or organised. Into which of the categories in Sequel I of this chapter would it fit?

(2)   What appear to be the characteristics of the atmosphere in Lorraine's class?

(3)   How do you distinguish between social chat in class and discussion about work? At what point does the former become worrying?

Refer to Chapter 6, Sequel II, and then consider the place of social conversation in theories of language development.

(4)   What signs of confusion and ignorance does Lorraine show during her day?

How would you, with a class of thirty, attempt to monitor such confusion with each of your pupils?

(5)   How do Lorraine's apparent needs differ from Manjit's?

In what ways would you try to meet both sets of needs?

(6)   What are the advantages and disadvantages of such regular activities as 'Eight a Day?'

Measure your views against those of Mrs Ridgway in Sequel II.

(7)   Part of Lorraine's day is occupied in topic work based on her school environment. Such an approach, with a variety of work based around one central topic, is popular in junior schools and many helpful books have been written about it, including:

Haggitt, T., *Working with Language* (Oxford: Blackwell, 1967).

Kent, G., *Projects in the Primary School* (London: Batsford, 1968).

Lane, S. M. and Kemp, M., *An Approach to Topic Work in the Primary School* (London: Blackie, 1973).

Lynskey, A., *Children and Themes* (Oxford: OUP, 1974).

Moon, C. and Raban, B., *Penguins in Schools: A Guide for Teachers* (Harmondsworth: Penguin, 1975).

Pluckrose, H., *Creative Themes* (London: Evans, 1969).

Rance, P., *Teaching by Topics* (London: Ward Lock Educational, 1973).

Students in teacher training might care to work in small groups and select a theme or topic which they believe to be appropriate for a specified age range (mixed-ability class), preparing a collection of suitable prose extracts, short stories, poetry, drama possibilities, library research tasks, pictures, objects, cassette tape, etc., with assignments of all kinds. The main objective would be to produce a box of stimulus material on the chosen topic.

Some students may be in a position to try out such material on teaching practice.

(8)   In the course of a working week, a teacher does many jobs other than teach. The NFER survey, referred to in Chapter 5, of 129 teachers in 66 different schools, provides the following breakdown, which I quote with their kind permission.

	The grouping of teacher activities		*The teacher's day*
I. TEACHING	A	Lesson instruction	e.g. instructing class, group or individual in lesson topic.
	B	Lesson preparation, etc.	e.g. marking; planning, professional reading.
	C	Teaching but detail not recorded	e.g. education visit.
II. ORGANIZATION	A	Organizing in classroom or school	e.g. allocating pupils to assignments; arranging distribution of equipment.
	B	Staff consultation	e.g. talking to head/ colleagues/advisers about professional matters.
III. CONTROL AND SUPERVISION	A	Discipline	e.g. reprimanding pupils.
	B	Supervision	e.g. escorting pupils along corridors; playground patrol; dinner supervision.
IV. CLERICAL/ MECHANICAL TASKS			e.g. clearing up spilt milk; marking registers; duplicating maps; collecting monies.

The grouping of teacher activities		*The teacher's day*
	A Individual pupil	e.g. joking with pupils; speaking to pupil about personal matter; talking to parent; dealing with unwell pupil.
V. PASTORAL	B Special occasions	e.g. concert, sports afternoon, school jumble sale.
	C Extra-curricular activity	e.g. football club, chess club.
	A Personal	e.g. chatting with colleagues about personal matters.
VI. PRIVATE	B Moving/waiting alone	e.g. walking along corridor, with no pupils present; waiting in classroom for pupils to arrive.
	C. Professional work not connected with school job	e.g. at lunch-time, marking books of evening class students.
VII. UNRECORDED		e.g. observer could not see/hear teacher.

The effect of such categorisation is to undermine the stereotype of the teacher as classroom practitioner only. Particularly when it is known that, according to this research, 42 per cent of the junior school (i.e. 7 to 11 years) teacher's day is spent away from the classroom. Hilsum and Cane observe:

> This ought to encourage those who study the teacher's operational role to direct their thinking beyond the classroom, to see the teacher as a member of a school staff, and to bear in mind that his classroom activities (and the learning situations provided for pupils) may be significantly influenced by his non-classroom teaching work.

What practical implications do you believe such information as this should have upon teacher training?
How can students become aware of their prospective responsibilities in this wider context, or is it merely something that will just happen as time goes by?

(9) Suppose Lucy (Chapter 4) and Lorraine (Chapter 5) swopped schools. On the basis of the evidence presented here, how might the differing atmospheres and curriculum styles affect each of them?

CHAPTER 6. PETER

(1) Discuss Peter's classroom environment and its potential.
Refer to Sequel I at the end of Chapter 6 and identify any items you do not understand. Do any items surprise you?
What important aids, if any, are missing?

(2) In what ways do teacher–pupil relationships in Peter's class appear to differ from those discussed elsewhere?

(3) Is Peter intellectually stretched during the day, or free-wheeling?

(4) What are the advantages and disadvantages in the children being able to choose their own sequence and place of work, as well as some of their tasks?

(5) How far would you agree with my comments on SRA work cards (both in this chapter and Chapter 4)?

(6) Look in detail at the questions on the SRA cards featured in this chapter and Chapter 4, and list the skills which those questions seem designed to test.

(7) Judging by the story, *A Harp of Fishbones*, what do you believe can be the value of fantasy for such children as Peter?

(8) Having read Sequel II to Chapter 6, select three pieces of writing by children in one of your recent lessons and identify their expressive, transactional and poetic parts.

(9) Let us suppose that the following Documents A and B were composed by two different schools in response to the same premises, based on notions of 'Language Across the Curriculum'. Read through them carefully and, in small groups, decide to what extent you agree with each of the points made.

Language Across the Curriculum: Discussion Document A

Starting Points

(1) Language and learning are inextricably linked; language competence and satisfactory attainment in all school subjects go hand-in-hand.

(2) All children need to develop adequate literacy (i.e. reading and writing) and oracy (i.e. listening, thinking, speaking) skills.

(3) All teachers have responsibility for such development.

School Procedures

Speaking

(1) Children should not talk in the corridors or in assembly, either before it starts or after it has finished.

(2) Staff should be addressed as 'Sir' or 'Madam'. Girls should be addressed by their Christian names and boys by their surnames.

(3) The teacher's language serves as a model for the pupil. Therefore, there should be no slang; no hesitation; no 'you knows'; no broad accents.
(4) Pupils gain in confidence by participating in set debates and by giving prepared two-minute lecturettes to the class.
(5) Learning a poem for speaking aloud is a good elocution exercise.
(6) Whenever a pupil speaks incorrectly, his attention should be drawn to the fact.

Reading
(1) Pupils should be tested on diagnostic and attainment tests at the beginning and end of each academic year.
(2) All should follow the set reading scheme and the class reader.
(3) Reading aloud from each subject textbook should be encouraged.
(4) Each pupil should keep a full reading record and write a brief summary of each book he has read.
(5) Each pupil should be encouraged to join the local public library and also to persuade his parents to take a good newspaper regularly.

Writing
(1) Handwriting practice should take place each week.
(2) There should be weekly spelling tests in English and other subjects, with words either drawn from work done during the week, or arranged in phonic groups. Each spelling error in any subject course work should be written out correctly three times.
(3) Only material with no technical errors should be displayed on the wall.
(4) SRA or other work card comprehension exercises should occur at least once a week.
(5) There should be a common marking policy as follows:
    (a) every technical error should be indicated by appropriate symbols such as: Sp. (spelling); Gr. (grammar); N.C.S. (not complete sentence) P. (punctuation).
    (b) numerical marks out of ten should be awarded on each piece of work for both effort and attainment.

Language Across the Curriculum: Discussion Document B

Starting Points
(1) Language and learning are inextricably linked; language competence and satisfactory attainment in all school subjects go hand-in-hand.
(2) All children need to develop adequate literacy (i.e. reading and writing) and oracy (i.e. listening, thinking, speaking) skills.

(3)   All teachers have responsibility for such development.

School Procedures

Speaking
(1)   The atmosphere should be such that all pupils may at any time feel free to say what they genuinely feel to be true.
(2)   Small group work in all subjects should be encouraged.
(3)   The potential value of the anecdote, and language directly from personal experience, should be recognised.
(4)   Transactional language needs to be preceded by firm foundations in expressive talk.
(5)   Strategies should be devised for pupils to engage in speculation in all subjects.

Reading
(1)   Reading should be recognised as one of the language arts and not necessarily the most important.
(2)   The importance of the textbook should be diminished. Reading of all kinds of different material relating to a topic should be encouraged such as: books; pamphlets; notices; newspapers; magazines; periodicals; documents; reference works; biographies.
(3)   Pupils should read to each other on occasions as well as to themselves.
(4)   Tapes should be made for weaker pupils unable to cope with certain kinds of reading matter.

Writing
(1)   Written work should, wherever possible, arise naturally from the task in hand and not be imposed on it.
(2)   There should be audiences for the pupils' written work other than that of teacher as judge.
(3)   Each piece of writing should, where possible, be a real means of communication.
(4)   Handwriting, spelling and technical accuracy should be regarded as unimportant if the essential message can be communicated.
(5)   Self-initiated work and a large measure of choice should be encouraged.

(10)   Throughout this book transcripts have been recorded, both of conversations and pieces of teaching. It is a disturbing, but illuminating experience for a teacher to see his spoken words in print. The following comments were made by students in

training, after they had scrutinised a transcript of one of their lessons.

Place each comment under one of these five headings, as an indication of the area in which the student's awareness increased:

(i)   Proportions of talk.
(ii) Own teaching style.
(iii) Questioning technique.
(iv) Knowledge of individuals.
(v)   Language process.

(a) 'In seven minutes, eighteen children were asked or offered answers to questions and seventeen gave answers. This is approximately two-thirds of the class present on that day' (Joy, with 9-year-olds).

(b) 'My question, "Can anyone suggest how we might go about it?" is an open question to get them to include their own original ideas' (Elizabeth, 8-year-olds).

(c) Said of one boy's contribution: 'He is thinking as he is talking, and forming his conversation around disjointed thoughts' (Rod, 9-year-olds).

(d) 'The transcript highlights the fact that the discussion is completely directed from the teacher. There is little pupil initiation or pupil to pupil interaction (Amy, with forty 7-year-olds).

(f) 'The way in which the lesson was set up and carried out conveys the basic assumption that I am the fountain of all knowledge and that they must accept the factual information passively. This, I admit, is disturbing' (James, 9-year-olds).

(g) 'The transcript shows I allowed Ian to have attention when he constantly demanded it. This was because he is brain damaged and does not always readily enter into discussions, as he usually finds the level of conversation too high for him' (Juliana, 8-year-olds).

(h) 'She is using her own language and not bothering to adapt it for the teacher' (says Steve, of 8-year-old Jane's description of 'horrible, sweaty, smelly pigs and stinking hens').

(i) 'This pupil (nicknamed by the other children "Rent-a-mouth") was just being silly here. I don't think he can help talking a lot; he just blurts it out and then apologises' (Bruce, 10-year-olds).

(j) 'My instructions are very unclear when I think about them afterwards...I find I'm always asking them if they understand. This is probably distracting for them' (Monika, 10-year-olds).

(k) 'There were thirty children present and only seven were involved in the discussion. I should have brought more in' (Alan, 9-year-olds).

(l) 'Reading through the transcript I notice that I have not really acknowledged the answers I was given, apart from repeating them so all children can hear. At times I could have extended the children's answers' (John, 9 to 11-year-olds).

(m) 'The questions are mostly closed, and serve the purpose of recalling information but do not in themselves allow for an expansion of the facts or for exploratory communication' (Anne, with forty 7-year-olds).

(n) 'I did not realise until I taped this, that all the questions came from me and not from the children' (Hugh, 9-year-olds).

(o) 'Teacher reinforces answer with "Yes", then twists it into what she really wanted the children to say' (Marion, 7-year-olds).

(p) 'Very perceptive child who doesn't take one of the leading roles in the group. She relates back to me a lot instead of to the rest of the group' (Alison, referring to 10-year-old Amanda).

Finally, a brief exchange which defies categorisation.

Picture the scene: student teacher Helen, talking with a class of 7-year-olds about silk worms.

Lee: Jesus tries to make cruel people kind people, doesn't he?
Helen: Yes.
Lee: It just won't work with Dracula.

Bibliography

Ausubel, D. P. *(1969)*. *Readings in School Learning* (New York: Holt, Rinehart & Winston).

Barnes, D. (1976). *From Communication to Curriculum* (Harmondsworth: Penguin).

Barnes, D. *et al*. (1969). *Language, the Learner and the School* (Harmondsworth: Penguin).

Beard, R. M. (1969). *An Outline of Piaget's Developmental Psychology* (London: Routledge & Kegan Paul).

Bennet, N. (1976). *Teaching Styles and Pupil Progress* (London: Open Books).

Blackham, H. (1976). *Moral and Religious Education in County Primary Schools* (Windsor: NFER).

Blackie, J. (1967). *Inside the Primary School* (London: HMSO).

Bloom, B. S. (1956). *Taxonomy of Educational Objectives. Handbook One: Cognitive Domain* (London: Longman).

Brandling, R. (1978). *Festive Occasions in the Primary School* (London: Ward Lock Educational).

Brearley, M. and Hitchfield, E. (1966). *A Teacher's Guide to Reading Piaget* (London: Routledge & Kegan Paul).

Britton, J. L. (1970). *Language and Learning* (Harmondsworth: Penguin).

Britton, J. L. (1971). 'What's the use?' in Wilkinson, A. M. (ed.), *The Context of Language, Education Review*, University of Birmingham, vol. 23, no. 3).

Brown, M and Precious, N. (1968). *The Integrated Day in the Primary School* (London: Ward Lock Educational).

Bullock Report (1975). *A Language for Life* (London: HMSO).

Cliff, P. and F. (1965). *An Infant Teacher's Religious Education Diary* (London: Hart-Davis).

Creber, J. W. P. (1965). *Sense and Sensitivity* (London: University of London Press).

Creber, J. W. P. (1972) *Lost for Words* (Harmondsworth: Penguin).

Dearden, R. F. (1968). *The Philosophy of Primary Education* (London: Routledge & Kegan Paul).

Dearden, R. F. (1976). *Problems in Primary Education* (London: Routledge & Kegan Paul).

Department of Education and Science (1972). *Movement: Physical Education in the Primary Years* (London: HMSO).

Dewey, J. (1966). *Democracy and Education* (New York: Free Press Education).

Flavell, J. H. (1963). *The Developmental Psychology of Jean Piaget* (London: Van Nostrand).

Gagné, R. M. (1966). *The Conditions of Learning* (New York: Holt, Rinehart & Winston).

Gardner, D. and Cass, J. (1965). *The Role of the Teacher in the Infant and Nursery School* (Oxford: Pergamon).

Gattegno, C. (1962). *Words in Colour* (Reading, Berks: Educational Explorers).

Gloyn, S. and Frobisher, B. (1975). *Teaching Basic Skills to Infants* (London: Goldman, R. J. (1964). *Religious Thinking from Childhood to Adolescence* (London: Routledge & Kegan Paul).

Goldman, R. J. (1965). *Readiness for Religion* (London: Routledge & Kegan Paul).

Grimmitt, M. (1974). *What to Do in R. E.* (Mayhew-McCrimmin).

Hilsum, S. and Cane, B. (1971). *The Teacher's Day* (Windsor: NFER).

Holm, J. (1975). *Teaching Religion in School* (Oxford: OUP).

Holt, J. (1967). *How Children Learn* (Harmondsworth: Penguin).

Holt, J. (1974). *Escape from Childhood* (Harmondsworth: Penguin).

Isaacs, S. (1930). *The Intellectual Growth of Young Children* (London: Routledge & Kegan Paul).

Jackson, P. W. (1968). *Life in Classrooms* (New York: Holt, Rinehart & Winston).

Jackson, S. (1968). *A Teacher's Guide to Tests and Testing* (London: Longman).

Jennings, J. (1977). 'History and environmental studies', *Trends in Education*, vol. 4 (Winter) (London: HMSO).

King, R. (1977). *Education*, 2nd edn (London: Longman).

King, R. (1978). *All Things Bright and Beautiful?* (New York: Wiley).

Lambert, I. M. (1976). *The Teaching of Reading* (Derby: Professional Association of Teachers).

Marsh, L. G. (1970a). *Alongside the Child* (London: A. & C. Black).

Marsh, L. G. (1970b). *Approach to Mathematics* (London: A. & C. Black).

Martin, N. *et al.* (1976). *Understanding Children Talking* (Harmondsworth: Penguin).

Maybury, B. (1967). *Creative Writing for Juniors* (London: Batsford).

Neill, A. S. (1939). *The Problem Teacher* (London: Herbert Jenkins).

Parry, M. and Archer, H. (1975). *Two to Five* (London: Macmillan).

Peters, R. S. (1966). *Ethics and Education* (London: Allen & Unwin).

Piaget, J. (1941). *The Child's Conception of Number* (London: Routledge & Kegan Paul).

Plowden Report (1967). *Children and Their Primary Schools* (London: HMSO).

Pumphrey, P. D. (1977). *Measuring Reading Abilities* (London: Hodder & Stoughton).

Rae, G. and McPhillimy, W. N. (1976). *Learning in the Primary School* (London: Hodder & Stoughton).

Rance, P. (1968). *Teaching by Topics* (London: Ward Lock Educational).

Rance, P. (1971). *Record Keeping in the Progressive Primary School* (London: Ward Lock Educational).

Reiss, C. (1975). *Education of Travelling Children* (London: Macmillan).

Richards, C. (ed.) (1978). *Education 3–13* (Driffield, Yorks: Nafferton Books).

Richards, J. (1978). *Classroom Language: What Sort?* (London: Allen & Unwin).

Ridgway, L. (1976). *Task of the Teacher in the Primary School* (London: Ward Lock Educational).

Sadler, J. E. (1974). *Concepts in Primary Education* (London: Allen & Unwin).

Sealey, L. G. W., and Gibbon, V. (1962). *Communication and Learning in the Primary School* (Oxford: Blackwell).

Sinclair, J. McH. and Coulthard, R. M. (1975). *Towards an Analysis of Discourse* (Oxford: OUP).

Torbe, M. (1977). *Teaching Spelling* (London: Ward Lock Educational).

Tough, J. (1976). *Listening to Children Talking* (London: Ward Lock Educational).

Treasure Chest for Teachers (Kettering, Northants: Schoolmaster Publishing Co. (latest edn, 1978).

Waller, W. (1932). *The Sociology of Teaching* (New York: Wiley).

Williams, A. A. (1970). *Basic Subjects for the Slow Learner* (London: Methuen).

Name Index

Index